RESPONSIBLE GOVERNANCE

The Global Challenge

ESSAYS IN HONOR OF CHARLES E. GILBERT

Edited by

John W. Harbeson
City University of New York

Raymond F. Hopkins
Swarthmore College

David G. Smith
Swarthmore College

UNIVERSITY
PRESS OF
AMERICA

Lanham • New York • London

Copyright © 1994 by
University Press of America,® Inc.
4720 Boston Way
Lanham, Maryland 20706

3 Henrietta Street
London WC2E 8LU England

All rights reserved
Printed in the United States of America
British Cataloging in Publication Information Available

Library of Congress Cataloging-in-Publication Data
Responsible governance : the global challenge : essays in
honor of Charles E. Gilbert / editors, John W. Harbeson,
Raymond F. Hopkins, David G. Smith.
p.   cm.
Includes bibliographical references.
1. Representative government and representation.   2. Responsibility.
I. Gilbert, Charles E.   II. Harbeson, John W. (John Willis).
III. Hopkins, Raymond F.   IV. Smith, David G.
JF1051.R48   1993   350.007'5—dc20   93–30822 CIP

ISBN 0–8191–9293–7 (cloth : alk. paper)

 The paper used in this publication meets the minimum requirements of American National Standard for Information Sciences—Permanence of Paper for Printed Library Materials, ANSI Z39.48–1984.

Charles E. Gilbert

ACKNOWLEDGEMENTS

This volume began with a seminar at Swarthmore College in June 1989 to commemorate the retirement after 35 years of distinguished service of Charles E. Gilbert. During the months and years preceding its publication, the papers at that symposium have been revised, supplemented by an additional chapter, and put into a common format with the assistance of Helen Hudson, editorial advisor at University Press of America.

The co-editors wish to acknowledge the patient help of each contributor. In addition, our task was made practically possible by the able editorial and word processing assistance of Ms. Mildred Wulff, Swarthmore College '95 and Ms. Phyllis Fry, Social Sciences Computing Coordinator at Swarthmore College. Completion would not have been possible without special efforts of Mrs. Nancy Maclay, secretary for Food and Public Policy.

Robert Putnam thanks Princeton University Press for permission to publish a chapter drawn from his book *Making Democracy Work*. Jack Nagel thanks John Wiley & Sons, Inc. for permission to publish "Psychological Obstacles to Administrative Responsibility: Lessons of the MOVE Disaster" which appeared earlier in the *Journal of Policy Analysis and Management*, Volume 10, 1991, pp. 1-23.

Finally, we acknowledge the contributions of many friends and collaborators of Charles Gilbert for whom he has been a very important intellectual influence, admired co-worker, and valued friend. Their support, garnered by the efforts of Maurice Eldridge, Director of Development at Swarthmore College, added to the technical and financial support of the College, including cooperation of Kathleen Grace, Director of the Bookstore, were invaluable in making the publication of this book possible.

Errors are the responsibility of the editors and authors alone.

JWH
RFH
DGS
Swarthmore Pennsylvania
June 1993

Table of Contents

Part I.
Introduction

1. Introduction 1
   J. Roland Pennock, Swarthmore College

Part II.
Responsible Governance in American Settings

2. Empowerment and Responsibility in the Organization of the future. 5
   David V. Edwards, University of Texas-Austin

3. Psychological Obstacles to Administrative Responsibility: Lessons
   of the MOVE Disaster. 21
   Jack H. Nagel, University of Pennsylvania

4. Federal Responsibility for Banking Reform and the Role of the
   State 45
   Eleanor D. Craig, University of Delaware

5. Toward Responsible Volunteerism: An Exploration of Operative
   Doctrines 57
   Jon Van Til, Rutgers University-Camden

6. Counting and Shaping the Right to Vote 69
   Roger B. Moore, San Francisco

Part III
Responsible Governance in International Settings

7. The Role of governance in Economic Development 101
   Raymond Hopkins, Swarthmore College

8. Institutional Change in Italy: The First Two Decades 121
   Robert D. Putnam, Harvard University

9. Economic Reform and Responsible Government in Africa 177
   John W. Harbeson, City University of New York

10. Responsible Transnational Corporations? 193
    Jonathan F. Galloway, Lake Forest College

11. Conscience in World Politics. 209
    Richard W. Mansbach, Iowa State University

12. References 225

13. Index 231

CHAPTER ONE

INTRODUCTION

J. ROLAND PENNOCK

Almost without regard to the various meanings of "responsibility," as identified by Charles E. Gilbert, it may safely be said that wherever a government exists, problems of political responsibility arise. And at no time has this been more apparent than today. The decline of government order in Somalia in 1991-92 provides a striking example how the lack of government shows the crucial need for some form of political organization to possess and exercise responsibility. Indeed this lack threatens, where it does not destroy, the very foundation of life. A look at the former Soviet Union, or at Yugoslavia, underlines the point. The case of the European Community illustrates both the great need for a responsible government on a multinational scale and the great difficulty of creating it. Worldwide, we see examples of a struggle between the forces making for unification and those struggling for fragmentation. What institutions are best able to exercise political responsibility in each case, and how can they be made viable?

In the case of more developed countries, like the United States, the struggles take a different form, fortunately for us, a more pacific form. But here too, we struggle, politically, over how much power should be concentrated in one political organ, or how much it should be decentralized, in order to create a government that will exercise power with maximum responsibility.

My task however is not to discourse on this subject but to introduce a group of essays that may shed light on certain aspects of this vast domain. A book in honor of Charles E. Gilbert might have been simply a miscellaneous collection of essays inspired by his teaching and his friendship. Or the essays, taken together, might have related to all of his published works. It is the former, but it is by no means simply that; and it is not the latter at all. Rather, the contributions that follow all have a bearing on the subject adverted to above, and this result was assured to by the editor's wise decision to have them related to one or both of Gilbert's seminal articles: "The Framework of Administrative Responsibility" *(The Journal of Politics,* Vol. 21, 1959, pp. 373-407) and "Operative Doctrines of Representation" *(The American Political Science Review,* Vol. 57, 1963, pp. 603-18). This focus gives the volume a certain unity that it might otherwise lack. True, this unity is not, and is not intended to be that of a single-authored book. Far from it. The chapters could be divided into the conventional fields of the discipline, and to a considerable extent this has been done. But that would require some straining of the conventional categories, not least because a unity of concern pervades the whole.

It is worth a few words to say something about this unity. It is twofold. In the broadest sense, it reflects Gilbert's ever-present, strong theoretical bent. He is never content with saying how things work; he wants to know why, what principles are involved and how they can be applied elsewhere for human betterment. He is concerned with values, and is not content with such fuzzy, all-encompassing terms as "responsibility" without analyzing them into the multitude of values that they comprise.

This brings me to the second aspect of the unity that characterizes this, in some other respects, diverse book. Its title, *Responsible Governing: the Global Challenge*, says it all. It could, to be sure, be spelled out a little (losing the virtue of brevity) into something like "Responsiveness, Representation, and Responsibility: the Three 'R's' of Liberal Democratic Government." I insert this too cumbersome title because it suits my present purpose. It shows the unity of concerns embodied in these contributions. Both of the first two "R's" are essential to the third. Representation is the formal, constitutional mode of securing responsiveness, providing supplement and framework, backbone indeed, for all the other modes. For a liberal democracy, at least, responsibility embraces both of the other "R's." Without them, it would be toothless; without it, they would be fruitless (poisonous, in fact).

It may be helpful at this point to remind the reader of Gilbert's list of values wrapped up in that word "Responsibility." They are: "responsiveness," "flexibility," "consistency," "stability," "leadership," "probity," "candor," "competence," "efficacy," "prudence," "due process," and "accountability."

Obvious though it may be not all values in Gilbert's list are in every situation mutually compatible. This is true even of what was designated above as "the three R's of liberal democracy." "Responsiveness" may clash with "responsibility" in several of its meanings. Even if by the former we mean responsiveness to demand rather than to need (a problem in itself), the potential dissonance is clear. Anyone who follows public opinion polls knows that one who tried faithfully to represent them would soon find him- or her- self in conflict with one or more of the values of responsibility, such as "consistency" much of the time.

Furthermore, the legislator who tries to respond to need, as was hinted above, may find that popular demand is not necessarily reflective of real need. This fact is what led Madison to stress our "true interests" and to argue for institutions that would "refine" and enlarge the public views, by passing them through the medium of a chosen body of citizens, and whose patriotism and love of justice will be least likely to sacrifice that interest to temporary or partial considerations *(The Federalist, No. X)*.

When we consider probity as a further element of responsibility, we gain further insight into the problem of the responsible representative seeking to be "responsive." We may gain some comfort in considering that the representative may take account of the intensity of popular demand -- some comfort but by no means complete reassurance; but perhaps enough to make it clear that the representative must be much more that a delegate. It also points to the need for more than one body to effectuate all of the elements Gilbert found in "responsibility."

Let me now turn from these general introductory remarks to more specific reference to what is to come. The volume is divided into two parts. In the first of these, Jack H. Nagel examines one of the most puzzling and dramatic events in the history of American municipal government, the tragedy of Philadelphia that grew out of the MOVE affair. It is the history of how an apparently competent and widely respected black mayor allowed a disaster of vast proportions to occur in a black, middle-class neighborhood in his city. Although the mayor's behavior seemed irresponsible and doubly paradoxical, Nagel has found a psychological study that, he believes, solves the mystery.

Next, we move to the federal and state levels, where Eleanor D. Craig examines banking policy. She believes, especially in the light of experience in

Delaware, that in this instance the federal government would have been acting more wisely if it had left the matter to the states, those laboratories of public policy in a democracy.

David V. Edwards, in the following essay, points to the need for further modification of existing institutions, providing new modes of management and leadership. Intentionally or not, he takes a cue from Felix Frankfurter who, in one of his oft-quoted opinions, declared that "responsibility is the great developer of men." Edwards maintains that authority and control of resource must be decentralized, and that empowering more individuals will lead to an increase in creativity and productivity. Governmental practitioners must not be content with following set procedures; they must concentrate on problem solving, infused with ethical action. It might be added that one could accept these goals and at the same time wonder whether decentralization, judged by its past record, would be likely to lead to ethical action.

Jon Van Til's contribution relates to Gilbert's article on "The Framework of Administrative Responsibility" in which he developed "operative doctrines of administrative responsibility." Van Til proceeds to apply these doctrines to the realm of voluntary associations, where he finds them just as helpful as they had proved to be in the political realm.

The following chapter ventures into the realm of jurisprudence. In this essay, Roger B. Moore, taking off from Gilbert's "Operative doctrines of Representation," examines the terrain opened by the Supreme Court when it, for the first time, recognized the question of the fairness of legislative apportionment as a justiciable one. Not only that, but it becomes apparent that this in turn leads, in the process of achieving an equitable result, to the modification of existing institutions, all in the way of shaping the polity in a way that "makes everyone count." Here the court was clearly seeking to pursue several of the goals of responsibility, such as responsiveness and accountability, although some critics have questioned whether, in departing so sharply from its own precedents, it was being adequately consistent.

Opening Part III, Raymond F. Hopkins points out that most of what are generally considered necessary features of democracy (or at least of responsible government, which he equates with good government), also play a wider role: they are conditions of economic development as well. These conditions, as Hopkins enumerates them, are: (1) openness, (2) the rule of law, (3) respect for human dignity, and (4) civic-mindedness. What is especially relevant for this volume is that they are cast in terms sufficiently broad and flexible to apply to countries whose political and governmental institutions depart in various respects from the patterns established by Western democracies. It is even possible to imagine that these tests might be applied to multinational and transnational organizations and to voluntary associations (both of which are discussed in later chapters), not to mention their more obvious applicability to the countries most in need of economic development.

Next, Robert D. Putnam presents a case study of the insertion of a new, elective layer of government, a regional government, between the central and local government, in a hitherto highly centralized polity (that of Italy). Among his interesting findings especially relevant to this book is that the elected councilors came to interpret their role less as being "responsive to " their constituents' views and more as being "responsible for" their welfare, thus placing major emphasis on one aspect of the concept of responsibility.

In the following chapter, moving across the mediterranean to Africa, we view the state of many, indeed most, of the countries as they are surveyed by John W. Harbeson. He locates responsibility for this sad state of affairs partly in their own governments and partly in the World Bank and the International Monetary Fund. The key point for the purpose of the present essay grows out of the diagnosis of the problem. In a nutshell -- and here one notes a similarity to the formula applied in Italy, as described by Putnam -- it is the failure to decentralize responsibility. However, he is arguing for something more than Italy has done. In modern management style, he wants cooperation to be widespread, not only crossing the boundaries between administration and politics but also tending to separate layers of government, and government and voluntary agencies, and private agencies, domestic or international. One wonders whether the call for more decentralization is prudent? Will the increase of flexibility be accompanied by adequate leadership at the national level? To me at least, such questions clearly can be answered only on the basis of a case-by-case study.

The proper role of nongovernmental organizations comes in for central attention in Jonathan Galloway's essay on Transnational Corporations those multinational legal entities that are now more or less losing all sense of nationality and are becoming truly transnational. Here, Galloway finds, and foresees increasingly, responsibility (especially in its leadership aspect) asserting itself through various local movements (such as environmentalism) but especially through those sprawling corporations that both take their character from and provide influence to many if not all parts of the world, in fine disregard for national boundaries. To whom, one wonders, are these transnational organizations accountable?

The final chapter of what will be known to his many admirers as "Chuck's book" is peculiarly fitted to honor a man so interested in and committed to the finest values. Entitled "'Conscience' in World Politics," this essay will bring a gleam of light to the most disenchanted. In it, Richard W. Mansbach sets out to establish the proposition that, as a rule, foreign policy leaders are instructed and powerfully influenced by something we call "conscience." Moreover, he has the audacity to provide us with eloquent arguments and irrefutable evidence in support of that proposition. Cheers for him and for the man who inspired it.

CHAPTER TWO

EMPOWERMENT AND RESPONSIBILITY IN THE ORGANIZATION OF THE FUTURE

DAVID V. EDWARDS

For organizations to be effective in periods of rapid and comprehensive change, the responsibilities of leaders and followers must be structured to foster creativity, innovation, and high productivity.[1] The traditional modes of administration -- management and leadership -- have become obsolescent in the face of unprecedented change and novel demands. To function effectively, organizations both private and public will increasingly need a new mode of administration - one that decentralizes authority and the control of resources as well as responsibility. I shall describe this new administrative mode, which I call empowerment,[2] in this essay.

Managers and leaders have been slow to adopt empowering structures and practices because they have been conditioned by both their training and their reward systems to fear the consequences of relinquishing control. At the same time, political scientists and organization theorists have been equally slow to see the need for empowerment and to recommend it, in large part because they too continue to think in traditional terms. In their cases, this means defining their own professional responsibilities as being limited to conceptual clarification and empirical study, thereby excluding from them the recommendation of reforms. Fundamentally descriptive and reactive, this approach ignores the essentially political nature of definition and the ethical responsibilities of the scholar.

What is required is for scholars, along with those who manage the public and private organizations they study, to come to a new understanding of their roles and responsibilities in the context of rapid and comprehensive change at all levels of social organization, from the family and the firm to global society. This understanding would best begin with recognition of the extent to which politics operates at what social scientists call the epistemological level in both the world of scholarship and the world of administration. Put another way, politics operates at the level of perceiving, experiencing, and discussing reality, as well as at the level of

---

[1] I am indebted to David G. Smith, John W. Harbeson, and Alessandra Lippucci for their extensive helpful comments and suggestions on earlier drafts of this essay. I may have empowered them to comment upon it. They certainly empowered me to create a much better essay than I could have written without their contributions.

[2] The term empowerment is increasingly popular in political, management, and helping profession circles, but is generally used in a much looser sense to refer to increasing someone's capacities, as I shall further explain below.

attempting to reconstruct it. Understanding this will enable those in both worlds - the academic and the practical-to discover how to become more effective and responsible.

The politics of definition

Political scientists and organization theorists have devoted considerable effort to analyzing the concept of responsibility in hopes of uncovering or clarifying its most appropriate meaning.[3] But arriving at such a definition - or any definition - is not so much a conceptual as it is an essentially political undertaking. Those who fail to take account of this fact may perpetuate particular definitions in changed historical contexts where they no longer perform a positive function. This is what has happened to many scholars and administrators who today operate with a dysfunctional concept of responsibility that severely limits the effective functioning of organizations in both government and business.

Definitions of key political terms are not "given by the subject"-nor are they given by the dictionary. Rather, they are largely determined and imposed by people who have their own particular prescriptive interests or projects,[4] and the authority to implement them. Because these definitions are crucial for those agendas - for what can be thought and what will be done - there are always efforts to dismiss or discredit competing definitions.

There is, in other words, a discernible connection between a definition and the action it is intended to legitimate.[5] This is what makes the selection of definitions and their imposition upon research subjects and/or colleagues a fundamentally political move. Given this realization, the responsible scholar should become aware of the likely consequences of his or her selections among competing definitions. Indeed, the responsible scholar will make his or her selection among definitions conscious of what that choice will enable him or her to do and taking account, insofar as possible, of the ethical implications of that choice.

Most social scientists remain unaware of this contingent or political nature of

---

[3] An intellectual father of this effort is Charles E. Gilbert. Unfortunately, his pathbreaking and underbrush-clearing analysis of the historical and intellectual bases of the concept, "The Framework of Administrative Responsibility," 21 Journal of Politics (1959), pp. 373-407, has not received the attention it deserves.

[4] This recognition has been nourished by the infiltration of Continental European social theory into Anglo-American social science. I have in mind here in particular the works of such provocative and insightful social theorists as Jean-Paul Sartre, Michel Foucault, Jacques Derrida, Jean-Francois Lyotard, and others commonly called post-structuralist and/or postmodern. Of course, they differ ferociously among themselves on many matters, but all have helped to heighten our appreciation of the essentially political nature of analysis. The major writings of these theorists are now widely available in English translations, and are too numerous to cite here.

[5] There is a growing tendency in political science to refer to key terms as "essentially contested concepts" subject to endless dispute. This approach was suggested by W. B. Gallie [in "Essentially Contested Concepts," 56 Proceedings of the Aristotelian Society (1955-56), pp. 167-98] and developed by William Connolly [in The Terms of Political Discourse (Princeton: Princeton University Press, 2nd ed., 1983)]. But this approach seems to undervalue the political nature and consequences of definitional disputes. It also fails to explain political disagreement, as Andrew Mason has argued [in "On Explaining Political Disagreement: The Notion of an Essentially Contested Concept," 33 Inquiry (1990), pp. 81-90].

definition and of its implication: the consequent necessity for conscious responsible choice among competing possible definitions. As long as they conceive of the task of political science as discovering, describing, and then explaining the truth about political reality, they can think of definitions as accurately or inaccurately capturing the essence of some aspect of reality, and evaluate them in these terms. By continuing to conceive of the act of definition as purely descriptive, they can sequester themselves from responsibility and help to perpetuate the myth that they are operating in an apolitical epistemological context. But they remain responsible for the historical consequences, whether they recognize this or not.

The definition of politics

This political approach to definition is actually an important part of a political approach to the broader practice of political science. I have argued elsewhere that the most fruitful way to understand the nature of politics is as dispute over claims to the authority to describe, explain, or interpret some aspect of the nature of reality.[6] The focus on claims to authority shifts our attention to the essentially problematic nature of political analysis and political action and encourages us to examine critically the grounds for such claims. When we do so, three things become possible.

First, we are able to demystify such claims to authority and then to evaluate them in terms of our own criteria for granting authority. Second, we are able to separate the assertions being made about the nature of reality from the allegedly authoritative grounds for belief in those assertions. This move then encourages us to make our own evaluation of the assertions about reality should we wish to do so. Third, we are increasingly able to consciously choose the image of reality that will most likely conduce to the developments we favor.

In the absence of such realizations, we will tend to accept the claims made by political authorities--whether actors or political analysts--allowing them to be imposed upon us by means of assertions that they are somehow privileged by being grounded in the historical record or in the considered reflections of an experienced actor.

The point is not that there is no historical record that we can use to arbitrate disputes about the nature of reality,[7] any more than it is that there are no experienced actors with useful expertise to whom we can turn. The point is rather that any decision to appeal to a historical record or to defer to expertise is a choice we make. And that choice carries with it responsibility because it contributes to the opening up of some possibilities and the foreclosing of others.

Reality remains subject to contingency and to choices actors make freely--that is, in a way not fully caused by circumstances. In this sense, what we

---

[6] David V. Edwards, Creating a New World Politics (New York: McKay, 1973) and The American Political Experience, four editions (Englewood Cliffs: Prentice-Hall, 1979, 1982, 1985, 1988).

[7] In fact, of course, the point is that there are limitless historical records, and each is itself fundamentally political. Thus, in a similarly political fashion, what becomes at issue is which historical record to accept as authoritative. Two of the more interesting recent analyses of "the politics of historiography" are Sande Cohen, Historical Culture (Berkeley: University of California Press, 1986) and Hans Kellner, Language and Historical Representation: Getting the Story Crooked (Madison: University of Wisconsin Press, 1989).

think of as reality is fundamentally at least somewhat indeterminate.[8] This view, which is certainly consistent with our everyday experience, implies that we will have choices to make about the image of reality we accept and in terms of which we act, and those choices will inform our actions and thereby tend to help shape the outcomes of those actions.[9] In other words, the fact of indeterminacy does not mean that we have no interest in, nor does it mean we bear no responsibility for, our action's outcome. When it comes to the making of history, doing nothing is generally worse than doing something. And even when we do something, indeterminacy may intervene and then will have to be dealt with.

It is crucial that, in choosing one course of action over another, we be prepared to alter our action as experience and practice demand. Equally crucial is our recognition that implicit in the choice of a particular course of action is the choice of an image of reality that justifies that choice and makes its pursuit possible. When events cause that image of reality to change, the course of action it justifies must also change. Similarly, when the course of action is forced to take a different turn, or is derailed, the image of reality on which it depends is called into question. We must then reassess our policy alternatives as well as the conceptions of reality that legitimate them.[10]

The point, then, is that reality is constituted and reconstituted over time by the actions of people who act in accordance with images they hold, whether consciously or nonconsciously, of the nature, limits, and possibilities of reality. Whoever effectively commends such reality images to actors will tend to inform or even control their actions. In other words, one's effective control is a function of the extent to which other actors subscribe to (that is, consider authoritative) the reality image one wishes to impose upon them. This explains the inordinate power of expert opinion in cases where others are not confident enough of their own experience to rely upon it or to challenge the experts.

Claims to authority are therefore the crucial element in "the politics of expertise."[11] They are also essential to the politician, the administrator, and the academic political scientist.[12]

The claims to authority currently made by the administrators of public and private organizations are suffering increasing erosion because obsolete administrative practices fail to foster the creativity, innovation, and high productivity

---

[8] For a stimulating argument to this effect, see G. L. S. Shackle, Imagination and the Nature of Choice (Edinburgh: Edinburgh University Press, 1979). See also my paper "Theorizing as Practice, or The Defensible Concept of Theory and Its Uses," presented at the 1989 annual meetings of the American Political Science Association in Atlanta, GA.

[9] I apply this argument to international relations in Creating a New World Politics.

[10] I shall return to these questions of practice below.

[11] See, among a growing number of studies, Frank Fischer, Technocracy and the Politics of Expertise (Newbury Park, CA: Sage, 1990).

[12] For consideration of the background phenomenon of professionalism, see Magali Sarfatti Larson, "In the Matter of Experts and Professionals, or How Impossible It Is to Leave Nothing Unsaid," chapter 3 in Rolf Torstendahl, et.al., eds., The Formation of Professions: Knowledge, State, and Strategy (Newbury Park, CA: Sage, 1990).

required for effectiveness and to contribute to humane development of workers.[13] It is past time to replace these obsolete practices with a new mode of administration that promises to achieve these organizational goals by combining effectiveness with social responsibility. Empowerment is this mode. Before turning to an examination of the mode of empowerment, I shall explain briefly some reasons why persisting modes of administration have failed and why these failures point to empowerment as the preferred alternative.

The modes of administration

The United States, many claim, is currently suffering from a lack of leadership, or at least from a shortage of leaders, in both the public and private sectors.[14] We may trace the political nature of such an assertion to the agenda or objective of those arguing this position. Most of them today call for increased creativity, innovation, and productivity in American business, industry, and government in order to meet the growing economic challenges posed by Japan and by an expanding united Europe.

However, there are others with different political agendas who argue that the fundamental problem is the quality of life in the workplace, and assert that improved performance of individuals in the private and public sectors alike depends on improving the work experience in ways that lead to greater job satisfaction. In other words, there are competing definitions of the problem. Not surprisingly, they produce competing solutions. They do, however, seem to agree on one thing: the importance of "liberating the reserve strength of human potential" by means of a "shift in philosophy from 'thing'-centeredness to a human ecological emphasis in which production is only a part of the whole"--in the words of one recent analysis.[15]

The widespread view that we suffer from a shortage of leadership is, I think, a product of three misconceptions: of the nature of the problems we face; of the nature and promise of leadership; and of the possible modes of administration.

Until recently, the generally favored mode of administration, in both the private and the public sector, was management.[16] Scholars and consultants long sought to strengthen the tools of scientific management in the private sector. This

---

[13] See Norman E. Bowie, "Empowering People as an End for Business," in Georges Enderle, et.al., eds., People in Corporations: Ethical Responsibilities and Corporate Effectiveness (Dordrecht: Kluwer Academic, 1990), pp. 105-118, for an argument that businesses should do good, and that in doing good they are likely to do well.

[14] The books in which this claim is made are by now too voluminous to cite. Among the already "classic" books are James MacGregor Burns, Leadership (New York: Harper & Row, 1978), Tom Peters and Nancy Austin, A Passion for Excellence: The Leadership Difference (New York: Random House, 1985), and Warren Bennis & Burt Nanus, Leaders: The Strategies for Taking Charge (New York: Harper & Row, 1985). More recent, though not novel, arguments include Craig R. Hickman, The Mind of a Manager, the Soul of a Leader (New York: Wiley, 1990), Bennis, Why Leaders Can't Lead (San Francisco: Jossey-Bass, 1989), and Nanus, The Leader's Edge: The Seven Keys to Leadership in a Turbulent World (Chicago: Contemporary Books, 1989).

[15] Sven B. Lundstedt and Thomas H. Moss, "The Future of Innovation Management," chapter 17 in Lundstedt and Moss, eds., Managing Innovation and Change (Dordrecht: Kluwer Academic, 1989), page 224.

[16] For a comprehensive survey of relevant literature and arguments, see John M. Brion, Organizational Leadership of Human Resources, 3 volumes (Greenwich, CT: JAI Press, 1989).

first took the form of permutations on a "Taylorism" based on a belief that workers by nature needed incentives (plums to climb after) and disincentives (whips to be cracked over them) in order to become more productive.[17] Eventually (to encapsulate the history of management theory and practice in much too brief a fashion) the permutations on Taylorism gave way to "McGregorism", an approach that relied upon rewards to workers to generate commitment and responsibility.[18] While the assumptions of McGregorism about human nature were diametrically opposed to those of Taylorism, they nevertheless had the same self-limiting character because the approach assumed a given human nature and sought to build a managerial (or perhaps a "therapeutic") technology upon it.[19] Increasingly, however, some social scientists are coming to think that it is better instead to act as if human nature were relatively plastic[20] and develop strategies and institutions specifically designed to foster a desired human practice.

The longstanding private sector managerial approach of seeking "technological fixes" has also flourished in the public sector in recent decades. Urban reformers, for example, first sought to replace machine politics with managerial administration. In recent years, disappointed by public professionalization, some have switched to advocating replacing public with privatized service provision. In a similar fashion, scholars of the presidency have debated whether the trend toward the persuasive or rhetorical presidency should be encouraged or constrained, proposing such fixes as changes in news conferences or changes in campaign practices.[21] And scholars focusing on bureaucracy have sought ways of making it function more responsively or creatively.[22]

Nonetheless, in recent years more and more observers of both the public and the private sectors have come to believe that a more fundamental and pervasive problem is a lack of vision, not only in the organizations' employees, but more importantly in their managers. Many suggest that this lack of vision requires more leadership. They have contrasted management with leadership in terms distinctly unfavorable to management. In one of the milder formulations, management consultant, business school professor, and sometime university president Warren Bennis has argued that "Managers do things right. Leaders do the right thing."

---

[17] The father of Taylorism was management consultant Frederick W. Taylor, who came to dominate management thinking before World War I, and whose characterization of human nature this is.

[18] The father of this approach -- "Theory Y" as he called it, to distinguish it from his term for Taylorism, "Theory X" -- was Douglas McGregor. See his book The Human Side of Enterprise (New York: McGraw-Hill, 1960).

[19] Others have continued to develop interesting approaches grounded in a positive concept of human nature. See Barry Schwartz, The Battle for Human Nature: Science, Morality, and Modern Life (New York: Norton, 1986) and Alfie Kohn, The Brighter Side of Human Nature: Altruism and Empathy in Everyday Life (New York: Basic Books, 1990), which summarizes a wide range of research.

[20] For an argument that this is so, see Peter Berger & Thomas Luckmann, The Social Construction of Reality (Garden City, NY: Doubleday Anchor, 1966).

[21] The debate continues. See, for example, Jeffrey Tulis, The Rhetorical Presidency (Princeton: Princeton University Press, 1988).

[22] See, for example, William T. Gormley, Taming the Bureaucracy: Muscles, Prayers, and Other Strategies (Princeton: Princeton University Press, 1989).

Bennis and Bert Nanus conclude a recent book with the assertion that "Without leadership...it is hard to see how we can shape a more desirable future for this nation or the world. The absence or ineffectiveness of leadership implies the absence of vision, a dreamless society, and this will result, at best, in the maintenance of the status quo or, at worst, in the distintegration of our society because of lack of purpose and cohesion."[23]

But this call for leadership to get vision fails to address the question of just what vision is needed. Students of politics have reason for pessimism when it comes to visionary leaders, for they are more likely to think of Hitler while the administrative theorist thinks of Lee Iacocca. In a global political context, the visionary leaders who achieve the greatest success seem often to be those who are the least responsible.

The danger, in a political context, is that when we look to others for a vision of what we should become as individuals, groups, organizations, or as a society, we abdicate our own responsibility in these matters and allow our conduct to be informed by that borrowed or imported vision. Such abdication of responsibility continues to be a severe problem for societies attempting to move from dictatorship to democracy. Nowhere is this more apparent now than in Eastern Europe and the successor states to the Soviet Union.

Developing a citizenry able to act democratically is inseparable from the development of citizen responsibility for the direction human and state action should take. The same holds for the private sector, where firms long led by authoritarian management have had great trouble adapting to the new corporate environment of today, let alone to more participatory modes of administration.

Another virtue typically imputed to leadership is its capacity to inspire subordinates. We know that people can be temporarily inspired to exert greater effort in whatever they are doing by even the most vapid exhortations--those typical of so many self-improvement programs, for example. We might think of this as a kind of inspirational "Hawthorne Effect."[24] We also know that people can be similarly inspired by shallow and pernicious exhortations in demagogic regimes or in negative political campaigns. So again the question becomes: inspiration to what end?

In any event, it is unlikely that leadership can save us where management has failed, because there are simply too many "leadership" positions for the available pool of leaders. The federal structure of the United States has produced more than 80,000 governments,[25] while the capitalist economy sustains or challenges uncounted millions of enterprises. Experts continue to disagree over whether leaders are born or made. But even if leaders can be made,[26] there are not enough schools of business, management, and public affairs to furnish the requisite numbers of leaders to staff the tops of our public and private sector organizations--assuming that these institutions know how to make leaders and are

---

[23] Bennis & Nanus, Leaders, op.cit., p. 228.

[24] The reference is, of course, to the famous experiment with changes in lighting at the General Electric plant in Hawthorn, N.J., in which it was found that *any* change produced an improvement in productivity temporarily.

[25] This includes some 3000 counties, 19,000 municipalities, 17,000 townships, 15,000 school districts, and 26,000 special districts within our 50 states.

[26] For an argument that this is possible, see Jay A. Conger, et.al., Charismatic Leadership: The Elusive Factor in Organizational Effectiveness (San Francisco: Jossey-Bass, 1988).

able to do so effectively.

If we accept the prevailing diagnosis that managers can barely manage and leaders are few and not always up to the tasks of providing vision and inspiring followers, what can we do to regenerate the public and private organizations upon which our society and those of others depend?

The politics of administrative modes

This question would not even be raised by a political science--or an administrative science--that envisions itself as merely descriptive and explanatory. Such a political science restricts its investigations in a period of decline to the process of degeneration instead of considering possible processes of regeneration. In so limiting its studies, it contributes to that degeneration by making it appear to be an objective feature of an objective reality. But political scientists are having increasing difficulty sustaining this image of an objective political science, given that even the physical sciences now recognize choice and perspective as integral to their investigations and to the reality they study--and thereby help to constitute.[27]

Even assuming that such objectivity were possible in the social sciences, its pursuit would be irresponsible, precisely because reality is being continuously created, sustained, and altered by the choices people make on the bases of their beliefs about what is possible as well as their beliefs about what is desirable. Thus if we as social scientists study what has happened in a far-from-ideal past and generalize it to the present and future in the form of "laws" about social causation, we will be inadvertently circumscribing the realm of the possible future in a way that could only be welcomed were we living in a steady-state utopia.

This suggests that social scientists should be seeking to develop new possible modes of administration that hold promise of coping with our current and projected difficulties rather than relying on older modes which tend to perpetuate or even exacerbate these difficulties.

This is what some business and management specialists have been trying to do. Two prominent new modes of administration that significant numbers of them have been advocating as models are Japanese-style management and entrepreneurship.

Some argue for the adoption of Japanese organizational devices and incentives to reshape the American workplace and the work experience.[28] But others doubt that Japanese corporate culture can be successfully transplanted to American firms because it differs so drastically from the larger American culture.[29] Moreover, to my knowledge no one has developed a plausible model for Japanese-style management in the public sector. And developments in Japanese

---

[27] For an interesting summary of this position with discussion of some of its implications for society, see Willis Harman, Global Mind Change (Indianapolis: Knowledge Systems, 1988), and David Ray Griffin, ed., The Reenchantment of Science: Postmodern Proposals (Albany: State University of New York Press, 1988).

[28] See William G. Ouchi, Theory Z: How American Business Can Meet the Japanese Challenge (Reading, MA: Addison-Wesley, 1981), and K. John Fukuda, Japanese-Style Management Transferral (London: Routledge, 1988).

[29] For one among a growing number of relevant empirical studies, see Robert E. Cole, Strategies for Learning: Small-Group Activities in American, Japanese, and Swedish Industry (Berkeley: University of California Press, 1989).

politics in recent years suggest that, in the absence of a public sector rectitude considerably greater than the Japanese now have, the imposition of the Japanese corporate culture on either sector might well hinder rather than foster the sort of responsible and creative political practices we seek.

What about entrepreneurship,[30] the other alternative model some support? Political and economic thinking on both the left and the right now tends to favor more individual initiative in mobilizing financial and human capital in ways that boost innovation which bureaucracy has squelched. This was a prominent rationale for deregulation and privatization in the Reagan years, and then for the subsequent interest in innovative "tools" for governmental coordination of private activity,[31] as well as for innovative modes of public sector governance.[32] Political scientists, too, have long been interested in the processes of "policy entrepreneurship". But so far no obvious way has been found to foster sufficient entrepreneurship to effect the transformation required to regenerate the public and private sectors to make them consistently productive and innovative. Even proposals of "intrapreneurship,"[33] which would foster such venturesomeness within large-scale bureaucracies, although bold on paper, have generally proved insufficiently attractive to administrators.

It appears that the crisis we face is sufficiently severe to warrant a more revolutionary response. And if this is true in the United States, how much truer must it be of the most highly bureaucratized and centralized state socialist countries in the world, which are currently attempting to restructure their political and economic systems to introduce elements of market decision and political democracy?

The politics of empowerment

A promising revolutionary response may well borrow elements from the various solutions critics are proposing. But at the heart of the response must be a new mode of administration capable of converting challenges into opportunities. This response must be able to capitalize on the inherent strengths in workers--both those called "labor" and those called "management"--to maximize creativity and innovation at all levels. Such a revolution will require more than expert management. It will require more than dynamic leadership. It will, I believe, require the conscious and effective use of the new mode of active administration that I call empowerment.[34]

---

[30] For an interesting study, see Robert F. Hebert & Albert N. Link, The Entrepreneur: Mainstream Views and Radical Critiques (New York: Praeger, 1982).

[31] See Lester M. Salamon, ed., Beyond Privatization: The Tools of Government Action (Washington: Urban Institute Press, 1989).

[32] See David Osborne and Ted A. Gaebler, Reinventing Government: How the Entrepreneurial Spirit Is Transforming the Public Sector (Reading, MA: Addison-Wesley, 1992).

[33] Gifford Pinchot III, Intrapreneuring (New York: Harper & Row, 1985).

[34] As I indicated above, the term *empowerment* has come into increasing favor in the business press and in the field of organization theory, among other places, in recent years. Unfortunately, it is usually used in a casual way to refer to any efforts to increase the effectiveness or the sense of efficacy of employees or managers. See, for example, Jay A. Conger, et.al., "The Empowerment Process: Integrating Theory and Practice," 13 Academy of Management Review 3 (July 1988), pp. 471-482; Peter Block, The Empowered Manager: Positive Political Skills at Work (San Francisco:

Empowerment in administrative terms involves a superior granting simultaneously to one or more subordinates three key elements: responsibility, authority, and discretionary resources. While it is true that managers in large firms, like those in large governments, have always practiced the delegation of responsibility, and often the devolution of resources, they have generally done so without granting the authority necessary to empower the subordinates. It takes the combination of all three elements--responsibility, resources, and authority--to maximize creativity, innovation, and productivity at lower levels of organizations.

Delegation, the conventional administrative practice, leaves authority in the hands of the one who delegates.[35] The administrator decides when to delegate, to whom, and for what purpose. The result is that delegation actually tends to limit the prospects of success by presuming that the superior knows what is needed, who should do it, and when it should be done, if perhaps not always exactly how it should be done.

On the other hand, the less frequent practice of devolution of authority and resources--but without responsibility--tends toward anarchy. Such delegation can only succeed when subordinates are so well conditioned that they do not take advantage of the unconditional freedom inherent in the granting of authority unconstrained by responsibility. But subordinates who are this well conditioned are also unlikely to be free-thinking enough to generate the creation and innovation now required.

What is now sometimes called "transformational leadership"[36] or "SuperLeadership"[sic][37] in its most effective moments may serve to elicit the best that superiors know to request. It may even elicit the best that subordinates currently know how to deliver. But this is unlikely to achieve the desired results in a time of serious challenges.

Thus, neither the delegation of responsibility nor the devolution of resources, nor even transformational leadership, is enough to enable American businesses or governments to convert the new challenges into opportunities they can exploit. The key is active participation,[38] but participation of a special sort that can enable subordinates to transcend not only corporate limits but also their own and their superiors' existing ideas.

The practice of empowerment

Empowerment as a mode of active administration is now being developed and practiced by creative and innovative administrators in organizations large and small, private and public, although they often have their own term for the practice.

Jossey-Bass, 1987); and Robert E. Quinn, et.al., "Education and Empowerment: A Transformational Model of Managerial Skills Development," chapter 16 in John D. Bigelow, ed., Managerial Skills: Explorations in Practical Knowledge (Newbury Park, CA: Sage, 1991). My use is more precise, developed and elaborated in an ongoing study of competing modes of administration.

[35] For a representative conventional argument for delegation, see James M. Jenks & John M. Kelly, Don't Do, Delegate! (New York: Franklin Watts, 1985).

[36] Noel M. Tichy & Mary Anne Devanna, The Transformational Leader (New York: Wiley, 1986).

[37] Charles C. Manz and Henry P. Sims, Jr., SuperLeadership: Leading Others to Lead (New York: Prentice Hall Press, 1989).

[38] See Edward E. Lawler III, High-Involvement Management: Participative Strategies for Improving Organizational Performance (San Francisco: Jossey-Bass, 1986).

These administrators are using empowerment to maximize their successes today and to expand their contributions to shaping the world tomorrow.

Consider the example of W. L. Gore and Associates. While William Gore was a research chemist at DuPont he learned two vital lessons: how to do relevant research and how not to do administration. He set up his own firm to manufacture a superfine fabric that is waterproof, but can still breathe. It is now used to line many of today's best shoes, because it keeps the foot dry by keeping moisture out and allowing perspiration to escape. This is but one of its many uses, which have also come to include antipollution filters, electrical cables, and synthetic veins in the human body. Gore knew he had developed a very promising product, but DuPont was not interested in his idea. So he decided to leave DuPont and set up a first-rate organization to develop, produce, and market his product.

Gore designed his company to avoid the obstacles that he knew from experience prevent traditional administrators from cashing in on creativity, innovation, and job satisfaction. At Gore, therefore, there are no titles and no hierarchy. This means no employees and no bosses. Everyone is an "associate." To work there, you must have a Sponsor. Your Sponsor orients you and helps you succeed at your first project, but you are the one who must pick that project. You are told to wander around and "Find something you'd like to do." Once you succeed at a first project, you get an Advocate Sponsor who follows your progress and helps a compensation committee of your peers decide on your salary.

Everything at Gore is organized around individual initiative and voluntary commitment. As Gore himself says, "We can't run the business. We learned over twenty-five years ago to let the business run itself. Commitment, not authority, produces results." Indeed it does. Gore now has more than 4000 employees. To keep the focus on individual initiative and commitment, Gore has preserved what he calls a "lattice" organizational structure. "Certain attributes of the lattice can be defined: no fixed or assigned authority, sponsors rather than bosses, natural leadership defined by followership, person-to-person communication, objectives set by those who 'must make them happen,' tasks and functions organized through commitments. We don't manage people here, people manage themselves.... People promote themselves here...every time they take on a new responsibility, every time they get a big sale, every time they come up with a big invention."

To preserve this lattice structure, Gore creates a new plant whenever the number of associates at a given location approaches 200. Plants are also dispersed geographically so that people do not get in each other's way. The result of all this "self-management" is an enthusiastic workforce and remarkable growth. As Gore himself summarizes it, "People given freedom within the necessary creative restraints become unbelievably enthusiastic, energetic, and creative, achieving things that seem virtually inconceivable."[39]

This is but one illustration of a phenomenon now becoming increasingly

---

[39] See "The Heart Has Its (Business) Reasons," The Tarrytown Letter (November 1984), pp. 10-14; John Simons, "People Managing Themselves," 10 Journal for Quality and Participation 4 (December 1987), pp. 14-19; Virginia J. Vanderslice, "Separating Leadership from Leaders: An Assessment of the Effect of Leader and Follower Roles in Organizations," 41 Human Relations 9 (September 1988), pp. 677-696; and Amy Wegner, "Gore: An Innovative Philosophy," 80 Management Review 1 (January 1991), pp. 5-6.

common in the private sector.40 Among other firms now practicing somewhat varying versions of empowerment are Quad/Graphics, a graphic printing company, and Herman Miller, an office furniture company. Quad/Graphics, which prints such magazines as Newsweek and The Atlantic along with catalogues and rock album inserts, challenges its people to manage themselves without plans or corporate budgets, and through that extra responsibility to achieve much more than managers could ever have believed possible. This approach, which employees refer to as "Theory Q" after founder Harry Quadracci, has resulted in annual growth of about 40 percent since 1978.41 Herman Miller, using a participative administrative system which its chairman Max DePree calls "covenantal relationships," has grown by about 30 percent a year for a decade.42 Empowerment is also being tried occasionally in the public sector as well.43 And versions of it are also being attempted, often with understandably greater difficulty, in developing countries.44

Every instance of empowerment at work is somewhat unique, precisely because it grows out of the practice of granting authority, responsibility, and discretionary resources to any members of the particular organization who seem potentially able to handle them creatively and productively. Furthermore, not only the organizational settings, but also the individual psychologies of potential participants, and the collective cultures of the organizations vary from instance to instance. It seems reasonable to suppose that each of these elements could prove critical to the success or failure of any effort to employ the empowerment mode, but relevant experience is still being accumulated and evaluated. It is therefore impossible to say with certainty at this point how generally applicable a solution to the problems that concern us empowerment will prove to be.

Empowerment has not yet been developed into a concise set of general principles that active administrators can adopt to change their practices in order to maximize organizational productivity and creativity.45 Social scientists interested in improving both public sector and private sector administration can, however,

---

[40] See, for example, Todd Vogel, "Where 1990s-Style Management Is Already Hard at Work," Business Week (October 23, 1989), pp. 92-100.

[41] See Ellen Wojahn, "Management By Walking Away," Inc. (October 1983), pp. 68-76; Beverly Geber, "Not Just Another Printing Shop," Training (May 1988), pp. 65-69; and Daniel M. Kehrer, "The Miracle of Theory Q," Business Month (September 1989), pp. 44-49. Kehrer elaborates in his book Doing Business Boldly (New York: Times Books, 1989).

[42] See Kenneth Labich, "Hot Company, Warm Culture," Fortune (February 27, 1989), pp. 74-78, and Max DePree, Leadership Is an Art (New York: Doubleday, 1989).

[43] See Lionel Topaz, "Empowerment -- Human Resource Management in the 90's," 30 Management Quarterly 46 (Winter 1989/1990), pp. 3-8.

[44] See, for example, Peter M. Ngau, "Tensions in Empowerment: The Experience of the Harambee (Self-Help) Movement in Kenya," 35 Economic Development and Cultural Change 3 (April 1987), pp. 523-538.

[45] Growing numbers of books misleadingly claim to do this. See, for example, Lorne C. Plunkett and Robert Fournier, Participative Management: Implementing Empowerment (New York: Wiley, 1991). All too often, as in this book (page 5), the term empowerment is used casually to refer to the vesting of responsibility in teams or individuals as a way of fostering participative management. The closest approach to a set of practical guidelines that I have found is Jay A. Conger and Rabindra N. Kanungo, "The Empowerment Process: Integrating Theory and Practice," 13 The Academy of Management Review 3 (1988), pp. 471-482.

contribute by attempting to develop increasingly general guidelines, as the relevant experience with the approach accumulates.[46]

What is especially interesting for our purposes is that some adopt empowerment because it promises heightened innovation and productivity, while others adopt it because they believe it is the right way to treat the human beings who constitute the workforce.[47] It is rarely the case that a particular mode of administration meets both criteria, so administrators have generally thought it necessary to choose between competing objectives or weight one significantly higher than the other.[48]

Choice points such as this are the occasions for most political battles. They confront the political scientist deciding what to study, just as they confront the administrator deciding how to operate. Faced with competing objectives, or competing routes to the same objective, the organizational actor or scholar must assess not only efficiency and such other group objectives as humaneness, but also the ethical values of the anticipated alternative consequences. This complicates decision considerably. A great attraction of empowerment is that neither the actor nor the scholar seems likely to have to make such a choice between competing objectives because both efficiency and humaneness seem to be consequences of this approach, and this should simplify ethical evaluation as well.[49]

The effective and ethical reflective practitioner[50]

The fact that political scientists concerned with organizations may affect the actors in those organizations in ways that then alter the subjectmatter they study compounds and complexifies the issues of ethical responsibility in both domains. These issues are further intensified by the fact that both sets of actors are operating

---

[46] The most promising mode of research for this project, developed most extensively in education and organization studies, is usually called "action research." See, among many relevant studies, Alfred W. Clark, compiler, Experimenting with Organizational Life: The Action Research Approach (New York: Plenum, 1976); Richard Winter, Action-Research and the Nature of Social Inquiry: Professional Innovation and Educational Work (Aldershot: Gower, 1987); and Renee T. Clift, et.al., eds., Encouraging Reflective Practice in Education: An Analysis of Issues and Programs (New York: Teachers College Press, 1990). See also the related but somewhat different approach of Chris Argyris summarized in his "Research as Action: Usable Knowledge for Understanding and Changing the *Status Quo*", chapter 9 in Nigel Nicholson, et.al., eds., The Theory and Practice of Organizational Psychology (New York: Academic Press, 1982), as well as in many of his books.

[47] For evidence of some connection between these two sets of considerations, see Steven L. Sauter, et.al., eds., Job Control and Worker Health (New York: Wiley, 1989), and DePree, op.cit.

[48] See Edmund F. Byrne, Work, Inc.: A Philosophical Inquiry (Philadelphia: Temple University Press, 1990).

[49] For an argument that empowerment is a way for managers to fulfill their ethical obligation to be responsible for the development of their employees, see Rabindra N. Kanungo, "Alienation and Empowerment: Some Ethical Imperatives in Business," 11 Journal of Business Ethics (May 1992), pp. 413-422.

[50] This section has benefitted greatly from suggestions and insistences by Alessandra Lippucci, who is really its coauthor.

in an indeterminate world which they in part create. The uncertainty inherent in such a situation raises practical problems for organizational actors and political scientists alike.

The first concern, which is of special import to traditionalist political scientists, is the uncertainty about the determinants of political phenomena. Such political scientists still generally think of themselves as offering truths about the causal nature of political reality. Yet if that reality is essentially indeterminate, they cannot have great confidence in what they propound as political knowledge and offer as advice to political actors.

The second concern, which follows from the first, is the uncertainty that attaches to ethical considerations that might be applied in the process of selecting which projects to undertake and how to do them. How can ethical considerations which are indeterminate reliably inform this selection process? Furthermore, if indeterminacy is a problem political scientists face in assuming responsibility for their own professional actions, how can they begin to advise other actors about their professional activities?

The only real option open to political scientists, in my view, is to build upon the guidelines Donald Schon has outlined in *The Reflective Practitioner*.[51] Reflective practitioners, in his terms, are professionals, such as city planners, architects, psychiatrists, and development advisors, who have learned to operate effectively in conditions of uncertainty. They do this by constructing hypotheses about causal relations that they then test in the course of carrying out their projects. In effect, they act without knowing and learn while doing. Political scientists, organizational theorists, administrators, and other actors can learn to do the same.

There are two critical components involved. The practice must be reflective in the sense that it incorporates learning while doing--experimentally developing and testing and revising as necessary hypotheses about what will work. But the practice must also be reflexive in the sense that it takes account of the fact that the practical social theorizing will inform or influence the practice of actors and so it must try to take these effects into account in advance--to build these likely future effects into the practical theorizing that guides action. The models for social theorizing relevant here are "self-fulfilling and self-denying prophecies" in sociology and politics[52] and "reflexive prediction" in economics.[53]

Thus the appropriate practice might best be termed reflexive reflective practice.[54] But if this is the best answer we have to the challenge of practical theorizing for administration and other political action in conditions of uncertainty, is it also relevant to the making of ethical judgments that I am arguing must accompany and inform practical theorizing?

In a sense, the questions of effective practical action and ethical action really collapse into the same problem which the reflexive reflective practitioner addresses

---

[51] See Donald A. Schon, The Reflective Practitioner: How Professionals Think in Action (New York: Basic Books, 1983).

[52] See, for example, Russell A. Jones, Self-Fulfilling Prophecies: Social, Psychological, and Physiological Effects of Expectancies (Hillsdale, NJ: Lawrence Erlbaum, 1977), and Rebecca C. Curtis, ed., Self-Defeating Behavior (New York: Plenum, 1989), esp. chapter 1.

[53] See Emile Grunberg, "Predictability and Reflexivity," 45 American Journal of Economics and Sociology 4 (1986), pp. 475-488.

[54] I develop this argument in "The Theorist as Reflexive Reflective Practitioner," a paper presented at the 1990 annual meetings of the American Political Science Association, San Francisco.

in the practical process of learning while and by doing.[55] Because this learning process is likely to be full of surprises which necessitate redefining the problem at hand and how best to resolve it, ethical considerations must necessarily be equally flexible and revisable. Thus reflexive reflective practice has little use for the sort of broad ethical generalizations developed by Kantians and others who focus only on intentions, on the one hand, or by utilitarians and others who focus only on consequences, on the other, to guide individuals in all circumstances.

At best, these ethical generalizations combine to comprise the reflexive reflective practitioner's ethical repertoire in the same way that scientific and other generalizations comprise his or her practical repertoire. They are, in other words, tools to think with, but they cannot function as blanket solutions to the particular problem at hand.

Of more practical relevance or suggestiveness is the ethical tradition of casuistry, in which ethical decisions are approached on a case-by-case basis.[56] What we have when we tackle a unique problem is a unique case. What is required is a "situated ethics" that unfolds as the "situated solution" unfolds.

Clearly the uncertainties and challenges of reflexive reflective practice are considerable, but they are also exciting. Political scientists, organization theorists, and other actors who see the merits of operating according to its ethical and practical principles will contribute to the historical process in a self-conscious and responsible fashion. They can no longer subscribe to the myth of objectivism that makes them unconscious and irresponsible contributors to history. The decision to "practice" political science and to "practice" organizational life combines problem-solving with ethical action. This unites political scientists and other actors in the common cause of advancing human civilization in principled progressive directions.[57]

The practical nature of this advancement leaves no place for traditional ideology--be it political or epistemological. The fundamental operative principle of reflexive reflective practice is that, for all the practical and moral constraints imposed upon it by the problem at hand, it remains fully open in its choice of conceptual tools and experimental approaches.

Thus reflexive reflective practitioners function most effectively in political, social and economic contexts that give the greatest scope to their free-thinking pragmatism. Ultimately the best measure of democracy in any context--be it an academic discipline, an organization, or a society--may prove to be the number of reflexive reflective practitioners it cultivates. And ultimately the greatest strength of the empowerment mode of administration may prove to be that it is the best way to foster reflexive reflective practice, and over time to make reflexive reflective practitioners of us all.

---

[55] For interesting examinations of the learning process in organizations, see Peter M. Senge, The Fifth Discipline: The Art and Practice of the Learning Organization (New York: Doubleday, 1990), and Hendrik van der Zee, "Designing the Learning Organization: Building Learning Abilities into Organizations," chapter 15 in Merrick Jones & Pete Mann, eds., HRD: International Perspectives on Development and Learning (West Hartford, CT: Kumarian Press, 1992).

[56] See Camille Wells Slights, The Casuistical Tradition (Princeton: Princeton University Press, 1981) and the interesting recent book by Albert R. Jonsen and Stephen Toulmin, Abuse of Casuistry: A History of Moral Reasoning (Berkeley: University of California Press, 1988).

[57] I develop these ideas further in "Ethics, Efficiency, and Reflexive Reflective Practice," a paper presented at the Second International Conference on Public Service Ethics, Siena, Italy, June 1992.

CHAPTER THREE

PSYCHOLOGICAL OBSTACLES TO ADMINISTRATIVE RESPONSIBILITY: LESSONS OF THE MOVE DISASTER*

JACK H. NAGEL

Introduction

On May 13, 1985, a confrontation between Philadelphia police and a cult called MOVE resulted in one of the most astounding debacles in the history of American municipal government. After massive gunfire, deluges of water, and explosive charges failed to dislodge the group from their fortified row house, police dropped plastic explosives from a helicopter onto a rooftop bunker. The bomb ignited an unexpected fire. Believing they could contain the fire, Police Commissioner Gregore Sambor and Fire Commissioner William Richmond decided to let the bunker burn. They miscalculated badly, and the fire raged out of control. Sweeping through three adjoining blocks, the inferno destroyed 61 homes and left 250 people homeless. Of the occupants of the MOVE house, one adult and one child fled through the flames into police custody. In the ashes were found the bodies of six adults and five children.

The MOVE tragedy severely damaged the reputation of Philadelphia Mayor W. Wilson Goode, who until then had been considered an effective manager, a rising star of national politics, and a symbol of hope for his city. In the aftermath of the disaster, a controversial grand jury decided not to bring criminal charges against the mayor and his chief aides, but condemned them for "morally reprehensible behavior."[1] The Philadelphia Special Investigation Commission (PSIC), appointed by the mayor himself, charged that "the Mayor abdicated his responsibilities as a

---

* For assistance in obtaining material, I am grateful to the staff of the Philadelphia Free Library. For comments or other help, I wish to thank (among others) John Anderson, Randi Boyette, G. Edward DeSeve, John DiIulio, William Grigsby, John Harbeson, Elizabeth Logue, William Marimow, William F. Nagel, Michael O'Hare, Marc Howard Ross, Henry Ruth, David G. Smith, and Robin Wagner-Pacifici. Special thanks are due my students in the Master of Governmental Administration program at the Fels Center of Government, University of Pennsylvania. The papers they have written on this topic and discussions of it with them have influenced my thinking on numerous points. I of course remain responsible for all errors and interpretations.

[1] Philadelphia Court of Common Pleas, 1988, p. 279.

leader," a condemnation shared by most informed observers.[2] With respect to the twelve values Charles Gilbert [1959] identifies with administrative responsibility, Goode and his key subordinates conspicuously failed to satisfy at least seven--responsiveness, consistency, stability, leadership, competence, efficacy, and prudence.

None of the many commentators ever satisfactorily explained why the previously impressive mayor was so irresponsible in this instance and in particular why his behavior contrasted so sharply with his reputation for hands-on management. Many observers subsequently avoided the incongruity by concluding that Goode had simply been "incompetent" all along. Whereas before MOVE he could do no wrong, after the disaster he seldom got credit for doing anything right. This paper will argue instead that, lamentable though it was, the mayor's performance exemplifies universal tendencies well understood by psychologists of decisionmaking. Analysis of the MOVE case therefore can suggest insights that may enable other administrators to recognize and control situations in which they too might otherwise succumb to irresponsible patterns of action and inaction.

The presentation that follows is organized into five sections: (a) a brief history of MOVE and its conflict with the City of Philadelphia; (b) a description of two central paradoxes in Mayor Goode's response to MOVE; (c) an explanation of both paradoxes using a standard theory about the psychology of decisionmaking; (d) a closer examination of three decisional conflicts that may explain why Goode had such difficulty dealing with this particular problem; and (e) reflections on lessons the MOVE disaster offers for the education of present and future public managers.

MOVE versus Philadelphia

The origins of MOVE can be traced to the early 1970s in the Powelton Village section of West Philadelphia, near the campuses of Drexel University and the University of Pennsylvania.[3] In this tolerant community, a haven for political and

---

[2] Philadelphia Special Investigations Commission, 1985, Finding 22; see also Findings 3, 15, 17, and 24, which use comparable language. The PSIC is generally known as "the MOVE Commission."

[3] This account draws on the following sources, in addition to the author's knowledge as a resident of West Philadelphia during the period described: Philadelphia Special Investigation Commission [1986], which includes a chronology; Philadelphia Court of Common Pleas [1988], which includes a history of MOVE; Anderson and Hevenor [1987]; Assefa and Wahrhaftig [1988]; Bowser [1989]; and Boyette [1989]. Charles Bowser and Michael Boyette were, respectively, members of the MOVE Commission and the grand jury. The eighteen days of hearings the MOVE Commission conducted in October and November 1985 are my principal source [Philadelphia Special Investigation Commission, 1985]. Transcripts are available in the Government Publications Department of the Philadelphia Free Library and the Urban Archives Center of Temple University. There is a volume for each day of hearings, with pages numbered separately within each volume for morning and afternoon sessions. I supplemented the transcripts by watching videotapes of key witnesses' testimony. (The hearings were televised live by WHYY-TV, the PBS station in Philadelphia.) As this chapter was about to go to press, Wilson Goode's autobiography was published in Goode W. Wilson with Joann Stevens, In Goode Faith (Valley Forge, Pa.: Judson Press). Although it contains fascinating material, I have cited his book here only when it supplies or substantiates factual details.

cultural rebels, a charismatic black handyman named Vincent Leaphart developed an anarchistic, back-to-nature philosophy, the main tenets of which were reverence for all animal life, rejection of "the [American] Lifestyle," and absolute refusal to cooperate with "the System." Aided by a white graduate in social work from Penn named Donald Glassey, who transcribed Leaphart's thoughts and taught them in a course at the Community College of Philadelphia, Leaphart attracted a "family" that eventually numbered at least forty members, most but not all of whom were black. At first they called themselves the American Christian Movement for Life, but they later shortened the name to MOVE. Following the example of Leaphart, who now referred to himself as John Africa, all the core members adopted the surname Africa, in honor of the continent where they believed life began.

As they put John Africa's philosophy into practice, MOVE generated frequent tension with landlords and neighbors, who complained about members' grossly unsanitary practices and their harboring of dogs, cats, rats, roaches, and flies. Beyond these spillovers of their peculiar lifestyle, MOVE members courted friction with authorities by confronting "the System" in all its manifestations, from the Philadelphia Zoo to Jimmy Carter. Using bullhorns to demonstrate and disrupt meetings, they perfected a vituperative rhetoric, profane and filled with sexual and racial provocation. When brought to trial, as they were literally hundreds of times, MOVE members acted as their own attorneys and clogged the courts by noncooperative, contemptuous tactics.

During the 1970s, a virtual feud developed between MOVE and the Philadelphia police. The mayor of Philadelphia was then Frank Rizzo, a former police commissioner famous for tough law enforcement. The majority of whites revered Mayor Rizzo's large and aggressive police department as a bulwark against crime and disorder, but political dissidents, blacks, and journalists accused the police of frequent brutality and disregard for civil liberties. As Anderson and Hevenor[4] observe, "MOVE demonstrators were frequently arrested, often harassed, and nearly always regarded with unconcealed disgust and contempt by Philadelphia policemen. With their unwashed, garlic-reeking bodies, dreadlocks, and impenetrable and obscene harangues, MOVE people were a constant affront to a police force that was (and is) largely white, ethnic ... and Catholic."[5]

After a melee in March 1976, when MOVE accused the police of causing the death of a MOVE infant, John Africa apparently decided to turn to armed resistance. By this time, core members of MOVE occupied a house owned by Glassey on North 33rd Street. Using loudspeakers fixed in trees, they frequently harangued their neighbors. Responding to complaints, city officials attempted to investigate code violations but were refused admittance. In September 1975, the city began the protracted process of enforcing the code through the courts. A judgment mandating inspections was obtaining in July 1976, whereupon MOVE constructed an eight-foot stockade around their compound. Heeding MOVE warnings that they would "cycle" (kill) their own children before submitting to inspections, the city refrained from enforcing the order. On May 20, 1977, mistakenly anticipating a city attempt to enter the premises, MOVE members brandished guns on the platform of their stockade. Shortly afterwards, Donald Glassey was arrested for filing false information when purchasing firearms. Turning informant to save himself, Glassey

---

[4] John Anderson and Hilary Hevenor, Burning Down the House: Move and the Tragedy of Philadelphia (New York: W.W. Norton and Co., 1987).

[5] See also the testimony of Laverne Sims (PSIC, 1985, 10/10 AM, pp. 65-77).

helped police seize MOVE guns and explosives at a location elsewhere in Philadelphia.

The stalemate in Powelton continued for nearly a year. On March 1, 1978, the city obtained court permission to blockade the MOVE headquarters for nonpayment of utility bills and refusal to admit inspectors. Police cordoned off a four-block area around the house and shut off gas and water. The siege appeared to have succeeded when intermediaries helped negotiate a settlement that was announced on May 3. MOVE surrendered weapons, allowed officials to inspect the Powelton property, and promised to vacate the house by August 1. In return, the city relaxed its blockade, freed eighteen jailed MOVE members on their own recognizance, and promised to drop all charges once MOVE departed from Powelton.

When August 1 came, MOVE refused to leave, because no one had found a site for relocation they would accept. On August 8, Police Commissioner Joseph O'Neill directed a carefully planned operation to drive the occupants from the house. Announcing each action in advance in order to protect MOVE women and children, whom they regarded as hostages, the police used a bulldozer, ram, and armored truck to breach the walls of the compound. A crane began demolishing the upper stories. Believing that all MOVE weapons had been confiscated in May, authorities were careless about concealing themselves. Suddenly, police saw a gun muzzle protruding from a basement window. After deluge guns flooded the basement, gunfire erupted, killing Officer James Ramp and wounding eight other policemen and firefighters. Following the exchange of shots, police poured in more water and smoke to flush out the occupants. As the MOVE members surrendered, officers beat and kicked Delbert Africa while news photographers recorded the action.

During the next five years, MOVE was visible to most Philadelphians only through a series of trials. In 1980, nine members were sentenced to lengthy prison terms for the murder of Officer Ramp; a tenth followed in 1982. In 1981, three police officers were tried for the beating of Delbert Africa and acquitted.[6] On May 13, 1981, Federal agents arrested John Africa and eight followers in Rochester, New York, where MOVE had owned houses since 1977. (At various times, MOVE also had enclaves in Richmond, Virginia, and Chester, Pennsylvania.) Defending himself and Alphonso Robbins Africa against bombmaking charges, John Africa won acquittal from a jury in Philadelphia in July 1981, after which he dropped out of sight.

As it turned out, the MOVE leader had not gone far. With a group of about a dozen adults and children, he was living in a house owned by his sister, Louise James, at 6221 Osage Avenue in the Cobbs Creek section on the western edge of Philadelphia, three miles from the site of the demolished house in Powelton.

Whereas the 33rd Street house had been a free-standing structure surrounded by a yard and located on a busy street, the new MOVE headquarters was a row house on a narrow, quiet residential street. These physical differences were to prove tactically important during the 1985 confrontation, but events in the two years preceding that catastrophe pivoted around social and political differences between the two neighborhoods. Nonconformist, racially mixed Powelton was a bastion of opposition to Mayor Rizzo. Its residents divided bitterly over whether the cultists or

---

[6] District Attorney Edward Rendell later blamed the acquittal on the invective and curses that Delbert directed at the judge and jury (PSIC, 1985, 10/22 AM, pp. 119-20). In 1992, Rendell succeeded Wilson Goode as mayor of Philadelphia.

the police were the more distasteful presence in their midst. One can easily imagine Frank Rizzo enjoying some amusement at their discomfort.

In 1980, barred by the City Charter from serving three consecutive terms, Rizzo was succeeded as mayor by the more liberal former Congressman, William J. Green, Jr. Fulfilling a campaign promise to Philadelphia's increasingly powerful black voters, Green appointed W. Wilson Goode as Managing Director, the city's chief appointive official. Goode, a former civil-rights activist, had previously served as executive director of the nonprofit Philadelphia Council for Community Advancement -- where he was credited with building more housing than all the city's housing agencies combined[7] -- and as chair of the Pennsylvania Public Utilities Commission. As Managing Director, Goode was in charge of ten operating departments, including police and fire. Hard-working, accessible, and highly visible, he soon became hugely popular among blacks and many whites as well. When Green announced in late 1982 that he would not seek a second term, Goode resigned to campaign for the mayoralty. In May 1983, he defeated Frank Rizzo in the Democratic primary, winning the votes of 98% of blacks and 23% of whites. In the November general election, he would face two white opponents.

The Cobbs Creek neighborhood was typical of Wilson Goode's bedrock political base. Its residents, almost all black, were generally stable working- and middle-class families. Most owned their homes and took pride in keeping them pleasant and attractive. By the fall of 1983, MOVE had become an intolerable affliction to this peaceful community. The home of Lloyd and Lucretia Wilson next door was invaded by insects that had spread from 6221. When the Wilsons sought to fumigate, Conrad Africa went berserk. "The bugs are our bothers and sisters. If you exterminate the bugs, you exterminate us," he berated Lloyd Wilson [PSIC, 1985, 10/9 AM, pp. 89-90]. In September 1983, following a dispute over a parking space, a MOVE male struck a neighbor named Butch Marshall to the ground, and three MOVE women bit Marshall on the face, back, and groin. After another assault in October, the neighbors circulated to city authorities a petition that complained about attacks, garbage, rats, a pigeon coop, animals, and MOVE's blocking of a common driveway behind the row.

As the neighbors "were reaching the breaking point," they met with State Representative Peter Truman.[8] Truman implored them not to do anything that would endanger the election of the city's first black mayor. If they would endure a few months longer, he assured them, Goode would solve their problem. Aided by the arrival of cold weather, which lessened health hazards and reduced outdoor interaction with MOVE, the neighbors waited. In November 1983, Goode won a resounding victory with 55% of the vote.

If Goode's triumph held promise of deliverance for the 6200 block, John Africa saw it as a different sort of opportunity, one that would produce intensified torment for the Osage neighbors. Obsessed with freeing his followers from prison, the MOVE leader believed that the mayor had the power to obtain their release and that the residents of Osage Avenue could persuade him to use that power. MOVE therefore embarked upon a campaign of what Goode later would call "psychological

---

[7] Roger Cohn, "Wilson Goode Has Something to Prove," Today Magazine, Philadelphia Inquirer (July 25), pp. 10ff.

[8] PSIC, 1985, 10/8 PM, p. 104. In Philadelphia at the time there were 28 districts for the lower house of the state legislature compared with only 10 councilmanic districts; thus the state representative was often the elected official closest to the people of a neighborhood.

warfare" against their neighbors, holding the block "hostage" in order to obtain as ransom the release of their ten convicted comrades. MOVE launched their campaign on Christmas morning, 1983. Beginning near dawn and continuing for eight hours, their rooftop loudspeakers blared an obscene diatribe that denounced the neighbors, the mayor-elect, and the System, and demanded freedom for MOVE prisoners. Eight days later, Wilson Goode became mayor of Philadelphia.

Two paradoxes

Mayor Goode's response to MOVE's challenge can be characterized by describing two patterns, both of which seem paradoxical. First, for sixteen months he avoided any significant action; but when he finally decided to enforce the law, the city mobilized against MOVE in less than a week and tried to execute a hastily prepared plan in the span of twenty-four hours. Second, although he was widely perceived to be an energetic, detail-oriented administrator, when he decided the city should act against MOVE, Goode had minimal personal involvement in both the planning and the execution of the attack.

Delay followed by haste

MOVE's war against the System, by way of their neighbors, continued through 1984 and the spring of 1985. In December 1983, they began fortifying their house by nailing boards across windows; the ramshackle effect contrasted starkly with the neat white trim and porches of the other houses. In October 1984 they started a rooftop construction that eventually became a bunker made of railroad ties, logs, and steel plates. Similar materials were placed against the interior walls of the house and basement. In May 1984, a hooded MOVE member brandished a shotgun on the roof, and the cultists began the practice of running across the row at night, waking frightened residents. Loudspeaker harangues were conducted daily for six to eight hours through the summer and fall of 1984. In these and other communications, MOVE members threatened the lives of President Reagan, Mayor Goode, judges, and any police officers who might try to enforce the law on Osage Avenue. A favorite tactic was to target a particular neighbor for a day, during which the unfortunate individual would be subjected to personal attacks filled with accusations of homosexuality, child molestation, promiscuity, or sexual inadequacy. As Bennie Swans of the Crisis Intervention Network later commented, "MOVE did not let up on those residents. They simply did not let up."[9]

Mayor Goode was aware of most of these developments. On March 9, 1984, Commissioner Sambor briefed him about the deteriorating situation on Osage Avenue. On May 28 and July 4, he met at their request with delegations of residents; they found the mayor knowledgeable about their plight and personally familiar with MOVE members, but unwilling to act. In June 1984, District Attorney Edward Rendell provided Goode with a memo outlining a legal strategy for disarming MOVE and abating the nuisance of Osage Avenue. Goode also received several phone calls from block captain Clifford Bond. On August 9, Lloyd Wilson came to City Hall to complain of an assault he had suffered the day before at the hands of Frank James Africa, while police officers watched from the corner. Goode "whisked" Wilson off to a side office, where he had a lengthy but unproductive conversation with Managing Director Leo Brooks and Commissioner Sambor.

---

[9] Philadelphia special Investigations Commision Hearings (1985: pp. 68).

Subsequently, Wilson and his family abandoned their home, driven our by vermin, noise, and fear from which their government would not protect them.

During this time city policy barred operating departments (including Health, Water, Human Services, Streets, and Licenses and Inspections) from carrying out their responsibilities with respect to MOVE, which they were told was "a police matter." For their part, the police maintained surveillance of the 6200 block, but refrained from intervention. They even discouraged state parole officials from serving outstanding fugitive warrants against two residents of the house, Frank James Africa and Larry Howard.[10] In response to the neighbors' entreaties, Goode took only two tangible actions: He extended the hours of nearby city recreation centers so residents' children could escape the loudspeakers, and he arranged psychological counseling to help the children cope with chronic tension.

Five of the MOVE Commissions's findings describe and condemn this protracted phase of inaction:

3. Mayor Goode's policy toward MOVE was one of appeasement, non-confrontation, and avoidance.

4. The Managing Director and the city's department heads failed to take any effective action on their own and, in fact, ordered their subordinates to refrain from taking action to deal meaningfully with the problem on Osage Avenue. . . .

6. In the first several months of his administration, the mayor was presented with compelling evidence that his policy of appeasement, non-confrontation, and avoidance was doomed to fail.

7. In the summer of 1984, the mayor was told that the legal basis existed at that time to act against certain MOVE members. Yet, the mayor held back, and continued to follow his policy of avoidance and non-confrontation.

8. From the fall of 1984 to the spring of 1985, the city's policy of appeasement conceded to the residents of 6221 Osage Ave. the continued right to exist above the law.[11]

To this indictment should be added two more charges. First, by tolerating MOVE's abuses, the city government for two years abdicated its most basic responsibilities to the law-abiding residents of Osage Avenue. As Clifford Bond put it, "I was placed in a position of feeling not as a citizen."[12] Second, by giving MOVE time to fortify their house, the policy of nonconfrontation made the task of dislodging the cult immensely more difficult when the mayor finally decided to act.

Sixteen months of delay abruptly gave way to fourteen days of hasty action in the spring of 1985. The shift in policy was precipitated by the neighbors. Unwilling to accept another summer of stench and harangues, they organized themselves as the United Residents of the 6200 Block of Osage Avenue and held a

---

[10] Philadelphia Court of Common Pleas, Report of the County Investigating Grand Jury of May 15 (May 15 1986, pp. 26).

[11] Philadelphia Special Investigations Commision, Findings, Conclusions and Recommendations. (1986:9, pp. 11-13).

[12] Philadelphia Special Investigations Commission, Hearings (1985: 10/9 AM, p. 4).

public protest meeting on April 25, during which several men announced they would respond to MOVE "in kind." At a May 1 press conference, the United Residents expressed their disgust with the city's inaction and requested intervention by Pennsylvania Governor Dick Thornburgh, a Republican. Coupled with new provocations by MOVE, these actions got the attention of the media, and editorialists demanded that the city meet its responsibilities.

On May 3, Mayor Goode convened a high-level meeting at which he asked District Attorney Edward Rendell to establish a legal basis for city action against the occupants of 6221. On May 5 Rendell's staff interviewed Osage residents in order to prepare warrants. At a second high-level meeting on May 7, Goode directed Commissioner Sambor to develop a plan that was to be carried out under the supervision of Managing Director Leo Brooks, a former Army major general.

Having anticipated action, Sambor had set up a planning group a week earlier. Remarkably low in rank for such a major operation, it consisted of three men who had served under Sambor in his previous post as commander of the Police Academy: Lieutenant Frank Powell, head of the Bomb Disposal Unit; Sergeant Albert Revel, a pistol instructor; and Officer Michael Tursi, the Department's top sharpshooter.

On May 9, with Managing Director Brooks at his daughter's graduation in Virginia, Sambor briefed Goode on the plan the three officers had devised. He recommended that warrants be served on Sunday, May 12, which was Mother's Day. Out of concern for the holiday, Goode authorized Sambor to proceed on May 13. On May 11, a judge issued warrants, and Sambor again briefed Goode. On the afternoon of May 12, police evacuated the neighborhood. Returning from Virginia that evening, Brooks heard on his car radio that the operation he was to head was underway. He arrived in Philadelphia in time to get a quick briefing from Sambor followed by a few hours' sleep.

At 5:35 a.m. on Monday, May 13, Sambor read an ultimatum to MOVE over a bullhorn, demanding that the four MOVE members named on the warrants surrender within fifteen minutes. MOVE used their own loudspeaker to reject the ultimatum in typical style, telling the police that their wives would be collecting insurance and sleeping with black men that night. When the fifteen minutes had expired, authorities directed water, tear gas, and smoke at the house, and its roof. According to the police, MOVE responded with gunfire, and officers retaliated massively, firing many thousands of rounds in the next ninety minutes. The debacle was underway.

As the MOVE commission and the grand jury pointed out, less hurried planning and execution might have prevented numerous errors and oversights. A full list would occupy many pages, so I shall mention just a few of the more egregious consequences of haste:

Commissioner Sambor and his planners made little attempt to draw on the resources of other agencies, inside or outside the city government; consequently, they failed to consider alternative strategies and deprived themselves of expertise -- such as the use of trained hostage negotiators -- that might have resulted in better implementation of their plan.

Goode, Sambor, and Brooks went ahead with the operation even though they knew that the mayor's directive to pick up the MOVE children before the assault had not been implemented. (MOVE adults usually took the children on daily outings to nearby Cobbs Creek Park, and as late as May 12, two of the children were observed outside the house). Thus they "clearly risked the lives" of six innocent children, five of whom subsequently died in the conflagration.[13]

The quick, secretive, informal planning process deprived the tacticians of crucial knowledge possessed by others in city government, including surveillance officers. As a result, to take just one example, they did not appreciate the extent of the interior fortifications that foiled their initial strategy of attempting to insert tear gas through the walls.

Contingency plans were not developed; the final, fatal decision to drop the bomb was the result of ill-considered improvisation. After the primary plan failed, officials were apparently determined to occupy the house before dark. When Brooks informed Goode of the bomb proposal by telephone at 5 p.m., the mayor paused only thirty seconds before approving the idea.

Insufficient attention was given to communication systems, resulting in slow, incompatible, or nonexistent communication channels between crucial actors -- police and the occupants of the MOVE house, police and fire units, the mayor and managing director, and the managing director and police commissioner. Slow communications may have prevented Goode and Brooks from reversing in time Sambor's and Richmond's decision to let the bunker burn.

Arms-length action by a hands-on Mayor

Until May 1985, both as Managing Director and as Mayor, Wilson Goode was perceived by the public as an incredibly hard-working, demanding, detail-oriented manager. Contemporary press descriptions give a vivid sense of his style: "He appears to be everywhere. . . He annoys a lot of people because he continues to ask questions until he gets an answer that makes sense."[14] "He loves to come down hard on details."[15] "His zeal is prodigious, his double digit days are legend. . ."[16] "Today, in Philadelphia, in the first year of Wilson Goode's first term of office, there is absolutely no doubt about who is in charge."[17] Indeed, one of the few criticisms of Goode in this happy period was that he delegated too little: "He seeks near-absolute control over his operating department."[18] "He has an aversion to delegating authority. He tries to do too much on his own."[19]

Goode's view of himself corresponded to the public image: "I want to know what the problems are in this city. . . I can't do that sitting on the 16th floor here, I

---

[13] Philadelphia Special Investigations Commission, Findings, Conclusions and Recommendations (1986), p. 6.
[14] Cohn, 1982, p. 27. The second sentence is a quotation from Shirley Hamilton, Goode's chief of staff.
[15] Mike Mallowe, "And Now, the Goode News," Philadelphia Magazine 71 [p. 139].
[16] Ron Javers, "On the Run: Lunch with Wilson Goode," Philadelphia Magazine 74 (April 1983), p. 8.
[17] Mike Mallowe, "The No-Frills Mayor," Philadelphia Magazine 75 (1984, p. 168).
[18] Roger Cohn, "Wilson Goode Has Something to Prove," Today Magazine, Philadelphia Inquirer (1982, p. 21).
[19] Mike Mallowe, The No-FrillsMayor," Philadelphia Magazine 75 (1984, p. 226).

really can't."20 "Someone has to be in charge. People through the government must know that the mayor is there giving directions. . ."21 "I'm a nuts-and-bolts person."22 Perhaps his favorite term was "hands-on."

However, after he authorized an armed confrontation with MOVE, Goode was anything but hands-on. He held only two high-level meetings to plan the operation. The May 7 meeting focused on the legal basis for action, and the May 9 meeting lasted less than thirty minutes. On both occasions, Goode prevented detailed discussion of the police plan. The contrast in styles was pointed out to the MOVE Commission by District Attorney Rendell:

> And I turned to the [Police] Commissioner and I said, "Are you going to use tear gas and water? And he said yes and started to explain a little bit, and the Mayor said . . ., "Look, I will leave that up to you all. Its your plan and execute it." In other words, he cut off discussion. . . . And I thought it was somewhat unusual. . . . I had known Wilson for the three years that he was Managing Director. I worked very closely with him . . ., and then while he was Mayor I had significantly contact with him. Wilson's management style has always been one where he got involved in all -- not in all of the details, but in certainly the significant details. And I thought that was . . . a little out of character. . . . 23

Rendell speculated that Goode wished to avoid leaks, that perhaps he "intended as soon as I walked out of the room to sit down and go over it blow by blow with the Police Commissioner."24 In fact, Sambor did brief Goode about the plan on May 11, but only because Brooks was out of town -- at all other times, including May 13, Goode and Sambor strictly followed the chain of command, communicating with each other only through Brooks. Goode seems not to have been deeply engaged in the May 11 meeting, for he recalled it as occurring over the telephone, whereas Sambor testified in detail that he went to Goode's office.25 Goode's last briefing was by telephone on the evening of May 12, when Brooks called him to relay the discussion he had just had with the Police Commissioner.

On May 13 itself, Goode heeded the advice of his staff and Brooks by staying away not only from Osage Avenue, but also from Brooks' command post four blocks north at the Walnut Park Plaza, the tallest structure in the area. As the operation began, Goode followed developments together with four black elected officials whom he had invited to this home in Overbrook, about two miles from Osage Avenue. Later, in his office at City Hall, he was understandably preoccupied with MOVE. Although the mayor frequently conferred by phone with Brooks,

---

20 Roger Cohn, "Wilson Goode Has something to Prove," Today Magazine, Philadelphia Inquirer (1982, p.13].

21 Mike Mallowe, "The No-Frills Mayor," Philadelphia Magazine 75 (1984, p. 168].

22 Mike Mallowe, "And Now, the Goode News," Philadelphia Magazine 71(1980, p. 139).

23 Philadelphia Special Invesrigations Commision, Hearings (1985, 10/22 AM, p.95).

24 In his autobiography, Goode writes that Managing Director Brooks prompted him to cut short the discussion because Rendell "talks too much," W. Wilson Goode with Joann Stevens, In Goode Faith (Valley Forge, PA: Judson Press, 1992).

25 In his autobiography, W. Wilson Goode with Joann Stevens, In Goode Faith (Valley Forge, PA: Judson Press, 1992) relocates the meeting to his office.

Goode's distance from the scene and the clumsiness of his communication links prevented him from exercising effective control over the terrible events of that day.

In short, as the MOVE Commission concluded, "The mayor failed to perform his responsibility as the city's chief executive by not actively participating in the preparation, review and oversight of the plan."[26]

Irresponsibility and decisional conflict

In 1977, eight years before the MOVE disaster, the psychologist Irving Janis and Leon Mann published a treatise called Decision Making.[27] In it, they outlined a model based on psychological conflict that economically explains the two central paradoxes in Wilson Goode's actions, as well as many otherwise puzzling subsidiary aspects of his behavior during this tragic episode.

Janis and Mann premise their theory on the idea that decisionmaking is not merely a cool intellectual process but also involves "hot" emotional influences. The need to make a decision is inherently stressful. Although moderate anxiety improves cognitive functioning, excessive stress can severely impair the quality of decision processes. The greatest stress occurs when all known options threaten to impose severe losses, especially if those losses are not merely "utilitarian" but include "highly ego-involving issues," such as severe social disapproval and/or self-disapproval.[28]

When a decision maker is faced with an emotionally consequential, no-win choice, how he or she copes with the problem depends crucially on two factors--hope and time. If the decision maker sees realistic hope of finding a solution superior to any of the risky options that are immediately apparent, then that person's efforts are likely to follow the desirable pattern Janis and Mann call vigilance, which is close kin to the familiar rational-comprehensive ideal. The vigilant decision maker canvasses a wide set of alternatives; considers the full range of goals and values involved; carefully weighs costs, risks, and benefits; intensively seeks and accurately assimilates new information; reexamines all alternatives before

---

[26] Philadelphia Special Investigations Commission, Findings Conclusions and Recommendations (1986, p. 16).

[27] Janis is better known among students of politics, policy, and management for his earlier work on "groupthink" [Irving L. Janis, Victims of Groupthinking (Boston: Houghton Mifflin, 1972)]. Elements of groupthink can be found in various official groups involved in the MOVE problem, but the full-blown syndrome does not appear, perhaps because the mayor's interpersonal style inhibited development of the requisite emotional cohesiveness. (Like other cults, MOVE itself exhibited a virulent form of groupthink.) Janis's work on organizational decisions has developed from the specific to the general. In Decision Making, he and Mann depict groupthink as a collective version of the broader phenomenon of defensive avoidance, which in turn is part of a "conflict model" based on psychological stress. In his latest book, Crucial Decisions (Janis, 1989), the conflict model becomes a component of a still more general "constraints model." The comprehensiveness of the constraint model is a virtue for some purposes, but I believe the paradoxical features of the MOVE case explained best by the conflict model.. Thus my account relies more on Decision Making than on Crucial Decisions.

[28] Irving l. Janis and Leon Mann, Decision Making: A Psychological Analysis of Conflict, Choice and Commitment (New York: The Free Press, 1977), p. 46.

settling on a final choice; makes detailed provisions for implementing the chosen course; and devotes special attention to contingency plans.[29]

If however, a decision maker loses hope of finding an acceptable option, he or she is likely to fall into either of two patterns of seriously defective search and appraisal. The first and more common syndrome, called defensive avoidance, typically occurs when there is no overwhelming pressure to change the existing policy even though its consequences are (like those of all other alternatives) highly unfavorable. The chief symptoms of defensive avoidance are procrastination, passing the buck and other ways of denying personal responsibility, and bolstering.[30] "Bolstering" is a process of cognitive distortion in which one "spreads" or exaggerates the value of the chosen course compared to alternatives by avoiding exposure to disturbing information, selective attention and recall, wishful thinking, oversimplification, rationalization, and denial.

Defensive avoidance "satisfies a powerful emotional need - to avoid anticipatory fear, shame, and guilt."[31] Its emotional benefit is a state of "pseudocalm", resulting from the decision maker's suppression of troubling thoughts and avoidance of stimuli that might evoke the painful dilemma.

When external pressures impose a deadline or threaten an imminent disaster if the existing policy is maintained, the state of pseudocalm is shattered and the underlying conflict breaks through to the surface, arousing unbearable emotional stress. In such circumstances, the decision maker is likely to respond with the pattern of behavior Janis and Mann call hypervigilance.[32] Responding to "the strong desire to take action in order to alleviate emotional tension," the hypervigilant decision maker "superficially scans the most obvious alternatives open to him. . . , hastily choosing the first one that seems to hold the promise of escaping the worst danger."[33] Like defensive avoidance, hypervigilance involves severely defective search and appraisal:

A person in this state experiences so much cognitive constriction and perseveration that his thought processes are disrupted. The person's immediate memory span is reduced and his thinking becomes more simplistic. . . . [T]he person in a state of hypervigilance fails to recognize all the alternatives open to him and fails to use whatever remaining time is available to evaluate adequately those alternatives of which he is aware. He is likely to search frantically for a solution, persevere in his thinking about a limited number of alternatives, and then latch onto a

---

[29] Irving l. Janis and Leon Mann, Decision Making : A Psychological Analysis of Conflict, Choice and Commitment (New York: The Free Press, 1977), p. 11.

[30] Irving L. Janis, Crucial Decisions: Leadership in Policymaking and Crisis Management (New York: The Free Press, 1989), p. 80.

[31] Irving L. Janis and Leon Mann, Decision Making: A Psychological Analysis of Conflict, Choice and Commitment (New York: The Free Press, 1977), p. 85.

[32] The choice of words is unfortunate, because the authors use "vigilance" for their ideal problem-solving process; thus, "hypervigilance" suggests too much of a good thing. The hyervigilant actor exhibits too much emotional arousal and too much haste, but no true vigilance.

[33] Irving L. Janis and Leon Mann, Decision Making: A Psychological Analysis of Conflict, Choice and Commitment (New York: The Free Press, 1977), pp. 47, 74.

hastily contrived solution that seems to promise immediate relief, often at the cost of considerable postdecisional regret.³⁴

An explanation for the first paradox of Wilson Goode's behavior toward MOVE should now be obvious. His delay/haste pattern is a textbook example of defensive avoidance followed by hypervigilance. The two stages are not really paradoxical, because they resulted from the same underlying decisional conflict. As Janis and Mann³⁵ observe, a "person's defensive avoidance pattern might abruptly change to hypervigilance if he encounters a new, dramatic danger signal." The mobilization of the Osage neighbors signaled to Goode that a continued policy of nonconfrontation would be fraught with new, unacceptable dangers -- a certainty of severe political embarrassment and a high probability of unofficial violence against MOVE. The mayor was forced to act, and in his state of hypervigilance, he accepted the first option presented to him -- the ill-fated proposal devised by Sambor's planners.

But why was the MOVE problem in particular so difficult for Wilson Goode to handle, when he had been able to deal effectively with many other issues in a distinguished career of public service? Janis and Mann³⁶ [1977, p. 75] contend that both vigilant and defective patterns of problem solving are within the repertoire of every decision maker. Anyone, they believe, can fluctuate from one pattern to another depending not only on the objective circumstances of action, but also on the relation of those circumstances to personal values and affiliations, which determine whether actions and outcomes will be conducive to self-esteem and social approval for a particular individual. To explain the second paradox, it will therefore be necessary to look more closely at Wilson Goode, as well as at the fine details of his decision processes with respect to MOVE.

The Mayor's decisional conflicts

Goode's testimony to the MOVE Commission, coupled with other evidence about his personality and values, suggest that the drama on Osage Avenue aroused within the mayor severe conflicts that he was never able to resolve. Instead he in effect fled from them, with the result that he virtually abdicated his responsibility as the city's chief administrator.³⁷ The mayor's conflicts may be summarized as three dilemmas: (1) MOVE's intransigence and irrationality appeared to necessitate the use of force that would almost surely end in bloodshed, but Goode saw himself as a peacemaker and a preserver of life; (2) to enforce the law against MOVE would require the mayor to depend on the Philadelphia Police Department, but the police might well be unreliable, among other reasons because his own relationship with them was uneasy and because many of them hated MOVE; (3) as a black man committed to a policy of respecting civil rights, Goode felt dissonance about authorizing official coercion of a black group; but MOVE's bizarre behavior must

---

³⁴ Irving L. Janis and Leon Mann, Decision Making: A Psychological Analysis of Conflict, Choice and Commitment (New York: The Free Press, 1977), p. 51.

³⁵ Ibid., p. 66.

³⁶ Ibid., p. 75.

³⁷ Although based as much as possible on published materials, the analysis that follows is necessarily inferential and speculative.

also have aroused in him anger that he would have difficulty acknowledging, given his religious values and self-image as a controlled person.

Blood on the hands of a peacemaker

At first glance, Goode's desire to avoid action against MOVE appears readily understandable. In retrospect, everyone saw Osage Avenue as a no-win situation. If the city refrained from confronting MOVE, the cultists would make life intolerable for their neighbors. If the city attempted to enforce the laws, MOVE would respond violently, producing a high probability of death. District Attorney Rendell described the effect of this realization on the emotions of participants in the crucial meeting:

> I have attended a lot of meetings since I have been in public life, but I never ever had attended a meeting that had the impact on me that my meeting on Thursday, May 7, 1985 did, when in fact the plan of action was signed, sealed and delivered; when the arrest warrants and the search warrants were approved, signed by a judge; when we had picked a time and date to act; when we knew it was going to occur. There was almost a dread in that room so thick that you could have cut it with a knife. Because, understand, every one of us in that room knew that someone -- there was an extraordinarily high likelihood that someone was going to die.[38]

Nevertheless, to some politicians the MOVE problem might have seemed a golden opportunity. Throughout history, leaders have won popularity by unleashing violence against unpopular enemies, foreign or domestic. By 1985, MOVE had alienated virtually everyone in Philadelphia. Confronting them would have cost Goode little if any support among his black political base, because the neighbors who were pleading for relief were not only black but also representative of his most reliable constituency. MOVE instead offered Goode an excellent chance to broaden his already impressive popularity, because forceful action against them in the name of law and order would have appealed most to those whites who were not yet part of his coalition.

Goode himself noted the political value of decisive leadership. Asked at the MOVE commission hearings whether his staff's advice that he stay away from the scene of action was "substantive or political or both," he replied:

> I thought it was substantive. I don't think that it .... had anything to do with politics. From my vantage point, both in foresight and hindsight, . . .it is far better for a Mayor to be perceived as being out there on the scene with hands-on than not to be and, therefore, from a political point of view I think I lose points. . . .[39]

In fact, despite the debacle, polls in the aftermath of May 13 showed strong public support for Goode's decision to act against MOVE. His approval ratings did

---

[38] Philadelphia Special Investigations Commission, Hearings (1985:10/22 AM, 34).
[39] Philadelphia Special Investigations Commission, Hearings (1985:10/15 AM, p.94).

not drop precipitously until the fall of 1985, when information revealed by the hearings made him appear inept, irresponsible, and evasive.[40]

True, as 1978 and the aftermath of 1985 showed, the public would be distressed at death to innocent parties -- police, firefighters, or MOVE children. Police officers and firefighters do, however, accept mortal risks as part of their jobs; and, forewarned by MOVE's treachery in 1978, they could more carefully protect themselves from gunshots.[41] As for the children, if Gocde had insisted on implementation of his explicit order to pick them up before commencing the operation, they probably could have been saved. Thus the people most likely to die in a properly planned and executed operation were MOVE adults. Most Philadelphians perceived them as dangerous, deranged, and incorrigible; their deaths in resisting legitimate authorities would have been mourned by few and welcomed by many.

Although the conclusion of this cold political logic might not have troubled most citizens, it appears to have been unacceptable for Wilson Goode. Perhaps the most revealing moment of his testimony to the MOVE Commission came when he was asked to describe his emotions as his office television showed the fire raging out of control:

> I went through very deep emotions at that time. I cried because I knew at that point that lives would be lost, and I knew that homes would be destroyed and I knew that despite all of our good intentions, that we had. . . an absolute disaster. And I can't explain to you or to anyone the kind of emotions that I went through, because everything about me is about preserving life and to know that any plan that I've had anything to do with would, in fact, bring about the cessation of life, was very tough.[42]

There are independent reasons for believing the sincerity of Goode's statement. Widely regarding as a deeply religious man, he has been a devoted and active member of the First Baptist Church of Paschall since 1955, serving during most of this time as a deacon and lay leader of the congregation. Well into adult life , he seriously considered entering the ministry. On his pastor's advice, he prayed for guidance. "I came away feeling strongly that I was called," he said later. "But it was a ministry of a different kind, a ministry of public service." An early profiler wrote, "His whole notion of public service is grounded in his faith, and he approaches his work at City Hall with almost an evangelical fervor."[43]

Indeed, most of Goode's career exhibits a marked inclination toward conciliation and peacemaking. As a community activist in the 1960s and early

---

[40] Amy Wilenz, "Goode's Intentions," Time 125 (1985: May 27, p. 22); William K. Stevens, "Mayor Goode's Once-Solid Path turns Rocky in Philadelphia," New York Times (October 23, 1985).

[41] On May 13, only one police officer was struck by a MOVE bullet, and a bulletproof vest saved him from serious harm. A policy of protecting firefighters from possible MOVE gunfire was one reason the fire spread so fast and so far. Having vowed that no firefighter would face gunfire, Fire Commissioner William Richmond deliberately chose to sacrifice property in order to save lives (Goodman, 1989).

[42] Philadelphia Special Investigations Commission, Hearings (1985: 10/15 PM, p. 95).

[43] Roger Cohn, "Wilson Goode Has Something to Prove," Today Magazine, Philadelphia Inquirer (July 25, 1982), p. 13.

1970s, "his low-key manner usually helped keep potentially explosive situations under control."[44] As a politician, he first unified the previously divided black community, then established an effective alliance with white liberals in the Democratic primary, and finally in the 1983 general election, through a series of conciliatory gestures, won the support of Frank Rizzo. Consequently, he carried 27% of the white vote, and Philadelphia during the first year of his term rode a wave of elation, smugly comparing its newfound racial harmony to the bitter divisions in Chicago and other cities. As mayor, many of Goode's early string of triumphs depended on his ability to build consensus and placate opposition. The few criticisms of Goode during this period centered on claims that he was too willing to appease opponents and too reluctant to lead in the absence of consensus. His own view was more positive: "I've had a charmed life as mayor because I've learned the arts of compromise and negotiation."[45]

A commitment to peacemaking is also consistent with the full pattern of Goode's dealings with MOVE. The disastrously little time and attention he devoted to planning the use of force contrasts strikingly with his extensive involvement in efforts to understand MOVE and to negotiate a solution[46]. When Managing Director, he met about fifteen times with John Africa's sisters, Louise James and Laverne Sims, both of whom had been involved with MOVE and were also the mothers of MOVE members." I always had a comfortable relationship with them, when we have shared together, where they have talked with me and I have listened a lot."[47] The open door continued after he became mayor. On July 31, 1984, when city officials were anticipating a confrontation with MOVE on the August 8 anniversary of the Powelton shootout, the two sisters requested a meeting and were given almost instant access. Goode told the MOVE Commission, " I literally jumped at the meeting because for the first time, I thought I had someone that I could talk to that could, in fact, avoid a conflict out there."[48] (Note how the procrastination of defensive avoidance vanishes when hope appears.) As late as May 9, Goode sandwiched in his fateful meeting with Sambor between discussions with community activists, through whom he hoped to arrange a meeting with Gerald Ford Africa:

> I then asked them to go back, to indicate to Gerald Ford Africa that I was willing to meet at any point that he decided, that he decided that he wanted to meet. I would come to his house. I would go to a neutral house...I would personally negotiate with him any type of release from the house that they were talking about, any movement they wanted to make at that time...After the optimism on Thursday, about noon, they got back to me that next day and said that there was a 360 degrees turn in the attitude of Gerald Ford Africa when they went back, and that he became profane towards them and said he would not meet with me under any circumstances ever for anything.

---

44 Roger Cohn, "Wilson Goode Has Something to Prove," Today Magazine, Philadelphia Inquirer (July 25, 1982), p. 27.
45 Amy Wilenz, " Goode's Intentions," Time 125 (May 27, 1985), p. 22.
46 William K. Marimow, "Two Images of Goode: Activism vs. Delegation," Philadelphia Inquirer (October 23, 1985), p. 1-A.
47 Philadelphia Special Investigations Commission, Hearings (1985: 10/15 AM, p. 29).
48 Ibid., p. 25.

And it was at this point that hope which I had of bringing about some negotiation in fact fell through.[49]

In directing his personal effort concerning MOVE toward negotiation, Goode was clearly playing to the area where he "felt familiar, resourceful and competent."[50] But such skills had probably developed precisely because they were so consistent with Goode's religious motivation and self-image. In contrast, to be "on the scene with hands-on" in managing a police operation against MOVE would be to risk coming away with blood on his hands---blood that might be politically advantageous but personally intolerable.

Unleashing an unreliable force

Thus, when the Osage neighbors precipitated Goode's final stage of hypervigilance, he kept the police operation at arms length, shielding himself from personal responsibility for the onslaught to come by entrusting the planning and execution to the police, whom he described time and again in the hearings as "experts" and "professionals." Goode's seemingly blind trust in his police force prompted this sarcastic interrogation by Commissioner Neil J. Welch, who had once directed the Philadelphia office of the FBI:

> WELCH: Now, we got a Mayor that's been a Mayor for a year or two and before that he was the Managing Director and certainly isn't the first time he's seen the Philadelphia Police Department and its personnel perform... [W]hat was your judgment as to the professional capability, the dependability, the quality and integrity of the Philadelphia Police Department to execute, to draft a plan and to execute, to draft a plan and to execute it successfully?
>
> GOODE: My judgment was that Greg Sambor had the ability within the parameters which I set forth, to go out and to develop a plan... It was my judgment that... being the kind of trained professional person and manager he is, that he, in fact, could do that... That when he finished that plan, he was to discuss that with Leo Brooks, who I felt with his 30 years in the armed services, as a Major General, could evaluate appropriately and properly that overall plan... So I left that meeting with full confidence that Greg Sambor and Leo Brooks could, in fact carry out the assignment given to them.
>
> WELCH: Mayor, you displayed great confidence in your Police Department and your Police Commissioner, as you have just outlined. This is the same department that has been or would have been under almost continuous federal investigation, had it not, for a period of some time?
>
> GOODE: That's correct.[51]

---

[49] Ibid., pp. 62-64.

[50] William K. Marimow, "Two Images of Goode: Activism vs. Delegation," Philadelphia Inquirer (October 23, 1985), p. 1-A.

[51] Philadelphia Special Investigations Commission, Hearings (1985: 10/15 AM, pp. 119--121).

Having had responsibility for the Police Department during most of the past five years, to admit the department's faults would clearly arouse dissonance for Goode; but it is inconceivable that he did not know, at some level, that his police were an unreliable instrument for this task. The Federal investigations to which Welch referred were not only for corruption, but for brutality and civil rights violations; and the mutual hatred between the police and MOVE was obvious, especially after the death of Officer Ramp and the beating of Delbert Africa in 1978.

In his initial attempt to solve the MOVE problem, Goode in fact sought to bypass the Philadelphia police. On May 30, 1984, just two days after his first meeting with a delegation from Osage Avenue, the mayor led ranking city officials to a session with U.S. Attorney Edward Dennis and representatives of the FBI and Secret Service. They rebuffed his argument that MOVE's threats against President Reagan and violations of their neighbors rights constituted grounds for U.S. intervention. Although consistent with the buck-passing pattern typical of defensive avoidance, Goode's attempt to enlist Federal authorities can also be interpreted as a prudent effort to find an armed force more detached, disciplined, and reliable than his own police.

Worries about controlling the city police were also present, though not emphasized, in the days before the final confrontation. At the May 7 meeting, prompted by Councilman Lucien Blackwell's strong warning about officers who might seek vengeance for 1978, Goode instructed Sambor to "handpick" the men who would serve in the Osage Avenue confrontation. (Sambor later claimed not to have heard such an order and in any case did not implement it. One of the gas-insertion teams included two officers who had been accused of beating Delbert Africa.[52] Goode ultimately admitted to the MOVE Commission that he doubted police fire control so much that he feared their bullets might endanger his own life if he went to the scene:

> COMMISSIONER AUDREY BRONSON: I understand that you felt that your life would have been at risk -- by whom?
>
> GOODE: Well, I have received a lot of information that simply people said to me, and I will share this candid discussion with you, that I should be careful of, first of all, of people who were MOVE sympathizers in the neighborhood, that with shots going on out there that a shot could easily go awry and hit me, that I should be--I should be--beware of even the potential for police shots going awry on the scene and, therefore there have been, as I was told, instances of the fact that commanders in the Army have, in fact, been mistakenly shot and I should be aware of those kinds of things and the people who talked with me simply persuaded me that, in fact, it would be a risk for me in the area.[53]

Although not explicit about who were "the people who talked with me," Goode later revealed that informants had warned him that "unkown members of my own police

---

[52] John Anderson and Hilary Hevenor, Burning Down the House: Move and the Tragedy of Philadelphia (New York: W.W. Norton and Co., 1987), p.115.

[53] Philadelphia Special Investigations Commission, Hearings (1985: 11/6 PM, p. 54).

force had targeted me for death if I came near Sixty-second Street and Osage Avenue." [54]

In short, part of Goode's reluctance to act against MOVE must have resulted from doubts, whether conscious or suppressed, that he could sufficiently control the use of force by the police. In the end he made no real attempt to manage the violence he had authorized. Perhaps, as many in Philadelphia believe, Goode rationally calculated that any such effort might fail and therefore deliberately distanced himself from a potential disaster in order to avoid legal or political responsibility. Such motives cannot be ruled out, but they do not adequately explain the string of cognitive distortions by which the mayor apparently avoided appreciating the reality of what his forces were doing. He told his breakfast guests that police were only firing over the roof of the MOVE house; he interpreted explosions he heard from his home as stun grenades; he thought that the "explosive device" would be placed on MOVE's roof rather than dropped from a helicopter; and he mistook "snow" on his television screen for water from firefighters' squirts.[55] Avowing these beliefs-- all unsupported by others' testimony-- would hardly help against criminal charges, and they only added to Goode's political vulnerability by subjecting him to ridicule. Such a consistent pattern of misperception seems more suited to deceive oneself than to deceive others, and better protection against self-condemnation than against the judgment of courts or voters. It therefore appears likely that deeper sources of ambivalence prevented the mayor from admitting to himself the full import of his decision to unleash official violence against MOVE.

Black against black: identification and anger

The foregoing is not meant to portray Wilson Goode as a pacifist or as one whose values are entirely antithetical to those of the police. After completing ROTC at Morgan State University, he served in the U.S. Army from 1961 to 1963, rising to the rank of captain and commanding a unit of 223 military policemen. His military experience made a deep impression on Goode. He has said that he learned more about management in the army than he did earning a master's degree in governmental administration at the University of Pennsylvania.[56] As mayor, he showed a marked penchant for appointing former military officers to high posts -- including Leo Brooks, a major general in charge of the Philadelphia Defense Personnel Support Center before Goode persuaded him to become Managing Director, and Gregore Sambor, a veteran and an officer in the reserves.

To Goode, however, the military seems to represent not so much legitimate violence as it does an organization the develops personal discipline and rewards it, regardless of race--in marked contrast to most of American society in his formative years. Early profiles of Brooks suggest the virtues that Goode most admires:
[A mutual acquaintance described Brooks as] "made out of the same mold as Wilson." Goode and Brooks shared poor childhoods in the South, Army-officer training and strong religious underpinnings. Brooks' father is a Baptist minister...Brooks also is a black man who, like his new boss, has achieved success

---

[54] W. Wilson Goode with Joann Stevens, In Goode Faith (Valley Forge, PA: Judson Press, 1992), pp. 217-8.
[55] Philadelphia Special Investigations Commission, Hearings (1985: 10/15 AM, pp. 74, 97; 10/15 PM, p. 111; 11/6 AM, p. 111; 10/15 PM, p. 31).
[56] In a conversation with the author in February 1981.

by making hard work his credo.57 At heart a traditionalist, Brooks believes in the old-fashioned virtues of hard work, self-discipline. . . and taking responsibility for one's own actions. To him, nothing exceeds the importance of family.58

To a black man with Wilson Goode's values, MOVE must have aroused deep and intense conflicts.59 On the one hand, as a former civil rights activist who had himself been arrested several times for demonstrations in Baltimore and Philadelphia and whose brother had been beaten by Philadelphia police,60 Goode must have had some lingering identification with MOVE. In 1978, much of the black and liberal communities had seen the MOVE problem as a racially motivated attack by the Rizzo administration on the rights of a predominantly black group. On one occasion, five thousand demonstrators marched around City Hall to protest the siege in Powelton; their chants linked MOVE with South African blacks as fellow victims of racial oppression. In 1984, U.S. Attorney Dennis, himself black, strongly warned city officials against violating MOVE's civil rights.61 Goode invoked his own concern for minority rights in explaining his reluctance to act:

> I think that if I was a different person, that perhaps I may have acted differently back in 1984. But I . . . do not feel that anyone who holds an office ought to use that office to infringe and violate other people's rights in order to achieve the overall good, and I guess I feel that way because I know that for so long in this country that laws were in fact, used to deprive blacks and women and Hispanics and others who were different, and therefore, I do not want, as mayor of this city to say to a group: Because you are different, because you don't comply with all the laws, therefore, I have the right, as the mayor, to simply go full speed and trample on you and all you rights . . .62

On the other hand, MOVE represented the antithesis of every standard by which Wilson Goode lived. They dwelt in filth; he was always well groomed. They lived communally; he had raised a family. They spewed profanity; he attended church every Sunday. They survived casually; he worked fifteen-hour days. They rejected the system; he aspired to run a major corporation. As they spurned his efforts to negotiate a peaceful solution, as they vilified him and threatened his life, the bizarre cultists must have aroused increasing anger in Goode. The impulse to vent this anger must have been strong, but his religious belief in preserving life and his self-image as a controlled person forbade yielding to it. "I've always felt that I

---

57 Russell Cooke and Hank Klibanoff, "Work is the Credo for New Managing Director," Philadelphia Inquirer (November 29, 1983), p. 12-A.

58 Hank Klibanoff, "The General," Philadelphia Inquirer (May 21, 1984), p. 4-B.

59 Much the same argument can probably be made for Leo Brooks, which may help explain why he too failed to fulfill his responsibility in the MOVE operation. Despite the advantages of similarity in promoting trust and comfortable personal relations, leaders take a great risk in depending excessively on key subordinates who are too much like themselves.

60 W. Wilson Goode with Joann Stevens, In Goode Faith (Valley Forge, PA: Judson Press, 1992), pp. 62-3, 118, 256.

61 Philadelphia Special Investigations Commission, Hearings (1985: 10/22 PM, p. 127).

62 Philadelphia Special Investigations Commission, Hearings (1985: 10/15 PM, pp. 97- 98).

have to be in control of me at all times," he once told an interviewer[63]; and another profiler got "the feeling that the emotion bottled up inside Wilson Goode is always close to eruption. You can see him almost counting to ten, thinking before he responds, calculating each sentence, crafting every phrase, then struggling mightily to reign in what might be rage."[64]

For a time, the mayor hoped that MOVE itself would assume the moral burden of precipitating violence. After receiving Rendell's memo justifying urgent action in June 1984, Goode delayed until August 8, the anniversary of the Powelton shootout, because reports indicated that MOVE planned a major confrontation with "the System" on that date. At the mayor's direction, the police prepared a plan for capturing the MOVE house,[65] and three hundred officers were assembled near Osage Avenue. Goode's choice of language in describing this incident is revealing:

> The August 8th plan was a reactive plan, was geared to go into effect only if certain types of aggressive behavior, aggressive steps were taken by MOVE members themselves. And therefore when they did not take any aggressive steps, nothing, in fact, was done at that time.[66]

The words "aggressive" and "aggression" recur frequently when Goode refers to the initiation of armed confrontation. It appears that he was willing in 1984 to do battle with MOVE, but only if MOVE were the aggressor, if MOVE bore the responsibility of having clearly initiated violence. To let deaths occur (or appear to occur) merely because of noise, stench, code violations, and unpaid utility bills was, to Goode, a morally unbalanced equation.[67]

On August 8, however, MOVE did nothing except take notes about the police preparations. After that day, Goode and other city officials entered a stage of full-blown defensive avoidance that lasted until May 1985. As the MOVE Commission observed about this period, "The policy of appeasement produced a rule of silence in City Hall, where information on the Osage Avenue situation was not disseminated and where city officials knowledgeable about the problems chose not to speak of them."[68] Goode and his colleagues were thus able to entertain the wishful hope that the Osage Avenue problem "would disappear" by ignoring the readily available knowledge that MOVE members were vigorously and visibly

---

[63] Roger Cohn, "Wilson Goode Has Something to Prove," Today Magazine, Philadelphia Inquirer (July 25,1982), pp. 10 ff.

[64] Mike Mallowe, "The No-Frills Mayor," Philadelphia Magazine 75 (December 1984), pp. 168 ff. Goode's emphasis on self-control was apparently a reaction to his father's violent rages when drunk. "I never wanted to lose control like my father, nor did I want to be like him when I grew up." [W. Wilson Goode with Joann Stevens, In Goode Faith (Valley Forge, PA: Judson Press, 1992), p. 27.

[65] This plan, prepared by Sergeant Herbert Kirk of the Police Academy, was the forerunner of the strategy employed the following May (PSIC, 1985, 10/11 PM).

[66] Philadelphia Special Investigations Commission, Hearings (1985: 10/15 PM, p. 59).

[67] Because some of his radical and civil libertarian supporters, both black and white, might have had the same attitude, Goode's calculation can be seen as both political and moral. As Sharifi (1990) observes, successful political leaders often mirror the potential reactions of key constituencies in their own concerns.

[68] Philadelphia Special Investigations Commission, Findings Conclusions and Reccommendations (1988: 10/15 PM, p. 13).

fortifying their compound.[69] Goode justified his policy of nonintervention on the grounds that no action should be taken "until such time as we worked out an overall plan that would be comprehensive in nature," but this argument was rationalization for avoidance, as is shown by the fact that he did absolutely nothing to force the creation of such a plan.[70] Indeed, the mayor had no contact with anyone concerning MOVE from August 9 until the end of April 1985.[71]

Goode's nine months of pseudocalm were then shattered by the United Residents' initiative, which revived what threatened to be an excruciating inner struggle. Rather than endure the tension during a protracted period of careful search and appraisal, the mayor sought to eliminate his conflict quickly by authorizing the police plan. Although he unleashed the violence of the police and perhaps in part vented his own anger through their vengeance, the use of force in this context was so dissonant with his self-image that he could not accept--psychologically at least as much as politically--the ownership that hands-on management would imply.

To shield himself form personal responsibility for violating crucial values, Wilson Goode thus abdicated his responsibility as an administrator. In so doing, he lost his best chance to control and minimize the inevitable violence. Because he was so reluctant to transgress his values, he permitted a series of events that in the end inflicted on them far greater damage than was necessary. The outcome has the irony of genuine tragedy. The preserver of life bore responsibility for eleven deaths; the builder of homes presided as sixty-one burned; the protector of rights permitted grotesquely excessive official violence.

Lessons for present and future managers

Perhaps the only consolation we can take from so awful a disaster is the hope that its lessons will help prevent future catastrophes. Thus the MOVE Commission concluded their report with no fewer than thirty-eight recommendations covering such matters as communication systems, assignment of authority and responsibility, policies for controlling weapons and explosives, strategic planning processes, interdepartmental coordinating groups, and so forth. Though the Commission's proposals may be sensible and worthwhile, from the perspective of the analysis offered in this paper, such advice misses the most fundamental lessons of the MOVE debacle.

Organizational systems, policies, and procedures are ultimately controlled and implemented by human beings. Effective communication will not occur when subordinates believe that their superiors cannot bear to hear the truth. Clear allocation of authority will be wasted on executives who, succumbing to painful quandaries, rationalize evasion of responsibility.

Programs for educating public managers should therefore devote much more attention to the psychology of decisionmaking, with a special focus on its prescriptive implications. For example, Janis[72] concludes his recent book by suggesting twenty sets of leadership practices that might help policy makers avoid pitfalls that often result in defective decisionmaking. As he observes, most of these

---

[69] Philadelphia Special Investigations Commission, Hearings (1985: 10/15 PM, pp. 76-7).

[70] Ibid., pp. 75-80.

[71] Ibid., p. 40.

[72] Irving L. Janis, Crucial Decisions: Leadership in Policymaking and Crisis Management (New York: The Free Press, 1989), Ch. 10.

recommendations will be costly to leaders and their support staffs in time, effort, and stress. Adjusting curricula to sensitize present and future decision makers to psychological factors will also demand new investments by schools, teachers, and students.

Dramatic examples like the MOVE disaster can help motivate such efforts, but in teaching the case during the past several years, I have found that students adopt their own avoidance strategies. Like the general public, their natural reaction is to debate, as one student put it, "whether moral bankruptcy or simple incompetence best explains this disaster." Whichever verdict is chosen, the effect is to distance oneself from the officials who are blamed for the debacle. The observer in effect is saying, "I would never be so evil, or so uncaring, or so inattentive, or so blundering as to permit such a horror!"

Interpreting the MOVE case in terms of a general theory such as the Janis and Mann conflict model elevates it from an idiosyncratic failure to a universal warning. Students can then move beyond emotional condemnation of a few officials to a sobering recognition of their own vulnerability to similar errors. The generality of the problem can be further emphasized by exploring parallel cases (though few will be so well documented as the MOVE incident). To take several recent examples, the delay/haste pattern appears to fit the British government's treatment of IRA strongholds in Belfast and Derry during the early 1970s, the Chinese government's response to the 1989 student demonstrations in Tienanmen Square, and the U.S. invasion of Panama to overthrow General Manuel Noriega.[73]

Once managers understand the dynamics of defensive avoidance and hypervigilance, what can they do to protect themselves? Because rationalization, denial, selective perception, and wishful thinking are so insidious, no one can be assured of immunity against defective decision processes. For this reason, Janis and Mann[74] recommend embedding preventive strategies in organizational standard operating procedures,[75] because "if anti-defensive avoidance procedures are not institutionalized but are rather left to the discretion of the leader or the members, they will be more honored in the breach than in the observance."

Nevertheless, it is not unreasonable to hope that individual awareness will also help. Relying on face validity rather than any systematic evidence of effectiveness, I would suggest the following strategy to managers who wish to reduce their vulnerability.

First, learn to recognize the behavioral symptoms of defective decisionmaking. For defensive avoidance, these include procrastination, buck-passing, and downplaying danger signals. Symptoms of hypervigilance include grabbing the first available alternative, neglecting contingency plans, and believing that action must be taken under extreme time pressure whether or not compelling deadlines exist. Wise managers will not only monitor themselves for these symptoms, but will also encourage trusted advisors to fight the battle for their minds by calling such tendencies to their attention.

---

[73] I owe these and other suggested parallels to a reviewer for the Journal of Policy Analysis and Management, which published an earlier version of this chapter.

[74] Irving L. Janis and Leon Mann, Decision Making : A Psychological Analysis of Conflict, Choice and Commitment (New York: The Free Press, 1977), p. 396.

[75] An example already well known in the policymaking community is the system of multiple advocacy recommended by Alexander L. George, "The Case for Multiple Advocacy in Making Foreign Policy," American Political Science Review 66 (1973), pp. 751--85.

Second, when these symptoms are observed, identify the central no-win dilemma or dilemmas.[76] Conflicts that impede effective decisionmaking are not always obvious and will vary from individual to individual. The desire to avoid responsibility and shield oneself from reality behind a screen of cognitive distortions becomes strongest when one's most central values are threatened, so the manager must heed the ancient injunction to "know thyself."

Third, learn to grasp problems firmly even when all options entail distasteful consequences for important values. The example of Wilson Goode shows that cherished virtues, if excessively protected, can be the source of tragic failure. Though vigilant problem solving and decisive management may induce stress, they are usually rewarded -- if not with unequivocal triumph, then at least by controlled damage and the respect that strong leaders are accorded. In contrast, the inferno on Osage Avenue should burn into our memories the lesson that however bad available alternatives seem, potential outcomes can be far worse if avoidance and hasty action permit a tough situation to deteriorate into a nightmare.

---

[76] One device that might help raise conflicts to consciousness is the decisional balance sheet, a kind of expanded cost-benefit analysis that includes not only utilitarian gains and losses but also the approval and disapproval of reference groups and oneself [Irving L. Janis and Leon Mann, Decision Making: A Psychological Analysis of Conflict, Choice, and Commitment (New York: The Free Press, 1977), Ch. 6. Note that the purpose is to recognize consciously the role of emotional influences, not necessarily to eliminate them.

CHAPTER FOUR

FEDERAL RESPONSIBILITY FOR BANKING REFORM AND THE ROLE OF THE STATES

ELEANOR D. CRAIG

Throughout the late 1980s the United States' banking system underwent dramatic changes. There was considerable deregulation and increased foreign competition. Nearly a quarter of the savings and loans became insolvent. The revolution in computers and communications changed the nature of many banking services. Some of the changes resulted from technological developments, while governmental actions caused other changes. Much of the governmentally induced change was initiated at the state level, partly due to the vacuum left by the lack of federal action and partly because the state governments seized initiatives to encourage economic development within their borders.

This leaves the question of whether the federal government acted responsibly in letting the fifty states set the course of U.S. banking, or whether the federal government deliberately allowed the states, in the words of Supreme Court Justice Louis Brandeis,[1] to act as "laboratories of democracy" which could try experiments with new solutions to economic questions? The entire nation could adopt successful experiments and forget the failures. A federal system of government could make changes that only impact a small part of the country and watch the results very carefully, prior to imposing those changes on the entire country.

Banking's challenge to responsible government at the federal level

The case for lack of government responsibility at the federal level in facing the banking issues of the late 1980s rests on the definition of "responsible government." Charles Gilbert, writing in the late 1950s, carefully defined responsible government.[2] His characteristics of what a responsible government does pose many questions for the recent banking reform. He said that a responsible government assumes a leadership role. Did Congress and the Administration take the necessary leadership in facing the Savings and Loan (S & L or thrift institutions) problems before the election of 1988? No, Congress and the President appeared to ignore the ever-worsening S & L problems to the long-run detriment of the taxpayer.

A responsible government provides efficacy and efficiency in administration. However, the federal government ignored market forces in dealing with banking

---

[1] David Osborne, Laboratories of Democracy (Boston: Harvard Business School Press, 1988), pp. 2-3.
[2] Charles E. Gilbert, "The Framework of Administrative Responsibility," The Journal of Politics, Vol. 21, #3 (August 1959), pp. 374-8.

problems in the late 1980s, using insurance coverage for deposit security rather than forcing the bank stockholders, depositors and managers to monitor their firms' financial health. Unlike other forms of business, the consumer cannot be the final judge of whether a bank grows or fails. The voice of private decision makers operating in free markets is silenced. The insurance coverage of our banking system has focussed on preventing failure rather than rewarding success. When insurance prevents banks from taking losses, competing institutions are suffocated and profits decline.

A responsible government uses a consistent approach to domestic problems and can resolve internal contradictions. Congress and the President allowed a deregulation of the deposit side of banks' balance sheets by removing the usury[3] ceilings and allowing banks to offer new investment products. Yet Congress and the President neglected to deregulate the asset side of the balance sheet, so banks could not compete in investment, insurance and real estate markets.

A responsible government should foster stability of results; policy should be predictable and follow established patterns. During the early 1980s many banks failed and were liquidated. However, when Continental Illinois, the eighth largest bank in the country became insolvent, the FDIC offered a $6 billion bail-out to prevent a "wide-spread" banking crisis. (The message sent was that the federal government's actions would be predictable unless those actions had any significant impact on big and powerful firms.) Why should depositors with large accounts at America's largest banks be given full guarantees when similar depositors at smaller institutions risk loss if the bank fails?

A responsible government follows due process equally in all situations. The jury is still out, but the bank inspections in certain regions of the country apparently have been far less rigorous than those in the rest of the U.S. Congressional influence and California state politics may have played a role in the errant inspections.

Responsible government is appropriately responsive. If restrictions on banking activity in fields like insurance and investments are obsolete in face of changed technology, the federal government could remove those restrictions. Rather, our federal government stood by and watched while some of the individual states removed those restrictions. The federal government tried to be responsive when the U.S. needed larger housing supply. Yet the government responded by restricting banks' lending practices, such as the thrift residential mortgage requirements and the Community Reinvestment Act mandating banks to earmark a portion of their home mortgage lending for the poor at preferential interest rates. The federal government would have been much more successful in enlarging the housing stock if it had given more market opportunities to the demanders of housing, e.g., housing vouchers for the poor.

Bank regulation imposed heavy costs

Many of the regulations facing the banks in the late 1970s imposed very high costs on both those banks and the users of the bank services. The federal government, by placing ceilings on the interest rates earned by deposits and defining only certain types of investments as eligible income earning opportunities, forced bank customers to look elsewhere for higher interest-yielding options. Because of the very high inflation rate during the late 1970s and the early 1980s, the market

---

[3] Interest rate maximums.

provided those high interest funds. Securities firms and other nonbank financial institutions developed money market mutual funds that paid more than triple the interest yields available in the bank demand deposit accounts. Consumers learned about those money market accounts, gave up the advantage of having their deposits in local banking institutions and willingly risked keeping their deposits in uninsured accounts. Corporate borrowers began borrowing from the securities markets through commercial paper, rather than using the banks, because the investment firms offered more readily available credit at lower rates.

Thus, the restrictions on the types of markets that the banks could enter and the prices they could charge were very expensive to the banks because they lost business. Those same restrictions were expensive to the low income bank customers and small businesses that didn't have the information and ability to move to nonbanks for deposits and loans.

Bank regulation into the 1980s

The banking reforms enacted by Congress after the Depression of the early 1930s guaranteed the safety of each and every bank and assured their profitability. Most of the measures restricted competition, limited prices and territory, and prohibited competition from other forms of business in offering demand deposits. Competition among banks was limited since the insurance guaranteed that each bank was as safe as the next one.

The structure that evolved was a dual banking system with regulatory power divided between the states and the federal government. Banks, depending on their mission and type, could choose a Federal Reserve charter as a national bank or a charter from the state where the bank was located. The duality of the regulatory structure permitted banks an escape route from arbitrary or discriminatory chartering or regulatory policies. Each bank has the option to switch to the alternative regulatory body.[4]

Throughout the Twentieth Century, each state determined its own bank branching rules, that is the number of offices each parent bank could open. The McFadden Act of 1927 (as amended in 1933) provided national banks the same branching rights as those of the state-chartered banks in their own states.

Bank holding companies were limited to "banking and other closely related activities" and were prohibited from making interstate bank acquisitions by the Bank Holding Company Act of 1956 and the Douglas Amendment to that Act. Bank holding companies could not branch across state lines unless a state explicitly invited their presence. Maine, a poor state and in need of capital, was the first state to take advantage of this provision in 1975. In 1980 South Dakota allowed limited purpose banks, which met certain capital and employment requirements, establish branches in their state.[5] Delaware followed with similar legislation the next year. (See case study that follows.) In 1982 New York passed nationwide reciprocal legislation and

---

[4] Advisory Commission on Intergovernmental Relations, "State Regulation of Banks in an Era of Deregulation," (Washington, D.C.: September 1988), p. 20.

[5] A constitutional challenge was adjudicated in the 8th District Circuit Court of Appeals, and found that South Dakota had violated the interstate Commerce Clause by restricting the business activities of the acquired national banks. The South Dakota legislature amended their Code by removing the restrictions, and thus the offending language. (Independent Community Bankers Association of South Dakota v. Board of Governors of the Federal Reserve System, January 28, 1988).

the New England states formed a regional reciprocal pact. Many other regions followed suit, but the New York banks were not included in any regional pacts. Some states like Arizona and Rhode Island and Louisiana permit nationwide entry. Forty-six states currently have some form of interstate branching.[6]

The Garn-St. Germain Act of 1982 and the Competitive Equality of Banking Act of 1987 allowed banks to acquire, across state lines, certain other banks that were in financial difficulty. Ailing Texas banks found a series of savior institutions, but there haven't been many rescue acquisitions in Louisiana. Of the more than 50,000 branches across the country, more than 7000 carry full service interstate branching powers.

Banking as a unique business

Is there any reason that banks are different from other business operations? Should the government impose stiffer regulations on banks and not let financial markets work for the general economic welfare? Are there special circumstances involved with banking that require the federal government to play a more active role than it would in the formation and regulation of other industries? Is the form of government regulation and control over banking likely to promote better results for the American economy than would less restrictive policies?

The FDIC in *Mandate for Change* argues that banks are "special" and require some government intervention for three reasons. First, banks keep depositors' savings and thus require some government insurance. Second, since most of the liabilities of banks are claims that can be requested on demand and most of the assets are not as liquid, banks are subject to "runs" and again need some form of insurance. Finally, banks are the mechanics of the payments system for U.S. commerce and the means by which the Federal Reserve conducts its monetary policy. This last special feature requires that the financial services industry, not each bank or even a narrowly defined banking system, remains healthy. Thus responsible government policy at the federal level seems to include some bank regulation.[7] Yet the types of regulations chosen and the "apparent willing relinquishing of its leadership role"[8] has left many opportunities for the states to deregulate the banking industry.

Benefits/costs of deregulation

Discussions of the benefits and costs of deregulating the banks, using an efficacy definition of government responsibility, usually focus on four areas: safety, service, competition, and the viability of small banks in a banking system dominated by multi-billion dollar institutions.

1) A deregulated banking environment will probably enhance bank safety. Deregulation will undoubtedly lead to bank consolidation. Larger banks have grown

---

[6] Dean F. Amel and Michael J. Jacowski, "Trends in Banking Structure since the Mid-1970s," Federal Reserve Bulletin, Vol. 75, #3 (March 1989), p. 133.

[7] Many serious banking students disagree. Catherine England argues that "banks are indeed special, but they are special primarily because of government policies. Banks and their customers have become increasingly dependent on continuing subsidies and protection provided by the government."

[8] R. Scott Foster, ed., New Economic Role of American States - Strategies in a Competitive World Economy (New York: Oxford University Press, 1988), p. 311.

big by diversifying, in terms of products and regions served. Small banks, loaded with local real estate mortgages in an economically declining area, suffer more than a larger bank offering a greater variety of services to a broader geographic market. The diversification has lessened the risk of bank failure.

2) Deregulation can enhance service levels. As the average bank grows and diversifies it will have more products to offer its customers. The bank will have larger borrowing limits and will allow greater access for the local borrower to the national money markets. Morris[9] found that when deregulated banking led to entry into banking markets, the markets became more competitive, and the banks offered more products at lower prices.

3) Discussions of bank deregulation highlight concerns over competition and the antitrust implications of bank mergers. Since the late 1970s, the banking system as a whole has become more concentrated at the state and national levels. In fact Amel and Jacowski[10] found that 80% of the states had seen a significant increase in concentration over the last ten years. This increase has occurred primarily through the merger and acquisition process enlarging the regional and superregional banks. In contrast, however, competition for banking services at the local level had increased. This competition is evidenced not only by the strength and market performance of many of the local banks, but also by the enhanced competition between those banks and other financial institutions.

4) Small banks still have a very important role to play in the deregulated environment. There is evidence on economies of scale, i.e. the level of activity that generates the lowest fixed costs per dollar of output. Clark[11] found that quite small banks, those with assets of less that $100 million, experienced the maximum economies of scale. Other writers, e.g., Hunter and Wall[12] found that average fixed costs are constant for asset sizes up to approximately $25 billion. Many of the smaller banks develop market niches and have long-standing relationships with a network of regular customers, e.g., automobile dealers who require regular loans on their inventories, commercial farmers who require seasonal loans, and the local construction companies that need financing for buildings in progress.

The bank deregulation has brought tremendous benefits to the economy. Curran[13] estimates that consumers have earned more than $100 billion in interest above what their receipts would have been under the old Regulation Q usury ceilings. Consumers also benefit from the discounted brokerage commissions offered by financial institutions. The increases in these fees are less than half of their earlier levels.

Banking in the 1990s compared with banking in 1980

---

[9] Charles Morris, "The Competitive Effects of Interstate Banking," Economic Review, Federal Reserve Bank of Kansas City (November 1984), p. 14.
[10] Amel and Jacowski, op. cit., p. 130.
[11] Jeffrey A. Clark, "Economies of Scale and Scope at Depository Financial Institutions," Economic Review, Federal Reserve Bank of Kansas City, Vol. 73, #8 (September/October 1988), p. 26.
[12] William C. Hunter and Larry D. Wall, "Bank Merger Motivations: A Review of the Evidence and An Examination of Key Target Bank Characteristics," Economic Review, Federal Reserve Bank of Atlanta, Vol. LXXIV, #5 (September/October 1989), p. 6.
[13] John Curran, "Does Regulation Make Sense?," Fortune (June 5, 1989), p. 181.

Many of the changes in banking, including the wide-spread deregulation, began at the state level and have spread throughout the country. Foster[14] compares this process in the 1980s with that of the 1930s when the New Deal drew heavily on the state and city initiatives from the previous decade. To date, the federal government has not validated the initiatives of the lower levels of government for deregulation in banking as it did with the social legislation initiated at the local levels before the New Deal. However, the federal government has ratified many of the state initiatives in providing banking services, e.g., governmental supervision of bank insurance, NOW accounts, interest earnings on checking accounts and disclosure rules on interest rates and fees.

Banking in the 1990s is international in scope. Lenders and borrowers shop for the best rates regardless of national origin. Many state and local governments have funded their capital programs with General Obligation bond sales denominated in yen and Eurodollars. The more concentrated foreign banking has the benefit of greater economics of scale. In 1992 the U.S. had 12,000 separate banks; Japan 76, Canada only 11, and Great Britain six "clearing" banks. Responsible government in the 1990's will have to deal with the competition from these very efficient foreign banks.

By the early 1990s, renegotiating much of the Third World debt mitigated some of their negative impacts. Banks have also accepted impossibility of payment on some of the loans. The economic recovery of some of those Third World debtor nations and the trade of some debt for assets of the debtor nation have also made the debt problems less severe. The only significant problems that remain are with Venezuela, Mexico, Brazil and Argentina and involve only five banks with these Third World debts at more than 40% of their equity.

The regulation-induced savings and loan crisis is ending. A more responsible government conclusion to the clearly emerging problems as the U.S. faced national elections would have reduced the costs to the taxpayers, estimated at nearly $250 billion in today's dollars.[15] Congress and the Reagan Administration made the political choice to ignore the impending crisis. In the 1990s healthy banks will assume most of the failed banks, their remaining assets and liabilities will be sold, and the S & L's that remain will behave more like commercial banks in their access to wider lending markets.

The technological advances that induced many of the changes in the banking industry through the 1980s will continue in the 1990s. The improvements in information processing and communications, particularly electronic funds transfers, have reduced the costs of entering new markets and greatly expanded the options for both bank customers and for the financial institutions themselves. Large corporations have had access to non-local banking connections for many years, but these technological improvements have opened national lending and banking services to small businesses and to individual households. Such features as automatic teller machines, point of sales systems, automatic clearing houses, credit cards and home banking have expanded the scope for both the customers and the banks. The delivery of financial services no longer requires a face-to-face encounter. In fact, there is a de facto branch bank hidden in every telephone, radio,

---

[14] Foster, op. cit., p. 329.
[15] If the bail-outs are funded with debt, adding interest to the direct costs will nearly double the total cost.

newspaper, television and mailbox.[16]

Nonbank competition will continue to grow in the 1990s. These alternatives will strengthen as long as the federal government over-regulates banks and puts them at a competitive disadvantage to the nonbank institutions offering similar services. These regulations include minimum levels of capital, reserve requirements, insurance fees, required lending for purposes inducing societal change and prohibitions on insurance sales and securities underwriting.

The deregulation that occurred at both the national and state levels will continue through the 1990s. The deregulation on prices both on the deposit side and on the loan side of the balance sheet, the geographic and product deregulation will persist. Absent another bout of serious inflation and high interest rates, the federal government should, if acting responsibly, continue to allow state experimentation without much direction. A high interest rate environment might encourage more federal intervention. If the intervention took the form of more regulation, the banks' financial woes would be exacerbated.

Delaware case study: responsible government at the state level

Delaware took the lead among the states in the early 1980s to deregulate the banking industry. The State's leaders deregulated interest rates, entry and the tax structure to encourage greater banking activity within the State borders. Delaware seemed to act in a responsible way, given the void left by the federal government and the poor performance in the State's economy.

In 1980 Delaware faced a question that would be critical to its economic future: Should the State, its political and banking leaders, agree to waive its protection under the Bank Holding Company Act and permit money center banks to move operations to Delaware? Even posing the question would have been unthinkable five years before. Since the Great Depression and the bank failures it generated, banking regulation was unquestioned. For four years, deciding where banks could locate, what banks could and could not do, and what interest rates banks could pay, was accepted doctrine in the U.S.

However, in 1980 inflation persisted at 13%, the prime rate reached 21%, the world economies were becoming increasingly integrated, communications technology was surging and competition for the financial services market was coming from many sources. These events put enormous pressure on U.S. banks. Banks looked for options to relieve the pressure. First they looked to Washington for relief from usury ceilings, location prohibitions, and restrictions on the type of services they could offer. Washington was not up to the challenge. Competing interests, bureaucratic intransigencies, and plain old politics paralyzed the reform process.

So the leading banks began to look for other solutions -- judicial solutions and state legal solutions. Citibank approached South Dakota to waive its interstate banking protection. Chase Manhattan approached Delaware and asked whether Delaware would consider permitting the money center banks to move operations there to enable them to escape from New York's usury laws and tax burdens? The question was hard. Delaware's political and business leaders met quietly for days to consider the answer. For Delaware bankers the questions were particularly difficult.

---

[16] Larry Frieder et.al., Commercial Banking and Interstate Expansion - Issues, Prospects and Strategies (Ann Arbor, MI: UMI Research Press, 1985), p. 89.

Why should they agree to permit these enormous banks in Delaware? Would not the new banks steal business? Would they not bring cut-throat competition? Finally, Delaware decided that it might very well be at the leading edge of an exciting opportunity. And Delaware answered "yes" to Chase, and the enabling legislation passed early in 1981. The results have been extremely positive, both for the economy of the State and also thus for the "old" Delaware banks.

Today the number of "new" bank employees exceeds the number of "old" bank employees. Last year "new" banks contributed 80% of the increase in assets, 70% of the increase in equity capital, and more than 50% of the increase in deposits generated by all Delaware banks. Total bank deposits in the State have grown 25% annually in the seven years since the "new" banks began to open in Delaware, compared to average annual growth rates of 5% during the same period before 1981. Bank deposits last year totalled $36 billion. The "old" banks have benefited, too. The three largest old banks all reported higher than average (when compared with the large regional banks) return on assets and return on equity for the last few years.

The "new" banks

Who are these 41 new banks? Why did they come to Delaware? What has been their economic impact on the State (and on the old banks)? There are 19 new banks that have Delaware offices as a result of the Financial Center Development Act, six new banks which came in response to the Consumer Credit Bank Act and the remaining new banks either acquired a bank in the State or opened for other specific reasons. The Financial Center Development Act, signed in 1981 by Governor du Pont, encouraged out-of-state bank holding companies to form Delaware subsidiaries if they had at least $25 million of capital stock and 100 employees in Delaware at the end of their first year. The new banks were only allowed one office and they had to operate "in a manner and in a location not likely to attract customers from the general public and to the detriment of existing Delaware banks."

The inducements for the new banks were twofold: 1) regulations on the level of interest rates and credit card fees were eliminated; and 2) regressive taxes were set on bank net income -- the marginal tax rate falls as bank income grows (to a lower limit of 2.7% for net income of more than $30 million). Major money center banks could export Delaware's market rates on consumer credit throughout the country and enjoy lower tax rates on their expanded profits. In this case a responsible government has enhanced competition and opened new markets.

The first new bank in Delaware was Morgan Bank (Delaware) which opened in late 1981 and now has much of its wholesale banking business located in the State. Another Morgan subsidiary, Morgan Christiana Corporation, operates deposit and check payment services for many of J.P.Morgan's operations from a second location. The second to open was Chase Manhattan Bank (U.S.A.) whose primary business is consumer credit cards. Chase now has $9.5 billion of assets in the State (2nd largest of all Delaware banks) and employs 1400 workers (the 25th largest employer in the State).[17] Of the remaining 16 Financial Center Development Act banks, seven are heavily committed to consumer credit, four are involved with commercial lending, four are primarily wholesale bankers, one primarily handles

---

[17] The largest by asset size is the American Express Centurion Bank, with assets of $9.6 billion and 450 employees. The largest employer is MBNA America Bank NA with 3800 workers and $5.6 billion of assets in the State.

cash management for its institutional customers and two have significant international operations.

Three other new banks openings in Delaware are of note. Lomas Bank USA, formerly a subsidiary of M Corporation in Dallas, opened in Delaware to market credit cards nationwide but has primarily targeted the Texas market. More than 50% of the credit cards in Texas are issued by non-Texas banks because that state has a usury ceiling that restricts credit card interest to twice the Treasury bill rate, or 7% today compared with nationwide market rates on credit cards averaging 18%. Barclays Bank of Delaware provides private label credit for White Consolidated Industries, an appliance firm. Bankers Trust (Delaware) was the last of the largest ten New York banks to establish a home in Delaware. Bankers Trust is marketing wholesale commercial loans across the country.

Six banks have entered Delaware under a different law, the Consumer Credit Bank Act of 1983, which allows firms to open credit card affiliates in the State with a minimum of $50,000 of capital, and requires that these firms use a credit card processor that employs at least 250 employees in the State within three years.

The State enacted two other laws to enhance its attractiveness as a financial center. The one passed in 1983 eliminates taxes on all international transactions of banks. The 1984 law allows banks to own export trading companies. Although there has been considerable interest, only one bank opened under these recent laws.

Delaware's deregulations also encouraged nonbank financial activity in the past few years. American Express and E.F.Hutton both offer commercial loans in the State. Beneficial National Bank employs 650 people in a credit card operation and Sears issues "Discover" credit cards through the Greenwood Trust Bank that Sears bought in 1984. J.C.Penney operates a retail bank in downstate Delaware, and Colonial National Bank was acquired by the Pennsylvania-based Teachers Service Organization to handle electronic funds transfer for their consumer finance business.

Why Delaware?

Delaware's progressive deregulation legislation for the banking industry and the lower tax rates were the prime elements attracting the new out-of-state financial institutions. Secondary growth has occurred because of the favorable economic climate that the banks discovered in Delaware. Most of the banks that located here within the first two years of the passage of the Financial Center Development Act have undergone major expansions. For example, Chase, Manufacturers Hanover, MBNA and Morgan have built large corporate structures here.

The new banks discovered Delaware's relatively low costs of living (4% lower than the U.S.average, 25% lower than New York City), low priced housing, high quality of education, plentiful recreational sites including ocean and bay activities, easy access to Philadelphia, New York, and Washington, D.C., and a very favorable labor climate. They have also found that it is easy to communicate with Delaware government that has been responsive to their needs.

To date, 46 states have passed laws permitting entry by out-of-state banks.[18] Many of those laws, however, are far more restrictive than Delaware's and allow entry only under very limited circumstances. Some states have allowed the large money center banks to purchase failing thrift institutions. Others have entered into regional banking compacts allowing cross-state acquisitions within carefully defined

---

[18] Exceptions are Iowa, Kansas, Montana and North Carolina.

geographic boundaries. Citicorp has probably been the most aggressive in taking advantage of the reduced barriers to entry and now can conduct retail banking business in offices in nearly every state.

Economic impact

The new Delaware banks have 18,000 full-time employees in mid 1992. Using an employment multiplier of 1.7, there have been a total of 30,600 direct new and induced jobs generated by the new banks. The spillover jobs extend throughout the State in all sectors, including manufacturing, construction, utility, trade, finance, service, and government employment. Since 1985, banking employment in Delaware has grown at an average annual rate of 15.8% compared with 3.3% for the U.S.and 2.0% in the neighboring states.

These new banks have generated considerable revenue for the State, both directly through the bank franchise tax, and indirectly through the enhanced income accruing to the newly employed workers. In 1980, before the Financial Center Development Act, bank franchise tax revenue was $2.2 million and contributed 0.3% of General Fund Revenue. For 1992 the bank franchise tax generated $61 million, nearly 5% of the State's General Fund.

And the old banks have benefitted as well. No old bank has gone out of business since 1981 and most have gained from the increases in employment and income experienced in the State. The banks' fear of an inadequate supply of labor has been quelled. Although there has definitely been some wage acceleration and higher turnover rates among bank personnel in the past few years, the State's labor force of 370,000 and more than a 1.3 million in the labor forces of Delaware and the contiguous counties in Pennsylvania, New Jersey, and Maryland have provided an ample labor supply. Most of the new banks report two or three well-qualified applicants for each position advertised.

The excitement in Delaware's economy is not exclusively due to the changes the State has made in banking legislation. The Financial Center Development Act was a significant contributor, but far from the only one. The innovative and dramatic results achieved in attracting major financial institutions, enabled the State's leaders to showcase Delaware's favorable overall business climate. Media coverage of the banking legislation and bank moves to the State in the nation's leading newspapers, magazines, and television shows was plentiful. However, the positive statements made by the bankers who have moved here and continue to expand in Delaware have been the State's best advertisement. This message has been received by executives not only in the banking industry but also in all lines of business across the country.

Conclusion

While the Reagan Administration denounced government's intervention in business practices, Delaware and other state governments played the role of economic innovators. They restructured their taxes, designed economic development incentives, and created new playing fields for the banking industry.

Changes in federal law to allow full interstate banking were anticipated several years ago. The pressure for this deregulation has been reduced by the record number of bank failures, although the two events are not connected. Banks can be strengthened if they are given greater flexibility to compete with the diversified financial services firms. The technological advances in banking, including electronic transfers, have and will probably force a great deal of de facto interstate banking.

transfers, have and will probably force a great deal of de facto interstate banking. Today, however, considerable uncertainty exists about the future federal government's role in banking. The federal government may merely ratify and legitimize the actions that the states have taken. Or federal government could preempt the states' banking powers particularly as the states expand bank activities into the fields of insurance, security underwriting and real estate.

Federalism in the U.S. does not give the states and the federal government equal power with respect to banking. The Feds have the primary power, especially as they construct possible antitrust challenges. States retained the branching powers, but there is a wide-spread perception that the federal government is in a strong position to assume all the other regulatory powers. If the deregulation that has occurred is making the banking system more responsible to the ultimate demands of the consumers and markets in general, why isn't the responsible role for the federal government one that ratifies the deregulatory successes that have occurred in the state laboratories of democracy? One of the fundamental problems of federalism in the U.S. has been the appropriate delegation of power. In bank deregulation, responsible governing might allow that power to remain in the state capitols.

CHAPTER FIVE

TOWARD RESPONSIBLE VOLUNTARISM: AN EXPLORATION OF OPERATIVE DOCTRINES

JON VAN TIL

The emergence of a third, or voluntary, sector of society confronts the political scientist with the challenge of analyzing the boundary between public and private action. Six traditions of political thought (idealist, utilitarian, formalist, pragmatic, participatory, populist) are applied in this paper to the study and practice of contemporary voluntarism.

The realm of voluntarism in society encompasses such phenomena as volunteering, citizen participation, nonprofit organizations, and philanthropy. Nine percent of all employment in U.S. society occurs in the voluntary and nonprofit sector,[1] and voluntary associations play key service and advocacy roles in such contemporary issues as abortion rights, housing the homeless, and restraining, or advancing, a variety of foreign and domestic policy initiatives.

In this paper I will consider the theory and practice of voluntarism (defined as organized action, uncoerced and deemed socially beneficial) in the various forms it takes as an operative doctrine (or guiding set of beliefs aimed toward action). It is my argument that among these operative doctrines are clusters that most closely approach the ideal of "responsible voluntarism," or a form of voluntary action that meets a set of widely agreed upon criteria for just and effective human activity.

Concepts of representation are conventionally seen as the province of political scientists, and I write as a sociologist who has long specialized in the study of voluntary action. Linking the theory and practice of voluntarism with those of governmental institutions requires some effort to oversee the fences that have developed between these disciplinary specializations.

Relations between governmental and voluntary organizations are complex in American democracy, and repay the attention of political scientists. It is, after all, through actions mediated by voluntary associations that much significant politically related participation occurs in society. Examples are as diverse as the abortion controversy, through demonstrations and the occasional fire-bomb; the agony over the homeless, through the divestment of public responsibility for housing to an overmatched (on that issue) "voluntary sector;" and the machinations of the Iran-Contra scheme, through the use of a nonprofit organization to advance administration goals of shipping arms illegally to the Nicaraguan opposition.

---

[1] See for reference Virginia Ann Hodgkinson and Murray S. Weitzman, <u>Dimensions of the Independent Sector: A Statitical Profile</u> (Washington: INDEPENDENT SECTOR, 1984). The nonprofit sector, as conventionaly defined, includes in its ranks many colleges, universities, and hospitals.

In many cases, deeply held views advanced by voluntary associations counter those held with equal fervor by other associations. There is as at least as much diversity in the third sector as in any other.

Government's role toward associations is itself manifold: it certifies some, but not all, associations as worthy of tax-exemption; it rewards some, but not all, nonprofit organizations with grants, contracts, and other official recognition; it relies on some, but not all, voluntary groups for the advancement of social or economic agendas of particular personal preference by elected leaders.

Political scientists have tended to focus their study of associations upon political parties, trade unions, and movement organizations which seek specific political reforms. This specialization has left the broader field of "third-sector" studies to an interdisciplinary collection of scholars in sociology, economics, and history (to list the most prominent fields).[2] Perhaps as a partial result of the relative absence of political scientists from the ranks of "voluntary and nonprofit" studies, the prevailing paradigm in this emerging scholarly field assumes a separation and even competitiveness between government and association.

Thus the leading peak association in the field emerged with the rather misleading name of "INDEPENDENT SECTOR." This association seems compelled by its name and the prevailing ideology of its supporters to sustain a normative conception of the "independence" of associations from government that belies both reality and the private good sense of its leaders. In the broader field of associational life, awareness by practitioners of the nuances of government-voluntary relations seems far greater than that which greets the differentiation of voluntaries from corporate organizations. The result is a confusion of the role of voluntarism in society that often sees associational leaders referring to themselves as practicing in the "private sector."[3]

These confusions seem to me both conceptual and theoretical, and also appear remediable by a strong infusion of political theory. But efforts to introduce such perspectives into "the sector" (as its leaders cozily refer to it) have been coolly regarded. The obligatory reference to de Tocqueville or Bellah[4] usually suffices to establish the worthiness of the sector's mission and actions; fuller discussion of the societal implications of its work, especially if ambiguous in relation to the production

---

[2] The Association for Research on Voluntary Action and Nonprofit Organization (ARNOVA), the major scholarly association in this field, counts among its members 35 social workers, 34 sociologists, 34 business administration faculty, and 31 public administration faculty but only 11 political scientists.

[3] It seems difficult to explain this preference in paradigm in terms of simple political ideology. "Third sector" leaders include at least as many identifiable "liberals" as "conservatives," if one recounts those who have entered the "revolving door" of sector leadership from governmental life. At Independent Sector there is John Gardner, whose cabinet experience was under Lyndon Johnson. Moderate Republicans also come to mind: George Romney at Volunteer: the National Center for Citizen Involvement, and David Mathews at the Kettering Foundation. The leading neo-conservative to take a leadership role in the sector is Leslie Lenkowsky, who directs a small policy studies center in Washington, D.C.

[4] Robert Bellah, et.al., Habits of the Heart: Individualim and Commitment in American Life (Berkeley: University of California Press, 1985).

of good, is typically absent.[5]

The social scientist retains the faith that knowledge is a basis for self-reflective action, and that such action will in some way advance the common plight of humankind. In that spirit of meliorist rationality, the present paper suggests that voluntarism must be tested by evaluative criteria before its social effect can be assessed. In this regard, the work of political scientist Charles E. Gilbert provides a useful conceptual base for the departure of this interdisciplinary essay.

In his paper, "Operative Doctrines of Representation", Gilbert [6] surrounded each of six conceptions of representation with a set of distinctive concepts, as follows:

1. The Idealist perspective is seen to take as its focus such concepts as:

Community as whole; collective interests; values; dialectic methods; leadership; expressive style; common concerns.

2. The Utilitarian perspective takes as its key concepts:

Individualism and individual choice; conservatism; limited government; interests; majority rule; concern with coercion; emphasis on economy and deemphasis of public sector.

3. The Formalist perspective emphasizes such concepts as:

Rationalism; formalism; constitutionalism; qualified individualism; rights; natural law; segregation of public and private; consensus.

4. The Pragmatic perspective places its attention on:

Group interests; urbanization; communication; regulation; expertise; experimentation; symbolic interactionism; process; problem-solving; public-private blurring.

5. The Participatory perspective looks at institutions that are:

Face to face; bear psychological meaning; and are oriented toward empowerment, equality, and social justice.[7]

6. The Populist perspective emphasizes:

Political equality; majority rule; translation of preferences into public policy; people.

---

[5] For my own effort to introduce a fuller discussion of these issues, see Jon Van Til, Mapping the Third Sector: Voluntarism in a Changing Social Economy (New York: The Foundation Center, 1988).
[6] Charles E. Gilbert, "Operative Doctrines of Representation," American Political Science Review, vol. 57 (September 1963), pp. 604-618.
[7] Jack H. Nagel, Participation (Englewood Cliffs: Prentice-Hall, 1987).

The role of voluntarism in democratic society has been explored in my earlier work, *Mapping the Third Sector*.[8] There I considered five traditions of democratic thought, loosely adapted from the work of Pennock and Putnam,[9] and related them to patterns of volunteered participation in society. These forms of democratic theory -- populism, idealism, pluralism, neo-corporatism, and social democracy (along with a sixth, constitutionalism) -- may be related to the six operative doctrines as follows:

THEORIES OF DEMOCRACY	OPERATIVE DOCTRINES
Populism	POPULISM
Idealism	IDEALIST
Pluralism	PRAGMATIC
Neo-corporatism	UTILITARIAN
Social democracy	PARTICIPATORY
(Constitutionalism)	FORMALIST

Applying the operative doctrines to the arena of voluntarism, we may first search for theoretical plausibility, and then a fit between theory and practice. In some cases we may find a doctrine particularly suited to a particular organization or leadership style. In other cases, the doctrines may be applied to suit a particular organizational phase or need.

Voluntarism as pragmatic, pluralist theory

Voluntary action is most often considered by its practitioners as part of a pluralistic system of decision-making, in which the common good is advanced by means of actions directed as well toward private advantage. Voluntarism is seen in the pluralist tradition as a way of accomplishing necessary societal affairs. It provides a way for individuals and groups to affect decisions without directly intervening in a governmental process. It also allows money to be transmuted into organization, and organization to partake in the exercise of power. The pluralist tradition has been applied to the study of voluntarism by such authors as Berger and Neuhaus, Schindler-Rainman and Lippitt, and Levitt.[10]

The weakness of pluralism lies in the advantages in wealth and power some groups enjoy over others. The tension between the noise required to raise an issue and the discomfort such volume occasions among the "regular players" is not easy to resolve. Within the nonprofit world, the tension between advocacy and service is of long standing. But Levitt's observation remains timely: "Since society is by nature

---

[8] Jon Van Til, Mapping the Third Sector: Voluntarism in a Changing Social Economy (New York: The Foundation Center, 1988).

[9] J. Roland Pennock, Democratic Political Theory (Princeton: Princeton University Press, 1979); Robert Putnam, Politicians and Politics: Themes in British and Italian Elite Political Culture (New Haven: Yale University Press, 1970).

[10] Peter L. Berger and Richard J. Neuhaus, "To Empower the People: The Role of Mediating Structures in Public Policy" (Washington, D.C.: American Enterprise Institute); Eva Schindler-Rainman and Ronald Lippit, The Volunteer Community: Creative Uses of Human Resources (Fairfax, VA: NTL Learning Resources Corp., 1975); Theodore Levit, The Third Sector: New Tactics for a Responsive Society (New York: AMACOM, 1973).

a complex compromise of its inhabitants, as things change some will believe that the compromises they are making are disproportionately high -- that there is inequity and therefore injustice."[11] These individuals will organize themselves in "New Third Sector" organizations to redress these perceived wrongs, Levitt notes, and those in power are well advised to listen and deal with them. But, he also notes, the noise and velocity of protest must be balanced by a respect for others.

In the pluralist literature on voluntarism one finds a litany of the pragmatic pluralist's values as Gilbert identified them: articulation of group interests; coping with the excesses of urbanization; establishing communication; assuring regulation; employing expertise; being willing to experiment; taking the role of the other; developing processes that both limit and resolve conflict; and blurring the boundaries between public and private actions.

Voluntarism in idealist theory

The idealist has long taken exception to the pluralist's contention that the simultaneous singing of many songs would lead to harmonious concert. From Rousseau to Lowi, idealists have been suspect of the particularism involved in association.

Idealists focus in their democratic theory on the role of dialogue and the building of a better and more holistic political community. Even when its thinkers -- such as T. H. Green, Bernard Bosanquet, and Mary Parker Follett -- saw voluntary action as a legitimate aspect of the good society, they tended to view dialogue as most significantly being engendered both within political and voluntary institutions.

Several influential contemporary idealists -- most prominently Sheldon Wolin and T. H. Lowi, fault voluntary action for its particularism. Lowi proclaims the virtues of constitutional democracy, and observes that private bureaucracies accrete about the provision of volunteering bureaucracies which themselves require public observation and regulation. The voluntary sector is handmaiden to a repressive and less than fully democratic society: it requires the "tempering" of the "excesses of pluralism"[12] and the distrust of interests and groups.[13]

Political idealists like Lowi and Wolin disparage voluntarism as they glorify the virtues of political life. But idealism is supported, nonetheless, as an operant doctrine of voluntarism by many organizational leaders and several prominent scholars. President Bush drew upon this tradition when he noted a "thousand points of light. And former foundation and university president Robert L. Payton views philanthropy as a core human value and a key institutional creation

The organization of efforts to make things better, or to make them less bad, is philanthropy. It begins with perception: someone has to see suffering and to recognize it for what it is. This requires imagination -- not simply the sensitivity of the observing novelist or anthropologist, but imagination linked to moral sentiment, moral sentiment linked to action. To these is added organization. . . .(I)t is within

---

[11] Theodore Levit, The Third Sector: New Tactics for a Responsive Society (New York: AMACOM, 1973).
[12] Sheldon S. Wolin, Politics and Vision (Boston: Little, Brown, 1960).
[13] Theodore J. Lowi, The End of Liberalism: Ideology,Policy, and the Crisis of Public Authority (New York: W.W. Norton 1969), p. 296.

the philanthropic tradition that the moral agenda of society is put forward.[14]

In practice, contemporary philanthropists describe their giving with the same blend of self- and other-interest that characterized the motivations of John D. Rockefeller and Andrew Carnegie, themselves inheritors of a Calvinist tradition of self-advancement through conspicuous self-abnegation.

The theory and practice of philanthropy rather fully encompass the idealist's central emphases as identified by Gilbert: community as whole, collective interests, values, leadership, expressive style, and common concerns.

Voluntarism in populist theory

A third tradition, that of populist theory, is typically more hospitable to voluntarism than is the idealist view. In the populist vision, what counts is the organized expression of heartfelt sentiment, the willingness to act on that sentiment, and the distrust of those who hold elite positions.

Historian Lawrence Goodwyn[15] sees the core vision of the Populist revolt of the late 19th century as: a profoundly simple one: the Populists believed that they could work together to be free individually. In their institutions of self-help, Populists developed and acted upon a crucial democratic insight: to be encouraged to surmount rigid cultural inheritances and to act with autonomy and self-confidence individual people need the psychological support of other people. . . .The Populist essence was. . .an assertion of how people can ACT in the name of the idea of freedom. At root, American Populism was a demonstration of what authentic political life can be in a functioning democracy.[16]

Contemporary populist theorist Harry Boyte has noted that voluntary participation may open "free social spaces that, under certain conditions, can turn into breeding grounds of insurgency."[17] A vibrant populism underlies the work of many voluntary organizations in contemporary society. Neighborhood organizations such as those organized in the 1970s by the National Association of Neighborhoods, and best exemplified by the ACORN organization in the 1980s, have aimed to empower citizens with a direct voice seen as unavailable to them through conventional political institutions.

The populist vision in voluntarism clearly involves the values identified by Gilbert: political equality, majority rule, translation of preferences into public policy; and the direct involvement of people in (to use another phrase that entered our discourse in the early '60s) decisions that affected their lives. This vision of voluntarism involves direct action, face-to-face organizing, and a critical estimation of the essentially private-regarding nature of megainstitutions, whether corporate or governmental. Voluntary associations, in this view, form an outpost of democracy in a world dominated by organizational elites -- a place where ordinary people can

---

[14] Robert Payton, "Teaching Philanthropy," in Jon Van Til, ed., Conflict, Change, and Consensus in Philanthropy: Confronting the Cutting-Edge Issues (1988), p. 119.

[15] Lawrence Goodwyn, The Populist Movement (New York: Oxford University Press, 1978), pp. 295-296.

[16] Lawrence Godwyn The Populist Movement (New York: Oxford University Press, !978), pp. 295-296.

[17] Harry C. Boyte, The Backyard Revolution: Understanding the New Citizen Movement (Philadelphia: Temple University Press, 1980), p. 63.

still make their influence felt.

Voluntarism and participatory social democracy

During the quarter-century, a great deal of public and scholarly attention has been paid to the doctrine of citizen participation. The Port Huron Statement was issued in the same year Gilbert published; the War on Poverty followed shortly with its call for "maximum feasible participation;" the National Conference on Citizen Participation was held in 1978; and the 1980s have seen the federal government rein in a wide set of participatory emphases.

I have chosen to focus on the participatory thrust toward social democracy in this section. I make this choice in light of the distinctive thrust of this perspective in practical political theory, and its obvious impact on academic thought over the past quarter-century.

Voluntarism is an ambiguous value to the advocate of participatory social democracy. Despite Amatai Etzioni's spirited defense of voluntary action in *The Active Society*, others have been more slow to rally to its cry. Michael Lerner notes that the spirit of volunteerism is not entirely foreign to the new democratic theory, though not its highest priority: "it is good to put iodine on scratches, but iodine will not cure a malignant tumor."[18]

The attractiveness of self-help to social democrats may reflect the belief that such "small groups," to use Lerner's phrase, can evolve into independent centers of political consciousness and action in times of social change. This faith in decentralized and spontaneous social action also underlies the social democrats' enthusiasm for grassroots movements. Michael Harrington writes directly of the need to take America's "most cherished conservative myth seriously: that the 'grassroots' should be a spontaneous, natural locus of political life. To make this old saw come true will take a radical reorganization of local and regional government in America -- and therefore a frontal assault on a bastion of undemocratic, conservative power."[19] And Walzer, in a felicitous phrase, writes of the "hollowing out of the state" that is achieved by citizen action in such a society. It is this view of democracy as continuing struggle by means of citizen volunteering that marks the social democratic perspective.

The participatory social democratic view of voluntarism emphasizes the themes of face to face interaction and psychological meaning identified by Gilbert, but extends this view to include the primacy of empowerment, equality, and social justice. These participatory values, analyzed in greater detail by Nagel,[20] form an important part of the contemporary theory of social democracy, and are fed, so its defenders contend, by a full and active or voluntary society.[21]

In the practice of American voluntarism, this flame is kindled by a set of organizational forces which fail to capture the support of major parties while they continue to influence them. The ideas of populism, often combined with idealist conceptions, remain persuasive in social science classrooms, Quaker meetinghouses,

---

[18] Michael P. Lerner The New Socialist Revolution: An Introduction to Its Theory and Strategy (New York: Dell, 1973), p. 240.
[19] Michael Harrington Toward a Democratic Left (New York: Macmillan, 1968).
[20] Jack H. Nagel, Participation (Englewood Cliffs: Prentice-Hall, 1978).
[21] See for reference Amitai Etzioni, The Active Society (New York: Free Press, 1968).

urban community organizations, and other interstitial loci of unfettered thought in our organizational society. While democratic socialism remains a "foreign ideology" to the American experience, it does seem to maintain enough of a hold in American thought to warrant its inclusion as an operant variant in the theory of voluntarism.

Voluntarism in utilitarian theory

Contemporary utilitarian theory may properly be viewed as taking, in one of its major forms, a distinctly conservative tack.[22] Perhaps its most pervasive statement is made in the form of the neo-conservative theory of privatization. Over the past quarter-century, neo-conservative theory and practice have risen to power and prominence in Western democracies.

To the neo-conservative, a major value of voluntarism is found in the tax savings it engenders, and not in its strengthening of democracy. The theory centrally focuses on those forms of organization that advance economic interests at the level of collaboration among elites. Such economically-inspired activity, however important, is neither voluntary nor democratic--in that it is remote from the rule of the people. Citizen participation plays a role in restoring traditional values of respect and decency in this theory, but the citizen activist is seen as preferring the pleasures of private life to the rigors of social politics.[23]

A related theory has been identified as neo-corporatist in some circles. Contemporary U.S. versions of neo-corporatist theory have been most prominently presented as normative by "neo-liberal" investment banker Felix Rohatyn. The neo-corporatist ideology abounds in discussions of "public-private" partnerships, and these discussions (as well as the packaged "deals" they lead to) also demonstrate the general absence of either citizen participation or voluntary action. Neo-corporatist theory prescribes a decision-making system in which the leaders of business and government meet as formally designated agents of their organizations to decide the great issues of economic policy, social distribution, and general welfare. The perspective of this theory, and the residual role it provides for the individual citizen (voter and trade union member) suggests that the theory stands somewhat removed from the "rule by the people."

In the hands of neo-corporatist thinkers like George Gilder or E. L. Savas, neo-corporatist theory advocates the "privatization" of public services, positing the development of private economies for the provision of formerly public goods. Building on the disenchantment with the bureaucratic state as service-provider, an influential contemporary critique of government has developed. The claim is forwarded that the state cannot perform as well as the market in certain activities, and that its role should be narrowly circumscribed. In such a view, voluntary action becomes part of an expanded "private sector," facilitating the reduction of public social service expenses, and calling upon the volunteered contributions of individual donors and actors.

The Utilitarian view has been most prominently presented in recent years by President Reagan's Task Force on Private Sector Initiatives. Wrapped in a mantle of glorification of the concept, two major themes of substance emerge: first, that voluntarism is a major source for the provision of social services, and second, that

---

[22] Charles E. Gilbert, "Operative Doctrines of Representation," American Political Science Review, Vol. 57 (September 1963), p. 606.
[23] Yale Burton Pines, Back to Basics: The Traditionalist Movement that is Sweeping Grass-Roots America (New York: Morrow, 1982).

decision-making in the voluntary sector should be the prerogative of a variety of "public-private partnerships." The Task Force came up remarkably short of suggestions as to how to accomplish its goals. Task Force member Richard Cornuelle,[24] a writer and former corporate official, noted that Reagan's statements on volunteerism often "carelessly" appealed "to a faith that was lost fifty years ago."

In the practice of contemporary "nonprofit organization" (to use the modish term of the 1980s that has come to replace "voluntary action" in everyday use within "the sector"), the emulation of business models and practices has become so widespread that the present author has suggested the establishment of an annual "George Babbitt Prize." This award, he offers, should be given to the individual "whose work most significantly advances the transformation of the voluntary nonprofit sector into a form indistinguishable from corporate 'business as usual.'"[25]

Formalist views of voluntarism

Formal views of voluntarism tend to center about the concept of "sector," of which four are commonly identified: business, government, voluntary, and household. On the basis of their membership in one of these formal organizational worlds, then, distinctiveness is attributed to an enterprise.

Such views, as Gilbert[26] noted, rely on "certain analytical concepts...from which it is difficult to eliminate the normative content." One such concept is certainly that of "the sector," which is often spoken of by associational leaders in hushed tones that imply the authority of their work.

In the work of James Douglas,[27] one finds a full-blown presentation of the formalist values of rationalism, constitutionalism, qualified individualism, rights, natural law, consensus, and, especially, the segregation of public and private.

My own work suggests the limitations of the formalist perspective. Seeing voluntarism as contained by a single "voluntary sector" in society,[28] I have argued, prevents us from recognizing that voluntarism can be an important force in the workplace and in government itself. Such diverse actions as those of the "whistleblower" or the "stipended volunteer" (say, in the Peace Corps) may be seen as instances of voluntarism. It has been my representation that only when the four sectors are viewed as components of a single structure, or political-economic society, that the most important functions of voluntarism begin to appear.

The contention that the voluntary sector is linked in manifold interdependence with governmental, corporate, and household structures has been asserted by Ostrander, Hall, Salamon, and others.[29] These views have proven controversial in the professional deliberations of the third sector, particularly among those organizationally tied to the advocacy of third-sector independence. The struggle between formalists and their critics is a central one in contemporary scholarship on

---

[24] Richard Cornuelle, Healing America (New York: G.P. Putnam's Sons, 1963), p. 177.
[25] Jon Van Til, "Op-ed: On the Babbit Prize," NonProfit Times (June 1989).
[26] Charles E. Gilbert, "Operative Doctrines of Representation," American Political Science Review, Vol 57 (September 1963), p. 609.
[27] James Douglas, Why Charity? The Case for a Third Sector (Beverly Hills: Sage, 1983).
[28] Jon Van Til, Mapping the Third Sector: Volunterism in a Changing Social Economy (New York: The Foundation Center, 1988).
[29] Lester M. Salamon, America's Non Profit Sector: A Primer (1987).

voluntarism.

Conclusion: toward responsible voluntarism

It seems clear that the six operational doctrines are alive and well in the third sector, and that each has its own strong intellectual and organizational adherents. It will require further study to detail the ways in which these doctrines are applied in associational life. In some cases, it is likely that an organization can be characterized as consistently following one or another doctrine; in others the doctrines may be applied in patterns reflecting different organizational tasks.

For the present, it may be noted that the fit between this schema and its earlier application to representation surely relates, in part, to the role that voluntary action itself plays in the representative process. It is by means of participation in associational life that Americans have located an important means of representing their most basic beliefs and advancing their most central interests. By affiliating themselves in voluntary nonprofit organizations, individuals are able to advance many of the goals conventionally ascribed to political representation.

Beyond its pluralist contributions, voluntary action in its populist and participatory modes contributes directly to the activation of individual and group concerns. Indeed, "communitarian" conceptions of voluntarism may be developed to address the widespread need expressed in modern society to blend rights and responsibilities in a responsive community. In that way, the idealist's goal of reflective action may also be advanced. These "active" conceptions of voluntarism may be contrasted with the more "passive" images provided by formalist and neo-corporatist conceptions. Here individuals are largely represented by elite forces, and do not actively involve themselves in the voluntary process.

Blending the participatory, pluralist, and idealist traditions, indeed, suggests the importance of borrowing another concept from Gilbert, and speaking of "responsible voluntarism" in an analogous way to his "responsible administration."[30] Such responsible voluntarism may be seen as a potential characteristic of every major societal institution. It might take the form of a particular dedication to work, or "whistleblowing" within a governmental or corporate bureaucracy, or working with neighbors to care for elders, install a stop sign, or restrain illicit drug sales within a neighborhood. It might include the twelve criteria Gilbert set forth for administrative responsibility: responsiveness, flexibility, consistency, stability, leadership, probity, candor, competence, efficacy, prudence, due process, and accountability.[31]

Voluntary and nonprofit associations form one important set of institutions in the organizational world of contemporary society. From Tocqueville to the very present (for example, Putnam's paper elsewhere in this volume), students of society have found in the intermediate association a source of participation, political competence, and legitimation.[32] It would seem altogether appropriate to hold such

---

[30] Charles E. Gilbert "The Framework of Administrative Responsibility," The Journal of Politics, Vol. 21 (1959), pp. 373-407.

[31] For a presentation of ten criteria for productive voluntarism, see Van Til, Mapping the Third Sector: Volunteerism in a Changing Social Economy (New York: The Foundation Center, 1988), Chapter 11.

[32] Neal Smelser, "Social Structure," Handbook of Sociology (Newbury Park, CA: Sage, 1988), p. 112.

associations to tests of effectiveness and responsibility. After all, if voluntarism is a force that includes the helping act of the altruist, the workings of the Red Cross organization to assure disaster relief, and the terrorist tactics of the Ku Klux Klan, it would certainly seem appropriate to be able to distinguish between "responsible" and "irresponsible" voluntarism.

Responsible voluntarism is an active, spontaneous, and challenging force in society. Its development might serve, therefore, as an organizing principle for the development of an active and participatory democracy in an era known for its complacency.

The kinship between political representation and voluntary action itself reflects the permeability of the boundary between the governmental and voluntary sectors. Just as there are competing theories of representation, so are there diverging views of voluntarism. The two sets of institutions aim toward common goals, but work through different organizational vehicles.

An additional kinship between the concepts is reflected their continuous requirement of examination, exploration, and elaboration. What Gilbert concluded of representation can be paraphrased precisely for voluntarism: since "voluntarism," despite its important role in philosophy and practice, is unlikely ever to meet with common understanding as a concept, the empirical study of voluntary action seems likely to be affected by commitments to these traditions; and their critical examination should therefore help to clarify research.

CHAPTER SIX

COUNTING AND SHAPING THE RIGHT TO VOTE

ROGER B. MOORE

Bridging the troubled waters

The question what is meant by representation seems of much less importance, given its ambiguity, than the question how it figures in one's approach to broader normative problems of politics.[1]
[2]From the number of imaginable cities we must exclude those whose elements are assembled without a connecting thread, an inner rule, a perspective, a discourse. With cities, it is as with dreams: everything imaginable can be dreamed, but even the most unexpected dream is a rebus that conceals a desire, or, its reverse, a fear.[2]

    This chapter explores how two sometimes awkwardly acquainted professions -- law and political science -- have shaped and might shape the quality and equality of representation in the United States. It discusses the relationship between the legal concept of "vote dilution" and normative problems of politics.
    By recognizing that a wide variety of local patterns and practices can impede the effective implementation of equal representation, vote dilution doctrine has provided racial and ethnic minorities with a powerful, if limited, means of entering a political system that has often been unwaveringly hostile to their presence.[3] But by asking how the abstract right to vote becomes operative in democratic political institutions, this doctrine is also something of a rebus: it mediates a conflict between those who desire broad political transformations to empower themselves in and

---

[1] Charles E. Gilbert, "Operative Doctrines of Representation," American Political Science Review, 57 (1963), p. 16.

[2] Italo Calvino, Invisible Cities, translated by William Weaver (San Diego, 1984), pp. 43-44.

[3] See, e.g., Thornburg v. Gingles, 478 U.S. 30 (1986). Gingles is the leading case interpreting the current version of Section 2 of the Voting Rights Act, 42 U.S.C. 1973. For useful overviews of political science and legal scholarship on minority vote dilution, see Bernard Grofman and Chandler Davidson, eds., Controversies in Minority Voting (Washington: 1992), and Chandler Davidson, ed., Minority Vote Dilution (Washington: 1984). Two other areas of vote dilution deserve mention, although they are not discussed in this essay. First, dilution issues arise when areas "targeted" under Section 5 of the Voting Rights Act must receive administrative preclearance for voting changes. See City of Rome v. United States 446 U.S. 156 (1980). Second, the Supreme Court has hinted in dicta that partisan gerrymandering may result in vote dilution under some limited circumstances. See Davis v. Bandemer, 478 U.S. 109 (1986).

within these institutions, and those who fear the consequences of these changes. Although their themes are sometimes not made explicit, vote dilution cases necessarily require both counting and shaping; "counting" to protect the right of citizens to an equally valued vote, and "shaping" to arrange representative institutions in a manner that ensures its citizens an equal opportunity to participate in the political process and elect candidates of their choice.

Beneath the formal language of dilution doctrine is a drama that resembles the distant and sometimes perilous travels of an explorer and her geographer. Wavering between boldness and timidity, the explorer sets out to reach the unfamiliar shores of "equal representation," but lives in constant fear of getting tangled in the "thicket" of politics,[4] or of being cast "adrift on uncharted seas" of history or social science.[5] The geographer carefully draws maps, checks statistics, and measures distances, but cannot identify the final destinations acting alone. Others suspiciously glance over their shoulders, concerned that they are either too reckless in their methods or too willing to leave the least powerful passengers behind. Some suspect that they have no interest in reaching the destination, while others live in mortal fear of what they will find when they arrive.

The questions raised in vote dilution cases sometimes embarrass students of democratic and constitutional theory by underscoring the stark contrast between the rhetoric of procedural equality and the crushing inequalities that pervade many aspects of political life. For minority voters who have suffered habitual exclusions from ordinary electoral politics, the idea of "voting rights" may seem strangely detached from the practical powerlessness they experience. Despite the legal right to vote and have each vote counted equally, minority voters may sense that political outcomes result from institutional forces that overwhelm their personal preferences. As both Charles E. Gilbert and Louis Hartz have reminded us, the images of democracy are not easily reconciled with political realities; rather, "by a sort of dialectic, democratic traditions tend to deny what is right under their noses."[6]

An emerging third generation of vote dilution doctrine is raising new opportunities to bridge the gulf between these images and realities. A first generation of vote dilution issues arose from geographic apportionment cases in the wake of Reynolds v. Sims, where the Supreme Court construed the Fourteenth Amendment's equal protection clause to mean that "the right of suffrage can be denied by a debasement or dilution of the weight of a citizen's vote just as effectively as by wholly prohibiting the free exercise of the franchise."[7] On one level, the principle of "one person, one vote" established in this case may seem purely arithmetic. However, Justice Warren's opinion also contained the germ of a more inclusive vision of equal representation, since it recognized that "each and every citizen has an inalienable right to full and effective participation" in the state's political processes, and to an "equally effective voice" in the election of

---

[4] Colegrove v. Green, 328 U.S. 549, 556 (1946).

[5] Mobile v. Bolden, 446 U.S. 55, 103 (1980), J. White dissenting.

[6] Gilbert, "Operative Doctrines of Representation," op. cit., p. 618. See also Louis Hartz, "Democracy: Image and Reality," in W. N. Chamber and R. H. Salisbury, eds., Democracy in the Mid-Twentieth Century: Problems and Prospects (St. Louis, 1960.)

[7] Reynolds v. Sims, 377 U.S. 533, 555 (1964).

representatives.8 While stating these principles in universal terms, the Court's remedy of arithmetically equal population districts did not address the meaning of these words for minorities who faced voting discrimination within these districts.

The first generation of vote dilution cases seemed largely unconcerned with institutional nuances of American politics that did not fit within the simple arithmetic of "one person, one vote." This inattention troubled members of racial and ethnic minorities who had long suffered from discrimination and often fared poorly in politics.9 These groups had good reason to fear that the redrawing of district lines and the at-large elections used to bring jurisdictions in technical compliance with "one person, one vote" would be used as occasions to plunder minorities' political power.10

Moreover, while the unprecedented success of the Voting Rights Act of 1965 against formal barriers to the franchise helped to prompt a "renaissance" in black political participation, this very success also prompted a renaissance in time-worn techniques that prevented minorities from translating these achievements into effective representation.11 These so-called "structural barriers" to voting equality -- which included the use of racial gerrymandering, winner-take-all at-large elections, and shifts from elected to appointive positions -- had helped undermine black political participation in the aftermath of the "first reconstruction" in the 19th century, and they threatened to have the same effect on the "second reconstruction" of the modern civil rights movement.12

In response to these concerns, a second generation of vote dilution doctrine began to address the special difficulties encountered by minorities -- principally racial and ethnic minorities -- who faced prolonged powerlessness because of

---

8 Ibid., p. 565.
9 Reynolds v. Sims itself epitomized this neglect, since the conflict that underlay the dispute involved a power struggle between rapidly growing white suburbs and a declining white "oligarchy" in rural counties with heavy black populations. In this pre-Voting Right Act case, few blacks were registered to vote. See James Blacksher and Larry Menefee, "At-Large Elections and One Person, One Vote: The Search for the Meaning of Racial Vote Dilution," in Davidson, ed., Minority Vote Dilution, op. cit., p. 203.
10 See Gordon Baker, "Gerrymandering: Privileged Sanctuary or Next Judicial Target?" in Nelson Polsby, ed., Reapportionment in the 1970s (Berkeley, 1971), p. 121.
11 Frank R. Parker, Black Votes Count (Chapel Hill, 1990), p. 1.
12 See J. Morgan Kousser, "The Undermining of the First Reconstruction: Lessons for the Second," in Davidson, ed., Minority Vote Dilution, pp. 27-46; Extension of the Voting Rights Act: Hearings before the Subcommittee on Civil and Constitutional Rights of the House Judiciary Committee, 97th Cong., 1st Sess. 2013 (1981), testimony of J. Morgan Kousser. On "structural barriers," see Armand Derfner, "Racial Discrimination and the Right to Vote," Vanderbilt Law Review, 26 (1973) 523-584.

factional domination.[13] Having only hinted at the available relief earlier,[14] federal courts expressly provided redress to victims of minority vote dilution. As recognized in a series of landmark federal cases, most notably White v. Regester[15] and Zimmer v. McKeithen,[16] courts were empowered to appraise a wide variety of local factors that influence opportunities for political participation and electoral inclusion.

The evidentiary factors described in White and Zimmer provided for a wide-ranging contextual exploration of local political opportunities, including characteristics of the local election system (such as the extent of racially polarized voting, successful minority candidates, and local voting practices that enhance the opportunity for discrimination against to minorities), characteristics of the political processes leading up to elections (such as the presence of racist appeals and the participation of minorities in parties' slating of candidates), and outside influences affecting the quality of representation (such as a history of discrimination against minority voting or political participation, the effects of discrimination in such areas as education, employment, and health, and officials' lack of responsiveness to minority needs).[17] These cases provided relief where the "totality of circumstances" demonstrated that African or Mexican Americans "had less opportunity than did other residents to participate in the political process and to elect legislators of their choice."[18]

Although these criteria provided minorities with a crucial new device to combat sophisticated forms of voting discrimination, they also generated fears that the federal judiciary would engage in the widespread restructuring of local election systems. The product of this fear -- the Supreme Court's notorious and short-lived Mobile v. Bolden decision[19] -- imposed a draconian intent test that undermined the

---

[13] Although most of these cases have challenged the use of winner-take-all at-large elections, a wider range of structural barriers to minority participation and election have also been the subjects of relief. See, e.g., Frank R. Parker, "Racial Gerrymandering and Legislative Reapportionment," in Chandler Davidson, ed., Minority Vote Dilution, op. cit., p. 85 (gerrymandering techniques of "cracking," "packing" or "stacking" the minority community).

[14] As early as 1965, the Supreme Court had suggested in dicta that, while multimember districts were not inherently unconstitutional, they might be invalidated if "designedly or otherwise," they operated "to minimize or cancel out the voting strength of racial or political elements of the voting population." Fortson v. Dorsey, 379 U.S. 433, 499 (1965).

[15] 412 U.S. 755 (1973).

[16] 485 F.2d 1297 (5th Cir. 1973) (en banc), aff'd sub. nom. East Carroll Parish School Bd. v. Marshall, 424 U.S. 636 (1976).

[17] For a helpful discussion of how evidence from political scientists is used in vote dilution cases, see Grofman, Mikalski, Noviello, "The Totality of Circumstances Test in Section 2 of the 1982 Extension of the Voting Rights Act: A Social Science Perspective," Law and Policy, 7 (1985), p. 199.

[18] White, 412 U.S. at 766-769.

[19] 446 U.S. 55 (1980).

evidentiary criteria used in these prior federal court decisions.[20] After extensive and sometimes virulent debate, Congress overwhelmingly voted in 1982 to amend the "nationwide" antidiscrimination provision of the Voting Rights Act, Section 2, to clarify that proof of discriminatory results is sufficient to prove minority vote dilution, and that proportional representation is not required as a remedy. In adopting the Section 2 amendment, Congress made direct reference to language and evidentiary criteria used in cases such as White and Zimmer.[21] Once a court identifies minority vote dilution in examining these criteria, it must use its equitable powers to completely remedy the problem.

Rejecting the "formalistic view" epitomized by the Bolden decision, Congress called upon courts interpreting the amended Section 2 to adopt "the functional view of `political process'," engaging in an intensely local appraisal of the factors derived from White and Zimmer.[22] If sensitivity to local circumstances was the great strength of this approach, impressionism was its weakness. Practitioners raised concerns that the factor-based approach had not clarified the priority it attached to particular factors or specified which configuration of factors would be decisive.[23] The most influential attempt to distill the essence of the results test has been the Supreme Court's seminal 1986 ruling in Thornburg v. Gingles,[24] which continues to define the interpretation of Section 2.[25]

In some respects, Gingles represented the triumph of second-generation vote dilution doctrine against renewed attacks. The Supreme Court invalidated most of a multimember redistricting plan that had resulted in minority vote dilution, rejecting attempts to transform the evidentiary criteria used to demonstrate racially polarized voting[26] and the extent of minority electoral success.[27] However, Gingles also subtly

---

[20] The Supreme Court's subsequent reading of the constitutional intent test in Rogers v. Lodge, 458 U.S. 613 (1983), avoided the harshness of the Bolden approach by noting that indirect evidence -- including the results of a districting scheme -- could be used as circumstantial evidence of discriminatory intent (ibid. at 618). In most circumstances, the question is now moot, since the statutory test under Section 2 of the Voting Rights Act,which had previously paralleled the constitutional standard, requires only proof of discriminatory results.

[21] 42 U.S.C. 1973. See S. Rep. No. 97-417, 97th Cong., 2d. Sess. (1982).

[22] Ibid., 30 n. 120.

[23] See James Blacksher and Lawrence Menefee, "At-Large Elections and One Person, One Vote: The Search for the Meaning of Racial Vote Dilution, in Davidson, ed., Minority Vote Dilution, op.cit., p. 216; Chandler Davidson, "The Voting Rights Act: A Brief History," in Grofman and Davidson, eds., Controversies in Minority Voting, op. cit., pp. 33-34.

[24] 478 U.S. 30 (1986).

[25] Bernard Grofman and Lisa Handley, "Identifying and Remedying Racial Gerrymandering," Journal of Law and Politics, 8 (1992), p. 347.

[26] Although no consensus was reached in Gingles on the specific statistical techniques used to demonstrate polarized voting patterns, a court majority upheld a finding of polarized voting based on evidence that blacks strongly supported black candidates and whites strongly supported whites. 478 U.S. at 58-61. A plurality held that a statistical correlation between the race of voters candidates selected was sufficient (ibid. at 63-70).

[27] A court majority rejected the contention that episodic successes of minority candidates automatically invalidate a dilution claim (478 U.S. at 74-76).

transformed the focus of dilution doctrine. Rather than merely referring to the multiple factors, a minority group challenging at-large elections must demonstrate three "necessary preconditions": that it is large and geographically compact enough to create a majority in a single-member district; that it is politically cohesive; and that bloc voting by the white majority is usually sufficient, in the absence of special circumstances, to defeat the minority's "preferred candidate."[28]

With its almost exclusive focus on "racial patterns in elections and demographics,"[29] Gingles ushered in a third generation of dilution doctrine, in which the geographer has attempted to steer the path toward equal representation in a simpler and more easily measurable direction. Although this turn responds to a yearning for easy mathematical rules to negotiate the complex territory of equal representation,[30] it has also invigorated the tension between conflicting sets of fears and desires. Some critics -- those questioning the voyage itself -- charge that dilution doctrine uses social engineering techniques to give minorities an unfair advantage in elections, hopelessly entangling courts in the much-feared "political thicket."[31] Other critics -- those questioning the destination -- contend that the new electoral focus signals a triumph of "tokenism" and a retreat from exploring sophisticated obstacles to equal participation in the political process, thus compromising the dream of a polity committed to full and effective representation for all its citizens.[32]

The third generation of dilution doctrine reflects deep ambivalences in American notions of voting rights, which evoke at the same time the desire for all to have an equally effective voice in the political process and the fear of institutional disorder that might arise if this ideal were fully implemented. The "brooding omnipresence" of proportional representation has long haunted vote dilution doctrine, since it exposes the tension between the rhetoric of procedural equality and the unequal power of losers in majority-rule districting systems.[33] While the fear of "proportional representation" and its effect on political institutions informs a huge amount of the resistance to proposed remedies for vote dilution, courts and commentators have often applied the term interchangeably to vastly different kinds of election systems. When remedial schemes employed in voting rights cases -- such

---

[28] Ibid., pp. 50-51.

[29] Laughlin McDonald, "The 1982 Amendments of Section 2 and Minority Representation," in Grofman and Davidson, eds., Controversies in Minority Voting, op. cit., p. 76.

[30] Pamela S. Karlan, "Maps and Misreadings: The Role of Geographic Compactness in Racial Vote Dilution Litigation," Harvard Civil Rights-Civil Liberties Law Review, 24 (1989), p. 179.

[31] Hugh Davis Graham, "Voting Rights and the American Regulatory State," and Timothy G. O'Rourke, "The 1982 Amendments and the Voting Rights Paradox," in Grofman and Davidson, eds., Controversies in Minority Voting, op. cit., pp. 177-196 and 85-117.

[32] See Lani Guinier, "The Triumph of Tokenism: The Voting Rights Act and the Theory of Black Electoral Success," Virginia Law Review, 77 (1991), pp. 1413-1514; Pamela S. Karlan, "Undoing the Right Thing: Single-Member Offices and the Voting Rights Act, " Virginia Law Review, 77 (1991), pp. 1-46.

[33] Sanford Levinson, "Gerrymandering and the Brooding Omnipresence of Proportional Representation: Why Won't it Go Away?" UCLA Law Review (1985), pp. 33, 257-278.

as single-member districts with heavily concentrated minority populations, or modifications of multimember districts that enhance the opportunity for minority influence -- are equated with the sorts of formal proportional systems used in many European countries, it is easy to miss the very different implications each of these methods may have for the institutions of representative democracy.

Beyond the question of election methods lies an even deeper source of tension: the troubled dialogue between rights and empowerment in a society where the conditions of politics are decidedly unequal. The fact that this dialogue must take place on the mine field of American race relations simply adds fuel to the fire. Because the images and realities of vote dilution doctrine are not easily reconciled, they sometimes have provoked cynicism as to whether voting rights can possibly take into account the institutional settings in which these rights may be effectively exercised. These cynical reactions can take two basic directions, each grounded in a particular constitutional theory and view of history. Although I will paint these reactions with broad brush strokes that border on caricature, I believe that each has had a powerful influence on attempts to steer the course of vote dilution doctrine. These directions may be termed the "complacent" view and the "tragic" view.[34]

The complacent view is rooted in formalist ideas of constitutionalism and a hostility toward the notion that terms such as "rights" are bound by time and circumstance.[35] This view contrasts the voting rights of the individual with claims predicated upon the powerlessness of particular groups. Although individuals may properly claim the right to cast a ballot and have it counted equally, group claims are presumed to lack legitimacy because they have no "core value" other than to guarantee proportional representation for politically unsuccessful minorities. Barring some clear evidence that government officials were motivated by racial or ethnic prejudice, institutional practices that submerge minority voting power (for example, replacing single-member districts with at-large election systems)[36] are regarded as neutral and natural parts of the political order. Attempts to remedy subtle forms of minority vote dilution are perceived to violate an individualist ethic of procedural equality, making some votes "count" more than others.[37] The inchoate assumption

---

[34] I have loosely adapted these terms from Drucilla Cornell, "Beyond Tragedy and Complacency," Northwestern Law Review, 81 (1987), p. 693. These reactions might also be described as "objectivist" and "relativist" in the senses used in Richard J. Bernstein, Beyond Objectivism and Relativism (Philadelphia, 1985).

[35] The socially constructed character of terms that define the boundaries of our discourse is, of course, a central theme in modern and postmodern social theory, articulated in the writings of Heidegger, Foucault, Derrida, and Kuhn, to name just several. See, e.g., Alan Megill, Prophets of Extremity (Berkeley, 1985).

[36] The tendency of at-large election systems to result in underrepresenting black citizens has been described as "one of the best-confirmed generalizations in the literature of political science." Richard Engstrom, "The Reincarnation of the Intent Standard," Howard Law Journal 28 (1985), p. 496. For a survey of pertinent studies, see Chandler Davidson and George Korbel, "At-Large Elections and Minority Group Representation," Journal of Politics 43 (1981), p. 982.

[37] These arguments were made repeatedly by the handful of senators who unsuccessfully opposed the "results test" amendment to the Voting Rights Act. For similar arguments in an academic setting, see Abigail Thernstrom, Whose Votes Count (Cambridge, MA, 1987); Kathryn Inglis

of the complacent view is that the "political process left substantially to its own devices" has come sufficiently close to racial justice so that further relief would provide minorities with "special protection."[38]

The tragic view operates as a reverse image of the complacent view. It is rooted in the antiformalist attack on traditional constitutionalism[39] and a suspicion that expressions of rights are inexorably bound by time and circumstance. Although the right to "equal representation" appears universal and inclusive, it is trailed by a silent ghost; the ghost of power justifying its own existence.[40] Legal definitions of this right, it is argued, serve mainly to legitimize the self-interest of the strong in dominating the weak, masking the instability and indeterminacy of existing allocations of power. In a world governed by the self-interest of the strong, discussions of "rights" convert real experiences into empty abstractions and may even frustrate "advances by progressive social forces."[41] Rather than delivering on its promise, "equal opportunity" in antidiscrimination law rationalizes an existing power structure that has successfully used legal rights-talk to immunize itself from real structural change.[42] The inchoate assumption of the tragic view is that racism has a symbiotic relationship with the institutions of American democracy,[43] frustrating attempts to establish a meaningful discourse between the pedagogy of rights theory and the "pedagogy of the oppressed."[44]

Taken together, the complacent and tragic views suggest that the explorer and geographer's voyage toward "equal representation" is doomed to run circles around a bitter and intractable neighborhood dispute, whose central characters are a stubborn patriarch portrayed by Leo Strauss and an impatient rebel portrayed by Friedrich Nietzsche. One clings desperately to the belief in the inherent justness of existing institutions, portraying challengers as nihilists who have no respect for a system of rights. The other suspects that rights are merely code words to rationalize

---

Butler, "Reapportionment, The Courts, and the Voting Rights Act: A Resegregation of the Political Process," University of Colorado Law Review 56 (1984), p. 1.

[38] Thernstrom, op. cit., pp. 5, 240.

[39] For a provocative survey of antiformalist themes in modern and postmodern constitutional scholarship, see Mark V. Tushnet, "Anti-Formalism in Recent Constitutional Theory," Michigan Law Review 83 (1985), p. 1502.

[40] The ghost's voice -- a familiar one in modern social criticism -- is that of Plato's foil Thrasymachus, arguing that "justice" reflects the self-interest of the strong. See Richard Wolin, The Terms of Cultural Criticism (New York, 1992), pp. 1-19. For an application to normative problems of American representation, see Elizabeth Mensch and Alan Freeman, "A Republican Agenda for a Hobbesian America?" Florida Law Review 41 (1989), pp. 581-622.

[41] Mark Tushnet, "An Essay on Rights," Texas Law Review 62 (1984), pp. 1363-64. See also Peter Gabel, "The Phenomenology of Rights-Consciousness and the Pack of Withdrawn Selves," Texas Law Review 62 (1984), p. 1563.

[42] See, e.g., Alan Freeman, "Legitimizing Racial Discrimination Through Antidiscrimination Law: A Critical Review of Supreme Court Doctrine," Minnesota Law Review 62 (1978), p. 1049.

[43] Derrick Bell, Faces at the Bottom of the Well (New York, 1992), p. 9; Jennifer Hochschild, "Race, Class, Power, and Equal Opportunity," in Norman E. Bowie, ed., Equal Opportunity (Boulder, 1988), pp. 75-101.

[44] Cf. Paulo Friere, Pedagogy of the Oppressed, translated by Myra Bergman Ramos (New York, 1988).

power systems, and proposes to speak bluntly in the language of power. Caught between the language of rights and the language of empowerment, vote dilution doctrine reflects the tension between "the essentialist permanence of natural law and the infinite plasticity of radical historicism."[45]

Although the tensions between rights and empowerment may prove to be intractable, I believe that these terms depend upon each other for meaning and provide no reason to abandon the exploration of "equal representation." Instead, the discussion of voting rights must be expanded to reflect the normative theories of politics implicit in various readings of voting rights. Neither the complacent nor the tragic view captures what is at stake in modern vote dilution decisions. The complacent view romanticizes the notion that there is some determinate and unchanging "individual right" to vote that is intelligible without reference to the political institutions that give it form and content. As it blinds itself to the variety of institutional characteristics that can shape the individual right to vote, it also neglects the historical and present obstacles that have thwarted the ability of racial and ethnic minorities to achieve equal opportunities to participate in the political process. At a more local level, this view drastically underestimates the barriers to minority political participation that persist in election schemes with a veneer of neutrality.[46]

While the tragic view exposes the complacent view's naivete toward problems of power and domination, it undervalues the significance of rights theories in the discourse on vote dilution. Hendrik Hartog has noted that there are three senses in which rights discourse may be used to realize constitutional aspirations: as a "trump" over competing claims; as a public duty to undo the structures that maintain oppression; and as a public duty for the government to "reconstruct itself or its relations to its citizens or lose legitimacy."[47] By raising questions about the relationship between the effective exercise of rights and the legitimacy of political institutions, vote dilution doctrine has embodied, at times, all three senses of rights. It is perhaps best understood as "an arena of struggle between contending and changing normative orders,"[48] one that has provoked -- and should provoke -- serious discussion of ways in which the institutions of representative government affect the exercise of political rights.

This essay's approach to vote dilution in this will not satisfy seekers a unitary definition of "equal representation" that transcends the problems of institutional context and the vagaries of normative political discussion. My response is simply that we cannot pretend these problems away by imagining that such a definition exists. In this regard, voting rights jurisprudence has much to learn from Charles E.

---

[45] Hendrik Hartog, "The Constitution of Aspiration and 'The Rights That Belong to Us All'," Journal of American History 74 (1987), p. 1026. A more extensive discussion of the Strauss/Nietzsche dilemma is found in Thomas L. Haskell, "The Curious Persistence of Rights-Talk in an Age of Interpretation," Journal of American History 74 (1987), p. 984.

[46] See, e.g., Chandler Davidson, "Minority Vote Dilution: An Overview," in Davidson, ed., Minority Vote Dilution, op. cit., p. 1; Pamela S. Karlan and Peyton McCrary, "Without Fear and Without Research: Abigail Thernstrom on the Voting Rights Act," Journal of Law and Politics 4 (1988), p. 751.

[47] Hartog, op. cit., p. 1020.

[48] Ibid., p. 1026.

Gilbert's pioneering essay, "Operative Doctrines of Representation."[49] Written in 1963, the same year that Justice Douglas rather cavalierly announced that the conception of political equality in American history "can mean only one thing,"[50] Professor Gilbert's essay revealed that political representation has no unitary meaning but can be approached from varying premises, each connected to particular normative traditions.[51]

Gilbert warned that generalizing about terms such as "representation" may obscure "the more detailed values at stake in action or discussion" and discourage "more pointed empirical inquiry relevant to those values."[52] In particular, those who try to make sense of the term must struggle with issues of "what is represented, and how; with the identification and evaluation of interests, and with the norms and sanctions affecting official behavior."[53] Understood this way, representation cannot be viewed simply as a numerical matter of aggregating private interests;[54] rather, it also involves the practical implementation of normative theories of democratic government. Its aims are not simply to count the polity, but also to shape the polity.

The "what" and "how" questions of representation pose several critical challenges for the future of vote dilution doctrine: first, to become sensitive to the institutional realities that often stand between the formal notion of a voting right and its effective exercise; second, to make sense of the judicial role in achieving a system that comes closer to equality in democratic representation; and finally, to identify and assess the more comprehensive institutional changes that may be necessary to bridge the gulf between the ideal of equal representation and the realities of political life.

This essay leaves many issues unexplored. It neither attempts to discuss more than superficially the development of case law and legislation on vote dilution, nor proposes a novel or elaborate framework by which courts may evaluate vote dilution claims. Instead, it explores the close connections between vote dilution issues and underlying problems in political theory. By exploring these connections, I hope to stimulate discussion about the values associated with equal representation and the institutional approaches best suited to realize these values.[55] Frank discussion of these relationships may also help to undo the "almost complete divorce" that plagues the categories of political science whose work sheds light on voting rights law. These include comparative politics, constitutionalism, domestic policy-making,

---

[49] Gilbert, op. cit.

[50] See Gray v. Sanders, 372 U.S. 368 (1963).

[51] The six traditions discussed in Gilbert's essay are: idealist, utilitarian, formalist, pragmatic, participatory, populist. See Gilbert, op. cit. An intriguing project -- one beyond the scope of this essay -- would be to survey voting rights cases for their affinities with these normative traditions.

[52] Ibid., p. 604.

[53] Ibid.

[54] Ibid., p. 616.

[55] While empirical political science will play a crucial role in this discussion, it must take account of the normative political theories associated with particular approaches. Unfortunately, many studies of elections and voting behavior have failed to address these connections. See Peter Natchez, Images of Voting/ Visions of Democracy (New York, 1985).

social choice theory, and political geography.56

My contention is that it is necessary -- and in a sense, unavoidable -- for courts to confront the normative political concerns inherent in the concept of vote dilution. Having determined that this is a necessary task, this essay explores the tensions between and within two themes, each of which captures a crucial aspect of what is at stake in vote dilution decisions.

The first theme may be labelled "counting the polity." This theme assumes that the goal of voting rights law is to implement the abstract right of all citizens to an equally valued vote. Implicit in this theme (though only partially acknowledged in the case law) is the assumption that a perfect system of voting rights would be the one that accurately aggregated all the private preferences expressed in elections. Although this theme emphasizes equal individual rights, it leaves ambiguous the institutional arrangements under which citizens' preferences are created, identified, and communicated.

Because of these ambiguities, a voting right cannot be defined solely through its abstract commitment to equality. Rather, as William Connolly has said of liberalism, "[i]t must be understood, as well, through the institutional arrangements it endorses. Its unity grows out of the congruence between these ideals and their institutional supports."57 Confronted with the problem of ensuring equal representation to minorities, courts and commentators have proposed various strategies to articulate a neutral way of engaging in the social ordering of equal voting opportunities. After discussing the three key approaches -- which I describe as the strategies of contextualism, containment, and proportionality -- I conclude that none of these have succeeded in insulating courts from the normative problems of politics. Courts cannot attempt to set rules for counting the polity without shaping the polity.

The second theme of "shaping the polity" recognizes that the right to vote implies institutions, and these institutions shape the character of representative government. This recognition, however, creates a need to account for the relationship between the individual's right to vote and the community in which it is exercised. Challenging the individualistic "Lockean consensus" of a previous generation,58 a new generation of theorists have attempted to reimagine the relationship between self and society in American public law. Drawing upon classical republican and civic humanist political theory, these theorists have argued the aim of jurisprudence is to promote civic virtue by restoring and perfecting an affirmative notion of freedom as self-government through politics.59 In this reading,

---

56 On the "almost complete divorce," see Arend Lijphart and Bernard Grofman, "Choosing an Electoral System," in Lijphart and Grofman, eds., Choosing an Electoral System (New York, 1984), p. 3.

57 William Connolly, "The Dilemma of Legitimacy," in William Connolly, ed., Legitimacy and the State (New York, 1984), p. 233.

58 Cf. Louis Hartz, The Liberal Tradition in America (New York, 1955).

59 See Section IV of this essay. The revisionist wave of constitutional theory has been described as "civic humanism," "modern republicanism," or "dialogic communitarianism." Its concerns have cut across a broad spectrum of recent legal scholarship, commanding the attention of such thinkers as Cass Sunstein, Frank Michelman, Drucilla Cornell, Richard Parker, Kathryn Abrams, and Gerald

the value of vote dilution doctrine is not simply to count the polity accurately, but to engage the previously dispossessed within an invigorated civic dialogue.

The theme of "shaping the polity" acknowledges that voting rights law influences the character of representative government. However, the classical dream of reasoned deliberation among equals committed to civic virtue seems far removed from the sharp conflicts and bitter racial divisions that are the legacy of American electoral systems and representative institutions. These differences have highlighted the normative problems of politics implicit in vote dilution doctrine, revisiting desires for more comprehensive minority empowerment and fears of its institutional consequences.

The third generation of vote dilution doctrine must confront these issues during a pivotal period in the history of racial and ethnic relations. While theorists and practitioners of politics and law are undoubtedly traveling in troubled waters, the future of representative democracy depends in part on their abilities to carefully scrutinize representative institutions to ensure that everyone may participate equally within the domain of civic discourse -- not simply in the selection of representatives, but in the representative process itself. In short, to translate the ideal of an equally effective right to vote into more than abstraction for those citizens who need it the most, jurists and political scientists must take seriously both the counting and the shaping functions of voting rights law.

Thorns in the political thicket

Methodological assumptions have political consequences.[60] What is actually asked of this Court in this case is to choose among competing bases of representation -- ultimately, really, among competing theories of political philosophy -- in order to establish an appropriate frame of government. . .for all of the states of the Union.[61]

The role of voting rights rules in shaping the character of political institutions has been widely discussed since the founding of the American republic.[62] However, the term "vote dilution" entered the constitutional vocabulary only after considerable struggle over the role of the judiciary in problems of politics. In large part, modern decisions are still tracing the footsteps of Felix Frankfurter, who both candidly acknowledged the "shaping" functions of voting rights decisions and rather awkwardly avoided having to discuss these functions.

Although Justice Frankfurter himself had recognized, in a landmark 1939 Supreme Court ruling, that the Constitution nullifies "sophisticated as well as simple

Frug, to name several. The so-called "republican revival" has drawn inspiration from historians that have challenged the Lockean consensus theory of American history, such as J. G. A. Pocock, Bernard Bailyn, Gordon Wood, and Robert Shalhope, and from communitarian political philosophers as diverse as Michael Sandel, Alasdair MacIntyre, Benjamin Barber, Richard Bernstein, and Jurgen Habermas.

[60] Catharine A. MacKinnon, Feminism Unmodified (Cambridge, MA, 1987), p. 56.

[61] Baker v. Carr, 369 U.S. 186, 300 (1962), J. Frankfurter, dissenting.

[62] See the comparison of Federalist and Anti-Federalist conceptions of voting rights in Sanford Levinson, "Gerrymandering and the Brooding Omnipresence of Proportional Representation," U.C.L.A. Law Review 33 (1985), p. 256.

modes" of voting discrimination,[63] this language initially arose in discussions of the disfranchisement of black voters. In contrast, cases raising issues about the value of one's fundamental right to vote under the Fourteenth Amendment -- such as legislative apportionment and other districting decisions -- were widely considered incapable of judicial resolution. Even during this period, however, a majority of justices never reached a consensus on the constitutional basis for avoiding such decisions.[64] Moreover, to preserve the distinction between disfranchisement and dilution, Frankfurter had to stretch the language of disfranchisement to cover extreme instances of racially discriminatory districting that today would be classified as vote dilution.[65]

Despite his endorsement of judicial intervention against sophisticated modes of submerging the votes of racial minorities, Justice Frankfurter's opinions on geographic malapportionment cases suggested that courts were powerless to counteract sophisticated modes of devaluing the fundamental right to vote. In Frankfurter's famous phrase, courts had no business wallowing in the "political thicket" of districting decisions, with their implicit dependence upon competing theories of representation.[66] Rather than resting on equal protection, Frankfurter believed that such decisions were rooted in the constitutional provision guaranteeing to states a "republican form of government."[67] For reasons that in retrospect seem to have undercut the purpose of the text, this "Guarantee Clause" has long been considered a nonjusticiable political question.[68]

One senses that beneath the murky discussion of "political questions" and the like,[69] Frankfurter was driven less by faith in the supreme wisdom of legislatures than by fear of delegitimizing the judicial role in political life. The most cogent statement of these fears in American voting rights law is Frankfurter's brilliant, if ultimately unpersuasive, dissenting opinion in Baker v. Carr.[70] Like Justice Oliver

---

[63] See Lane v. Wilson 307 U.S. 268, 275 (1939).

[64] In Colegrove v. Green 328 U.S. 549 (1946), three of the seven participating justices characterized apportionment as a nonjusticiable "political question." Justice Rutledge, who disagreed with this group on the issue of jusiticiability, cast the deciding vote against intervention on the ground that the Court should not overextend its equitable discretion.

[65] See the famous Tuskegee de-annexation case, Gomillion v. Lightfoot 364 U.S. 339 (1960).

[66] Ibid., p. 556.

[67] U.S. Constitution, Article IV, Section 4, cl. 1.

[68] A strong body of modern constitutional history and theory has challenged the conventional wisdom that the Guarantee Clause is best understood as a nonjusticiable political question. Such an interpretation undercuts two crucial values embodied in the clause: popular accountability of government decision-makers; and deliberative government decision-making. See Comment, "The Guarantee of Republican Government: Proposals for Judicial Review," University of Chicago Law Review 54 (1987), p. 231. See also Note, "The Rule of Law and the States: A New Interpretation of the Guarantee Clause," Yale Law Journal 93 (1984), p. 561 (arguing that the traditional rule misconceived the Framers' theories of federalism).

[69] Learned Hand observed with characteristic candor that the "political questions" doctrine has always been a "stench in the nostrils of strict constructionists." Learned Hand, The Bill of Rights (Cambridge, MA, 1958), p. 15.

[70] Baker v. Carr 369 U.S. 186, 300 (1962), J. Frankfurter, dissenting.

Wendell Holmes before him, Frankfurter reacted to the key insight of antiformalist jurisprudence -- that legal categories are socially constructed rather than "found" -- by becoming profoundly skeptical of the capacities of courts to endorse any baselines for evaluating the performance of the political process.[71] In essence, Frankfurter feared that any attempt to police the factional domination of electoral politics would merely reduce the Court to a faction. Much as Holmes had rejected the notion that the Constitution should enter the realm of economic theory, Frankfurter rejected the notion that the Constitution should enter the realm of political theory.

Although Frankfurter and Holmes elegantly described the "countermajoritarian" dangers of unelected courts overtaking the essential functions of democratic institutions, their impassioned defenses of the democratic process sometimes obscured the harsh voice of power justifying its own existence. In what may have been the nadir of his judicial career, Giles v. Harris, Holmes denied federal jurisdiction to literate blacks who were prevented from registering to vote, reasoning that if the state was so determined to keep blacks from voting, court action to ". . .add a name on a piece of paper. . ." would do little to stop them.[72]

Frankfurter's crucial insight was to recognize that discussions of procedural fairness in election systems inevitably involve comparisons of approaches to normative problems of politics. His crucial shortcoming was to assume that nonintervention provided a simple "escape hatch" that placed the judiciary above the fray of these normative problems. On the contrary, by declaring courts powerless to address sophisticated voting rights problems, Frankfurter begged the question of the philosophical basis for judicial deference to legislative decisions. The traditional basis for judicial deference -- faith in the underlying fairness of political processes -- is circular in vote dilution cases because the point of the suit is to challenge the legitimacy of these processes. This circularity places litigants in a double bind: courts will not intervene because democratically elected representatives are presumed to have the sole right to engage in political theory; but the elected representatives also will not intervene because the beneficiaries of an illegitimate election scheme cannot be expected to vote themselves out of office.[73]

Oddly enough, the charge of "countermajoritarianism" in judicial review of vote dilution has persisted in the jurisprudence of the Voting Rights Act long after Congress made it an express duty of courts to make local appraisals of voting discrimination.[74] Shouldered with this responsibility, courts must determine how to address the "what" and "how" questions of representation implicit in dilution doctrine. According to the late Robert G. Dixon, the most insightful scholar to confront the first generation of vote dilution problems, "[t]he ultimate rationale to be

---

[71] Cass Sunstein, "Lochner's Legacy," Columbia Law Review 87 (1987), p. 905.

[72] Giles v. Harris 189 U.S. 475, 487-88 (1903).

[73] Carl Auerbach, "The Reapportionment Cases: One Person, One Vote -- One Vote, One Value," Supreme Court Review 1964 (1964), p. 2. Where such circularities are present, deference to the legislative outcome merely amounts to power justifying itself, or "might makes right." See, e.g., Note, "Political Rights as Political Questions: The Paradox of Luther v. Borden," Harvard Law Review 100 (1987), p. 1135.

[74] See Karlan, "Undoing the Right Thing," op. cit., pp. 12-14.

given for Baker v. Carr and its numerous progeny is that when political avenues for redressing political problems become dead-end streets, some judicial intervention in the politics of the people may be essential in order to have any effective politics."[75] Modern vote dilution cases take the question one step further by asking, "effective politics for whom?" As Dixon recognized, courts cannot simply look the other way. What is needed is "a fresh dialogue on the basics of representative democracy among both political theorists and constitutional lawyers."[76]

Counting the polity

The concept of "we the people" under the Constitution visualizes no preferred class of voters but equality among those who meet the basic qualifications (Justice William O. Douglas).[77] By using the most popular and democratic rhetoric available to explain and justify their aristocratic system, the Federalists. . .contributed to the growth of that encompassing liberal tradition which has mitigated and often obscured the real social antagonisms of American politics (Gordon S. Wood).[78]

Although few modern supporters of the "complacent" approach vote dilution will openly disavow the "one person, one vote" standard, they often assert that this standard is procedural and individual, while protection against minority vote dilution is illegitimately substantive and collective.[79] This assertion understates the complexity and range of options present in the first two generations of dilution doctrine, and the possibilities available for the third.

The great accomplishment of Reynolds v. Sims and other first-generation vote dilution decisions was to recognize that judicial intervention was the only avenue available to overcome an impasse in the legitimacy of democratic government. But rather than meeting Frankfurter's challenge to address the normative problems that accompany the implementation of equal representation, the majority opinions in these cases seemed instead to recycle the formalist fiction that the governing standard was "found" and therefore above politics.

For Justices Warren, Douglas, and Black, the principle of "one person, one vote" had an ethereal quality; it was the "holy grail" toward which the spirit of American democracy has always aspired.[80] However, this historical premise simply homogenized wildly diverse American viewpoints concerning the relationship

---

[75] Robert G. Dixon, Democratic Representation (New York, 1968), p. 8.
[76] Ibid., p. 22.
[77] Gray v. Sanders 372 U.S. 368, 380.
[78] Gordon S. Wood, The Creation of the American Republic, 1776-1787 (New York, 1969), p. 562.
[79] See Larry Alexander, "Lost in the Political Thicket," Florida Law Review 41 (1989), pp. 568-569.
[80] Reynolds v. Sims 377 U.S. 533 (1964), J. Warren; Wesberry v. Sanders, 376 U.S. 1 (1963), J. Black; Gray v. Sanders 372 U.S. 368 (1963), J. Douglas. The "holy grail" metaphor is borrowed from Robert G. Dixon, "The Warren's Court's Crusade for the Holy Grail of One Man, One Vote," Supreme Court Review 1969 (1969), p. 219.

between voting arrangements and democracy.[81] As Willmoore Kendall once noted, riding men out of town on a rail is as rooted in the American tradition as is democratic participation.[82]

Needless to say, the idea of "one person, one vote" is crucial to the institutions and aspirations of representative democracy. However, the concept is not self-defining. Having supported the right of citizens to an equally effective vote "counted at full value without dilution or discount,"[83] the first generation of vote dilution cases provided only a very impressionistic account of the political settings in which this equality principle was to be applied. Indeed, the remedy offered in Reynolds v. Sims -- arithmetically equal population districts -- was incapable of meeting the opinion's apparent goals.[84] From a standpoint of voting power, the analysis ignored other structural aspects of election systems, such as the number of seats per district, that may affect voting power much more than population disparities among districts.[85]

All the first-generation vote dilution decisions slighted the difference between stating procedural equalities in the abstract and constructing political institutions that treat people equally. It is not clear that every form of procedural inequality is inherently objectionable; as Charles Beitz has noted, few "feel insulted or degraded by the patent inequality of representation in the U.S. Senate."[86] In contrast, racial or ethnic minorities who find themselves consistently shut out of effective political influence in an at-large election system, despite its compliance with "one person, one vote," may feel severe insult and degradation. To understand the contrast between the form and substance of political equality, voters must be viewed not as unconnected individuals, but as citizens in a community.[87]

The early "one person, one vote" opinions did not clarify whether the "full value" of a vote had any meaning for members of unsuccessful minority groups. Where a bare majority forms a fixed coalition that consistently defeats a losing coalition with sharply different interests, mere reliance on "one person, one vote"

---

[81] For useful discussions of the historical inaccuracies in reapportionment jurisprudence, see Charles Miller, The Supreme Court and the Uses of History (Cambridge, MA, 1969), p. 141 and Alfred Kelley, "Clio and the Court: An Illicit Love Affair," Supreme Court Review 1965 (1965), p. 119.

[82] Kendall is quoted in Garry Wills, Inventing America (Garden City, N.Y., 1978), p. xii.

[83] Reynolds v. Sims 377 U.S. at 565-66.

[84] For example, it would not prevent group configurations from making the strategic value of votes vary dramatically among districts with equal population; nor would it prevent a minority from controlling the state legislature (e.g., if a bare majority elected each legislator and a bare majority of legislators controlled legislative outcomes). See Jonathan Still, Voter Equality in Electoral Systems (New Haven, Yale dissertation, 1971), pp. 115, 130.

[85] Ibid., p. 110. See also Rein Taagepera and Matthew Soberg Shugart, Seats and Votes (New Haven, 1989), p. 55.

[86] Charles R. Beitz, "Procedural Equality in Democratic Theory: A Preliminary Examination," in J. Roland Pennock and John W. Chapman, eds., Liberal Democracy (New York, 1983), p. 86.

[87] Majority rule theories are incoherent when premised on "aggregated atomistic activity." See Elaine Spitz, Majority Rule (Chatham, New Jersey, 1984), p. 271.

would seem to make "a travesty of the equality principle."[88] Recognizing that the problem of minority subjugation would require the courts to engage in substantive political discussion, some academic commentators decried the "web of subjectivity" in the first generation of vote dilution cases.[89] But the most perceptive of these academic critics, Alexander Bickel, also recognized that dilution cases raise crucial questions about the legitimacy of representative institutions. Acknowledging the powerful role of groups in political action, Bickel argued that government's legitimacy must rest upon "more than the teetering knife-edge of the momentary majority."[90]

Courts and commentators often distinguish between the first and second generations of vote dilution problems by designating them as "quantitative" and "qualitative," respectively.[91] Dilution stemming from geographic malapportionment is described as "quantitative" because it is measured from a numerical baseline ("one person, one vote") that uses simple arithmetic -- "sixth grade" arithmetic, according to some detractors -- to compare the relationships between seats and individual votes in various election districts.[92] In contrast, minority vote dilution is often described as "qualitative" because no similar arithmetic baseline is used. Instead, these cases typically require "a blend of history and an intensely local appraisal" of the "design and impact" of the challenged election system on the participatory and electoral power of the group that has issued the challenge.[93]

The categorical distinction between "quantitative" and "qualitative" vote dilution cases is misleading. It inaccurately presumes that the first group of cases inhabit an objective domain of individual rights that is beyond "mere politics," while the second group injects courts into the murky domain of interest group power struggles. In fact, both types of cases illuminate the relationships between rights and politics. The conflict between urban and rural blocs in the early apportionment cases might be -- and often was -- portrayed as a murky conflict between competing interest groups.[94] Conversely, minorities raising the second type of dilution case may argue, quite plausibly, that their claims transcend the realm of "mere politics," because they are pointing to institutional barriers that have impeded their equal and

---

[88] J. Roland Pennock, Democratic Political Theory (Princeton, N.J., 1979), p. 8.

[89] See Alexander Bickel, The Supreme Court and the Idea of Progress (New York, 1970), p. 45.

[90] Alexander Bickel, "The Supreme Court and Reapportionmant," in Nelson Polsby, ed., Reapportionment in the 1970s (Berkeley, 1971), p. 60.

[91] See, e.g., Karlan, "Maps and Misreadings," op. cit., p. 178.

[92] Describing the mathematics in first-generation dilution decisions as "simplistic" would be something of an understatement. See Robert G. Dixon, "Reapportionment Values and Representation Practice: The Eschatology of One Man, One Vote," in Pennock and Chapman, eds., Nomos X: Representation (New York, 1968), p. 178. For a sensitive modern discussion of the complexities embedded in the relationship between seats and votes, see Taagepera and Shugart, op. cit.

[93] See White v. Regester 412 U.S. 755, 769 (1973); Thornburg v. Gingles 478 U.S. 30, 78 (1986).

[94] See, for example, Herbert Wechsler, Principles, Politics, and Fundamental Law (Cambridge, MA, 1961), p. 13; Phil Neal, "Baker v. Carr: Politics in Search of Law," Supreme Court Review 1962 (1962), p. 252.

effective enjoyment of the fundamental right to vote.

The distinction between quantitative and qualitative dilution cases also mistakenly assumes that the first group of cases is susceptible to a quantitative standard of evaluation, while the second group is incapable of such precise resolution. In fact, the purely quantitative approach taken in the geographic apportionment cases reflected in part a failure to comprehend the "fully political" nature of all districting decisions.[95] Implicit in these rulings were assumptions about the character of democratic represent ation. Moreover, the second group of cases could be measured from a simple arithmetic baseline as well: like "one person, one vote," various forms of proportional representation might provide a conceptually vacuous but easily measurable standard of evaluation. Objections to proportional representation, though common among American jurists and political scientists, are rarely stated in the language of procedural equality. Instead, these objections tend to focus on the fragmentary or destabilizing effects such systems are sometimes alleged to have on other democratic institutions, particularly the party system.[96]

Since minority vote dilution cases have focused on the disempowering results that various political systems and techniques have had on particular groups, they pose a critical challenge to those who conceive of voting rights simply as a matter of accurately counting preferences expressed in elections. For adherents of this view, the shift in focus from abstract individuals to group associations is troublesome because it creates a need for courts to define an outer boundary around the "legitimate" political process without participating in the normative problems of politics. Put another way, it creates a need for courts to find a neutral way to engage in the social ordering of equal voting opportunities. As Aviam Soifer has noted, this perspective assigns to courts a role much like Bogart's character in Casablanca: "tough and neutral and above the fray," but also able to deliver the system from threats to its integrity in moments of crisis.[97]

Although several strategies have been advanced to provide a neutral way of ordering equal voting opportunities, none have successfully insulated courts from the normative problems of politics. The first approach -- that of contextualism -- was at the heart of the approach to minority vote dilution that evolved in federal courts prior to 1980 in cases such as White and Zimmer, marked by a localized, multi-factor assessment of the conditions affecting equal opportunities in politics and elections.[98] The contextualist strategy embodies a critical insight, because it recognizes the importance of local variations and designs in the structuring of elections and democratic institutions. But since it lacks a precisely defined end point, contextualism relies heavily on the tools of the geographer; it recognizes that a dilution suit is "an interdisciplinary exercise where lawyers and academics learn

---

[95] Dixon, Democratic Representation, p. 69.
[96] See, e.g., Davis v. Bandemer 478 U.S. 109, 147 (1986), J. O'Connor concurring in judgment.
[97] Aviam Soifer, "Complacency and Constitutional Law," Ohio State Law Journal 42 (1981), p. 383.
[98] See, e.g., White v. Regester 412 U.S. 755 (1973); Zimmer v. McKeithen 485 F.2d 1297 (5th Cir, 1973)(en banc), aff'd sub. nom. East Carroll Parish School Bd. v. Marshall 424 U.S. 636 (1976).

from each other."[99]

Understood as a method to correct defects in the way that localities devalue minority votes, this strategy has strong parallels to the "process-based" theories of judicial review articulated by John Hart Ely and Jesse Choper.[100] Under these theories, judicial intervention against minority vote dilution is justified as an antitrust-like check on the political process to ensure that the "channels of political change" remain equally open.[101] However, this approach also fails in its attempt to construct a neutral boundary around the "legitimate" political process that shields courts from the normative problems of politics.[102] Since there is no easily identifiable Archimedean point at which political opportunities have been equalized, the contextual strategy revisits the conflicting desires and fears that are implicit in the concept of equal representation. Put another way, the "neutral" boundaries Ely and Choper place around the "channels of political change" are impossible to implement without a controversial assessment of the conditions of politics.[103]

The underlying assumption of the channel-clearing strategy appears to be that an understandable and judicially manageable set of relatively minor repairs can restore an equilibrium point of "equal opportunity," in which the majority can no longer oppress the minority. But theorists defending this perspective have displayed an understanding of pluralist coalition-building that is seriously outdated in its failure to recognize the institutional conditions that often place pressures on individual choices, whether by frustrating their articulation or even interfering with their formation.[104]

In short, the strategy of contextualism introduces, but stops short of fully confronting, the problems posed by power relationships operating within a pluralist context.[105] To delve further into these conditions would be to invite an assessment of normative political problems and of how well-equipped courts are to

---

[99] Peyton McCrary and J. Gerald Hebert, "Keeping the Courts Honest: The Role of Historians as Expert Witnesses in Southern Voting Rights Cases," Southern University Law Review 16 (1989), p. 101.

[100] John Hart Ely, Democracy and Distrust (Cambridge, MA, 1980); Jesse Choper, Judicial Review and the National Political Process (Chicago, 1980).

[101] See Joan Hartman, "Racial Vote Dilution and the Separation of Powers," George Washington University Law Review 50 (1982), p. 689.

[102] David G. Smith, "Liberalism and Judicial Review," in J. Roland Pennock and John W. Chapman, eds., Liberal Democracy (New York, 1983), p. 222.

[103] See Richard A. Posner, "Democracy and Distrust Revisited," Virginia Law Review 77 (1991), p. 650.

[104] See Richard Parker, "The Past of Constitutional Theory -- and its Future," Ohio State Law Review 42 (1981), pp. 223, 242-244. As Professor Parker points out, Ely and Choper offer a 1950s version of American pluralists such as Charles Lindblom and Robert Dahl, without discussing their more pessimistic recent writings. Charles Lindblom, Politics and Markets (New York, 1977), Robert Dahl, Dilemmas of Pluralist Democracy (New Haven, 1982).

[105] See, e.g., David Couzens Hoy, "Power, Repression, Progress: Foucault, Lukes, and the Frankfurt School," in Hoy, ed., Foucault: A Critical Reader (New York, 1986), p. 123; Fred R. Dallmayr, Polis and Praxis (Cambridge, MA, 1984), p. 77; Michel Foucault, Power/Knowledge (New York, 1980), p. 131; Steven Lukes, Power: A Radical View (London, 1974).

address particular types of problems. Only by directly engaging these concerns can voting rights doctrine become "a comprehensible and enriching element of political discussion."[106]

With its emphasis on local specificity, the contextualist strategy generated fears that courts were no longer above the political fray. The Supreme Court's reaction to this fear -- Mobile v. Bolden[107] -- imposed a strategy of containment that virtually abdicated judicial scrutiny over sophisticated forms of minority vote dilution. In form, Justice Stewart's plurality opinion imposed an extremely strict intent test on minority plaintiffs and drastically restricted the kinds of circumstantial evidence from which they could draw inferences of discriminatory intent. In practice, Stewart's opinion was a textbook example of failed judicial formalism: his attempt at preserving judicial neutrality against "gauzy" sociology resulted in more indeterminacy and confusion than the test he had sought to replace.

To its defenders, most notably Abigail Thernstrom, intent-based approaches contain vote dilution doctrine within a definable judicial framework that is "simple, principled, and tight."[108] However, Bolden opinion demonstrates how the veneer of "neutrality" can mask deeper assumptions about the social ordering of election systems. He rejected a challenge to Mobile's at-large election system on the ground that it had been adopted in 1911 as a "praiseworthy and progressive" reform to combat municipal corruption rather than as an attempt to exclude black voters, who already had been disfranchised in Alabama. If Stewart had gone below the surface of this comic excuse for history, he would have discovered that the "benign" justification for the election scheme was itself enmeshed in prejudice. Municipal reforms such as at-large elections were often defended as reducing the "corrupt" power of blacks (some of whom still managed to vote) and recent immigrants, who were widely perceived as too ignorant for responsible civic participation and as easy prey for ward bosses.[109] When paired with Reynolds, the Bolden approach seems especially cruel: while white majority voters can appeal to primitive arithmetic to enforce their equal voting rights, nonwhite minorities must overcome a presumption for the status quo that is almost Kafkaesque.

Subsequent events have negated the legal force of Bolden, since Section 2 of the Voting Rights Act was amended to disavow any intent requirement and to restore the pre-Bolden multi-factor test.[110] However, the decision reflects a familiar theme in antidiscrimination jurisprudence: the attempt to rationalize the existence of unequal opportunities as "readily explainable" on grounds apart from race, even when the alternative grounds themselves reflect a legacy of racial exclusion.[111] Rather than protecting courts from the "political thicket" or upholding some "core value" of

---

[106] David G. Smith, "Liberalism and Judicial Review," in J. Roland Pennock and John W. Chapman, eds., Liberal Democracy (New York, 1983), p. 222.
[107] Mobile v. Bolden 446 U.S. 55 (1980).
[108] Thernstrom, op. cit., p. 75.
[109] Bradley Rice, Progressive Cities (Austin, 1977), p. 88. On remand, a district court in Bolden found, after exhaustive historical testimony, that even the Supreme Court's draconian intent test had been met. Mobile v. Bolden 542 F.Supp. 1050 (S.D. Ala. 1982).
[110] See 43 U.S.C. § 1973; S.Rep. No. 97-417, 97th Cong., 2d Sess. (1982), p. 15.
[111] This is the intellectual strategy of Plessy v. Ferguson 163 U.S. 563 (1896).

individual voting rights, intent-based approaches reflect murky and psychologically naive notions about the way that racial exclusion operates in political institutions.[112] One recurrent danger is that Bolden-like assumptions about formal neutrality may be regenerated within the context of the statutory results test. The essence of this approach is not intent as such, but a containment strategy that limits the evidentiary criteria for showing vote dilution by appealing to fears of institutional disorder. Consequently, the containment theory has arisen in recent attempts to limit the types of evidence permitted in showing racially polarized voting,[113] and to assert an exception to vote dilution doctrine for single-member offices.[114]

The doctrinal move in Thornburg v. Gingles, with its key focus on prospects for minority electoral success, represents an attempt to mediate between the indeterminacy of the contextual strategy and the insensitivity of the containment strategy. It is perhaps best understood as a "realistic politics of the second-best" defined in opposition to extremes.[115] Charges that the proportional representation by race is now the national standard seem hyperbolic in light of evidence that blacks still hold only 1.5 percent of elected offices and Hispanics hold less than one percent, despite having 12 and 7 percent of the populations, respectively.[116] It is clear, however, that Gingles has accencntuated the judicial focus on drawing remedial district lines in a manner that enhances minority election prospects.[117]

The districting remedies practiced in Gingles and its progeny raise an inevitable comparison to a more formal strategy of proportionality. Some commentators have long held that some form of proportional representation must be adopted as the logical corollary to incorporate minority representation within the principle of "one person, one vote."[118] If the principle of equal counting is the

---

[112] See Charles Lawrence, "The Id, the Ego, and Equal Protection: Reckoning with Unconscious Racism," Stanford Law Review 39 (1987), p. 371.

[113] Some judges and commentators have attempted to impose a "voters' intent" requirement on Section 2, by insisting that voting is not racially polarized unless voters were motivated by race and not some other "neutral" requirement. See Engstrom, "The Reincarnation of the Intent Standard," op. cit. Although no clear majority delineated the proper methods of proof, Thornburg v. Gingles seems to have rejected this approach, since the Supreme Court affirmed a district court finding that accepted standard bivariate studies as proof of polarization rather than delving into voters' motivations. For recent discussions of this controversy, see James W. Loewen and Bernard Grofman, "Recent Developments in Methods Used in Vote Dilution Litigation," Urban Lawyer (1989), 21: 589; Bernard Grofman, "Expert Witness Testimony and the Evolution of Voting Rights Case Law," in Grofman and Davidson, eds., Controversies in Minority Voting, p. 197.

[114] See Karlan, "Undoing the Right Thing," op. cit., pp. 1-45.

[115] Bernard Grofman and Chandler Davidson, "Postscript: What is the Best Route to a Color-Blind Society?" in Grofman and Davidson, eds., Controversies in Minority Voting, op. cit., p. 316.

[116] Laughlin MacDonald, "The 1982 Amendments of Section 2 and Minority Representation," in Grofman and Davidson, eds., Controversies in Minority Voting, op. cit., p. 82.

[117] See, e.g., Jeffers v. Clinton 730 F.Supp. 1996 (E.D. Ark. 1989)(three-judge court), aff'd 112 L.Ed.2d 656 (1991).

[118] See, e.g., Note, "The Constitutional Imperative of Proportional Representation," Yale Law Journal 94 (1984), p. 163; Gerald Goulder, "The Reconstructed Right to Vote," Capital University Law Review 9 (1979), p. 32.

benchmark of equal representation, the Millian notion that the "first principle of democracy" is "representation in proportion to numbers" has a strong intuitive appeal.[119]

But judged simply as a matter of equal counting, proportional representation is as unintelligible as the district system without an underlying theory of representative democracy. As a method of making votes count more equally, proportional representation depends upon the way in which choices of representatives correspond with legislative decisions. It would seem to imply what might be called a "mirror image" theory of representation, in which interests expressed within the representative body are expected to form a photorealist picture of the exogenously determined interests of the constituents.[120] However, if representatives are "bound" to reflect their constituents' premises in such a precise way, and if the majority never agrees with the minority, the proportionally represented minority will lose every time the legislature votes.[121] Consequently, the more candid defenders of proportionality have conceded that its strongest case lies in its encouragement of diverse deliberation within representative institutions, not its satisfaction of the mathematics of preference aggregation.[122]

The point here is not to praise or bury proportional representation, but to emphasize that it cannot be justified by some pre-institutional notion of "equal counting. Not even the more formally equal methods of choosing representatives are able to overcome basic problems associated with the formation and aggregation of preferences on policy outcomes. Since citizens' preferences are shaped partly in reference to the constrained range of choices within the political system, it may be circular to defend the structure by pointing to these system-generated preferences.[123] Even if the preferences of individual voters are presumed to be exogenous, it is unclear whether any voting system can effectively combine the various signals that voters register in elections. The literature on "social choice" theory has become an embarrassment to anyone attempting to justify a routinely complex choice by appealing to its uncoerced satisfaction of preferences.[124]

---

[119] John Stuart Mill, Utilitarianism, On Liberty, and Considerations on Representative Government (New York, 1980), p. 260. The fact that Mill also favored plural voting for an elite class of electors illustrates the point that even proportionality is a matter of perspective.

[120] See Bruce Ackerman, "The Storrs Lectures: Discovering the Constitution," Yale Law Journal 93 (1984), p. 103; Hanna Pitkin, The Concept of Representation (Berkeley, 1967), p. 60.

[121] "[P]roportional representation does not so much eliminate 'vote-wasting' as alter its form and timing. The votes of the supporters of parties excluded from the governing coalition, then, will be wasted just as minority party members' votes are now wasted." Peter H. Schuck, "The Thickest Thicket: Partisan Gerrymandering and Judicial Regulation of Politics," Columbia Law Review 87 (1987), p. 1371. On the problem of "equally effective votes," see Grofman and Scarrow, "The Riddle of Apportionment: Equality of What?" National Civic Review 70 (1981), p. 242.

[122] Cass Sunstein, "Beyond the Republican Revival," Yale Law Journal 97 (1988), p. 1588.

[123] Cass Sunstein, "Constitutions and Democracies," in Jon Elster and Rune Slagstad, eds., Constitutionalism and Democracy (Cambridge, England, 1988), p. 348. This is the problem of "adaptive" or "endogenous" preferences. See Jon Elster, Sour Grapes (New York, 1983).

[124] See, e.g., Niemi and Riker, "The Choice of Voting Systems," Scientific American 234 (June 1976), p. 21.

Social choice literature suggests that "there probably is no single nondictatorial method of aggregating preferences of an electorate that will reliably produce a choice which satisfies minimal consistency and rationality standards."[125] When social choice problems are taken into account, proportional representation systems do not appear to be any more successful than districting schemes in yielding an accurate aggregation of private preferences expressed in elections.[126] In some especially bleak accounts, social choice theory turns us into Hobbesians: having abandoned hope for the "most fair" election system, we settle for any system that will produce a stable government and avoid civil war.[127]

The "root notion of representation," at least as it is commonly understood, simply ignores the problems of aggregating interests.[128] For those who view the idea of equal representation solely as a method of accurate counting, this deficiency would be cause for despair. However, as Charles Gilbert has reminded us, "representation" is important primarily in reference to approaches toward normative problems of politics.[129] In order to take seriously the idea that voting rights should be equally effective, courts cannot avoid shaping the polity.

Shaping the polity

We need, but fear, community.[130]

A sense of futility hangs over the discussions of vote dilution problems in the preceding section. Proponents of judicial intervention point to the breakdown of ordinary political processes but have little to say about the justification for courts to consider normative problems of representation. Opponents of intervention point to the premise that courts should not wallow in the political thicket, but they have little to say about their justification for doing nothing when ordinary political processes have broken down. Taken together, these perspectives suggest that, although something is rotten in the state, neither the judicial nor the political branch of government can break the impasse without violating the terms of their own legitimacy. The internal structure of this crisis might be described as the "Madisonian dilemma":[131] how may democratic institutions contain faction without themselves descending into factionalism?

---

[125] Michael E. Lavine and Charles R. Plott, "Agenda Influence and its Implications," Virginia Law Review 63 (1977), p. 561.

[126] William Riker, "Electoral Systems and Constitutional Restraints," in Lijphart and Grofman, eds., Choosing an Electoral System, op. cit., p. 106.

[127] Ibid., p. 107.

[128] Gilbert, op. cit., p. 616.

[129] Douglas Rae, "Reapportionment and Political Democracy," in Reapportionment in the 1970s, op.cit., pp. 95-96.

[130] Duncan Kennedy, "The Structure of Blackstone's Commentaries," Buffalo Law Review 28 (1979), p. 217.

[131] See Robert Bork, "Neutral Principles and Some First Amendment Problems," Indiana Law Journal 47 (1971), pp. 2-3; Paul Brest, "The Fundamental Rights Controversy: The Essential Contradictions of Normative Constitutional Scholarship," Yale Law Journal 90 (1981), p. 1063.

Although the amended Voting Rights Act has resolved the "countermajoritarian" problem of constitutional legitimacy by requiring judicial remedies against vote dilution, a statutory variation on the Madisonian dilemma emerges as courts address the "what" and "how" issues of equal representation. Since these issues are juxtaposed with concerns about racial and ethnic discrimination, dilution charges call into question the legitimacy of representative institutions for members of the groups who most desperately need meaningful inclusion in the life of the polity. Decades after Gunnar Myrdal first used the term, racial and ethnic relations remain the "American dilemma," marked by a pronounced tension between the high values espoused on a general plane and the political exclusion often evident on more specific planes.[132] Although the Voting Rights Act has contributed invaluably to minorities' inclusion in politics,[133] the legacy of exclusion has continued with a vengeance in many localities. In a significant number of areas, the phenomenon of racial or ethnic bloc voting has combined with characteristics of representative institutions to reduce the minority population to a perpetually powerless underclass.[134] Under these circumstances, the complacent approach to the political thicket -- for courts to do nothing -- promises "nothing less than a society where political power is perpetually stratified along racial lines."[135]

Legal scholarship on the subject of minority vote dilution has finally started to emphasize a theme submerged in a previous generation of doctrine: the relationship between judicial approaches to vote dilution and normative problems of politics. Rather than conceiving of the court's role as merely to provide for the accurate aggregation of private preferences expressed in elections, these new approaches have suggested directing Section 2 of the Voting Rights Act toward promoting the "civic inclusion" or "interactive participation" of previously excluded minorities in the deliberative functions of representative government.[136] Unlike the first generation of approaches to vote dilution, these analyses do not blind themselves to the institutional consequences of the rights theories they espouse. Rather, they seek to combine a sensitivity toward pluralist power relationships with an aspiration toward deliberative democracy. In large part, these objectives draw inspiration from the emerging family of constitutional theory that seeks to restore some ethos of "civic republicanism."

Although their aims and influences are varied, civic republicans converge in

---

[132] See Gunnar Myrdal, An American Dilemma (New York, 1944).

[133] See, e.g., Kenneth H. Thompson, The Voting Rights Act and Black Political Participation (Washington, 1982); John A. Garcia, "The Voting Rights Act and Hispanic Political Representation in the Southwest," Publius 16 (1986), p. 49; Joel A. Thompson, "The Voting Rights Act in North Carolina: An Evaluation," Publius 16 (1986), p. 139; Laughlin MacDonald, op.cit., p. 73.

[134] See, e.g., Frickey, "Majority Rule, Minority Rights, and the Right to Vote: Reflections Upon a Reading of Minority Vote Dilution," Law and Inequality Vol. 3 (1985), p. 209.

[135] Note, "Geometry and Geography: Racial Gerrymandering and the Voting Rights Act," Yale Law Journal 94 (1984), p. 204.

[136] See Karlan, "Maps and Misreadings," op.cit. (theme of "civic inclusion"); Kathryn Abrams, "'Raising Politics Up: Minority Political Participation and Section 2 of the Voting Rights Act," New York University Law Review 63 (1988), p. 449 (theme of "interactive participation").

their dissatisfaction with the isolationist individualism of conventional constitutional theory and their desire to invigorate a conception of community life as constitutive of the self rather than hostile to the individual.[137] The civic republican argument is based in part on a revised understanding of American constitutional history and in part on a revised appraisal of constitutional possibilities.

The historical argument draws on a growing body of modern historiography that has challenged the individualistic "Lockean consensus" of a previous generation. New historians of the Revolutionary Era have detected a fragile and unstable interplay between the secular accommodations of the Lockean tradition and the communitarian virtue of an earlier "civic humanist" tradition.[138] In civic humanist thought, "the development of the individual toward self-fulfillment is possible only when the individual acts as citizen, that is as a conscious and autonomous participant in an autonomous decision-taking political community. . ."[139] Rather than existing as an abstract, universal ideal, civic virtue depends on mastery of the politics of the moment, in which factions threaten to corrupt the polity by falsely associating their selfish interests with the good of all.

The survival of civic virtue requires an institutional setting in which no group rules exclusively and none is merely dependent on another.[140] This setting reflects a tension between two premises of American constitutionalism: the government of the people by the people and the government of the people by laws.[141] Instead of viewing government merely as a device to aggregate and satisfy the preferences of the individual, the civic humanist aspires toward "mutuality within difference":[142] a shared social context for public life that forms a bridge between citizen and society. American public law may move the polity nearer to this bridge by considering laws and rights as both the "free creations of citizens" and the "normative givens" of a public-regarding political process. (Frank Michaelman has described this approach

---

[137] Representative examples of civic republican constitututional theory include Frank Michelman, "The Supreme Court, 1985 Term -- Foreword: Traces of Self-Government," Harvard Law Review 100 (1986), p. 1695; Cass Sunstein, "Beyond the Republican Revival," Yale Law Journal 97 (1988), p. 1539; Kathryn Abrams, "Law's Republicanism," Yale Law Journal 97 (1988), p. 1591; and Richard Parker, op.cit. The conception of community as constitutive of self is drawn from Michael Sandel, Liberalism and the Limits of Justice (New York, 1982), p. 150. For critical appraisals of modern republicanism, see Richard H. Fallon, Jr., "What Is Republicanism, and is it Worth Reviving?" Harvard Law Review 102 (1989), p. 1695, and Terrance Sandalow, "A Skeptical Look at Contemporary Republicanism," Florida Law Review 41 (1989), p. 523.

[138] See J. G. A. Pocock, The Machiavellian Moment (Princeton, 1975); Gordon S. Wood, The Creation of the American Republic (Chapel Hill, 1969); Bernard Bailyn, The Ideological Origins of the American Revolution (Cambridge, MA, 1965); Robert E. Shalhope, "Toward a Republican Synthesis: The Emergence of an Understanding of Republicanism in American Historiography," William and Mary Quarterly 29 (1972), p. 49; Joyce Appleby, "Republicanism in Old and New Contexts," William and Mary Quarterly 43 (1986), p. 20.

[139] J. G. A. Pocock, Politics, Language, and Time (Chicago, 1989 ed.), p. 85.

[140] Ibid., p. 88.

[141] Frank Michelman, "Law's Republic," Yale Law Journal 97 (1988), pp. 1500-1501.

[142] Hanna Pitkin, Fortune is a Woman (Berkeley, 1984), p. 301.

as "jurisgenerative" politics).[143] For politics to work fairly and effectively, the legal order must shape institutions capable of both empowering individuals to participate in community life and preventing factions from stifling participation.

Civic republican constitutional theory illuminates the connection in voting rights law between counting the polity and shaping the polity; between the justice of standards for equal representation and the institutional settings in which they are situated. By focusing on these connections, it has renewed discussion of the "characteristic tensions in the normative conceptions of democratic politics" latent in voting rights cases.[144] At the same time, these theories raise substantial fears for those suspicious of the authoritarian tendencies of republics. In the past, civic republicans have sometimes defended maintaining the purity of their dialogue by restricting participation to self-sufficient property owners,[145] by requiring allegiance to a civil religion,[146] or by excluding divisive social or economic issues from the realm of public life.[147]

The central hermeneutic difficulty is to restore the ethos of community inclusion in a large, fractured modern polity whose widely varied citizens share no common conception of the public good, or even of the ground rules for deliberation about the public good. A danger remains that factional intrigue will capture the government by posing as civic virtue. Misgivings with this approach are similar to those Charles Gilbert raised against "idealist" notions of representation:

> We tend to mistrust its ambiguity about leadership and responsiveness, to doubt that the same subtle dialogue and ethical argument are possible in the great society and in the small group and to emphasize, therefore, the electoral sanction and the specifics of instrumental representation rather than the diffuseness of expressive representation; we set more by substance and procedure than by style; we suspect that unitary claims often mask sinister interests.[148]

A central danger in civic republican political analysis is its tendency to romanticize the deliberative process in representative institutions, obscuring the power struggles that are likely to persist even if some minorities find their way onto decision-making bodies. In Joyce Appleby's telling phrase, the tendency of the civic humanist revival has been to obscure underlying struggles for empowerment, allowing "the reality of power relations to fade away "much like the Cheshire cat, leaving nothing behind but the smile of culture."[149] Serious exploration of the power struggles shaping the quality and equality of community life reveals

---

[143] Michelman, "Law's Republic," op.cit., pp. 1504-1505.
[144] Frank Michelman, "Conceptions of Democracy in American Constitutional Argument: Voting Rights," Florida Law Review 41 (1989), p. 444.
[145] See Pocock, Politics, Language, and Time, op.cit., p. 93.
[146] E.g., Rousssseau.
[147] E.g., Hannah Arendt.
[148] Gilbert, op.cit., p. 606.
[149] Joyce Appleby, Liberalism and Republicanism in the Historical Imagination (Cambridge, MA, 1992), p. 135.

conflicting sets of fears and desires.

For racial and ethnic minorities that have experienced exclusion from ordinary pluralist politics as well as estrangement from the community, proposals to invigorate civic virtue evoke mixed feelings. While the vision of a genuinely inclusive community is inspiring, fears remain that the abstraction of "civic virtue" may be used to erase the "rights" for which they have struggled as a group seeking empowerment.[150] As applied to the subject of minority vote dilution, voting rights discourse has played an important, though incomplete, transformative and emancipatory role. This discourse gives credence to minority aspirations that combat "the experience of being excluded and oppressed,"[151] while also providing a rough way to measure the practical consequences of these rights in political institutions. Accordingly, "great care must be taken to ensure that the liberating baby is not thrown out with the liberal bathwater."[152]

Minorities have strong reasons to fear that, as was the case during the Progressive Era, terms such as "restoring virtue" or "reducing corruption" may be used to resist their attempts at inclusion in civic discourse. Especially in communities that have a history of exclusionary politics, the slogan of "civic virtue" may simply allow those in power to rationalize the exclusion or token participation of minorities rather than risk the instability or incivility their inclusion might create.

Modern supporters of the "complacent" view of voting rights have used the imagery of community to suggest that race-conscious remedies to vote dilution have had a "segregative" and divisive effect on public life.[153] By identifying citizens in terms of their factional affiliation, remedies based upon group representation are sometimes viewed as entrenching social divisions.[154] While these are serious charges, discussed further in the next section, the complacent theorists' formulation of the argument presupposes that a nonsegregative, nondivisive community life is possible in the absence of remedies that empower the previously excluded.[155] As I have argued, the likely effect of doing nothing in some communities would be to accept a future of permanent racial or ethnic stratification. Where the political institutions in place have consistently excluded a minority from effective participation, remedies that break this impasse may be the only way to make

---

[150] See H. N. Hirsch, "The Threnody of Liberalism: Constitutional Liberty and the Renewal of Community," Political Theory 14 (1986), pp. 437-438; Derrick Bell and Preta Bansal, "The Republican Revival and Racial Politics," Yale Law Journal 97 (1988), p. 1609.

[151] Kimberle Williams Crenshaw, "Race, Reform, and Retrenchment: Transformation and Legitimation in Antidiscrimination Law," Harvard Law Review 101 (1988), p. 1357.

[152] Alan C. Hutchinson and Patrick J. Monahan, "The 'Rights' Stuff: Roberto Unger and Beyond," Texas Law Review 62 (1984), p. 1486.

[153] See O'Rourke, "The 1982 Amendments and the Voting Rights Paradox," in Grofman and Davidson, eds., Controversies in Monirty Voting, op.cit., p. 108.

[154] Comment, "The Limits of 'Liberal Republicanism': Why Group-Based Remedies and Republican Citizenship Don't Mix," Columbia Law Review 91 (1991), p. 606.

[155] See Laughlin MacDonald, "The 1982 Amendments of Section 2 and Minority Representation," in Grofman and Davidson, eds., Controversies in Minority Voting, op.cit., pp. 77-79.

coalition-building possible.¹⁵⁶

While they also criticize the post-<u>Gingles</u> fixation upon the single factor of minority candidates' electoral success, supporters of enhanced minority empowerment fear that existing remedies to vote dilution underestimate the resilience of barriers to coalition-building. Having identified the consequences of racially polarized voting in general elections, vote dilution theory has often ignored the tendency of these same polarized patterns to reproduce themselves within representative bodies. ¹⁵⁷ Some advantage may inhere in simply having the voice of the "other" within the deliberative body.¹⁵⁸ But as Lani Guinier has noted, unless obstacles to equal representation are addressed throughout the political process, elected minority officials may serve as little more than "spokesmodels" for political equality.¹⁵⁹

In order to avoid using community to rationalize exclusion, modern civic republicans must emphasize the most enduring contribution of the liberal tradition: "the legitimate aspirations of the individual, of every individual, to be <u>included</u> in the common good."¹⁶⁰ In this sense, the theme of shaping the polity intersects the theme of counting the polity. The success of attempts to fuse these themes depends upon finding practical ways to institutionalize the aspiration to treat citizens equally, both as participants in politics and as subjects of public policy.¹⁶¹

In important respects, concerns of the most insightful communitarian republicans and pluralist liberals may converge on the need for legal theory to take into account the institutional settings conducive to equal representation. Just as the former would argue that meaningful inclusion of minorities is necessary for the sort of <u>undominated</u> normative dialogue they seek in the polity,¹⁶² the latter would seek a

---

¹⁵⁶ See Davidson, "The Voting Rights Act: A Brief History," in Grofman and Davidson, eds., <u>Controversies in Minority Voting</u>, <u>op.cit.</u>, 49; Comment, "Vote Dilution, Discriminatory Results, and Proportional Representation: What is the Appropriate Remedy for Section 2 of the Voting Rights Act?," <u>U.C.L.A. Law Review</u> 32 (1985), p. 1249.
¹⁵⁷ Guinier, "The Triumph of Tokenism," <u>op.cit.</u>, p. 1126.
¹⁵⁸ See Edward W. Said, "Foucault and the Imagination of Power," in Hoy, ed., <u>Foucault: A Critical Reader</u>, <u>op.cit.</u>, p. 153 ("...it is sometimes of paramount importance not so much <u>what</u> is said, but <u>who</u> speaks").
¹⁵⁹ <u>Ibid.</u>, p. 1079.
¹⁶⁰ John D. Caputo, <u>Radical Hermeneutics</u> (Bloomington, Ind., 1987), p. 254. For an attempt to fuse republican concerns with this aspect of the liberal tradition, see Sunstein, "Beyond the Republican Revival," <u>op.cit.</u>
¹⁶¹ Charles R. Beitz, "Equal Opportunity and Political Representation," in Norman E. Bowie, ed., <u>Equal Opportunity</u>, <u>supra</u>, p. 167.
¹⁶² Civic republican legal scholars often emphasize that empowerment of the dispossessed is necessary to achieve the "undistorted" dialogue that makes political life meaningful. These theories often draw on the political philosophies of Jurgen Habermas and Richard Bernstein. See, e.g., Drucilla Cornell, "Toward a Modern/Postmodern Reconstruction of Ethics," <u>University of Pennsylvania Law Review</u> 133 (1985), p. 291. For criticisms of Habermasian notions of communicative rationality, see Connolly, <u>op.cit.</u>, p. 237 and Dallmayr, <u>op.cit.</u>, p. 249.

similar inclusion to ensure a vibrant political interaction among diverse groups.[163] Unless these institutional concerns are addressed, it may be difficult to "expect the victims of discrimination to respect the political channels seeking redress."[164]

Toward a third reconstruction

The question is not "whether equality," but "which equality."[165]

It's "winner take nothing" that is the great truth of our country or of any country. Life is to be lived, not controlled; and humanity is won by continuing to play in the face of certain defeat. Our fate is to become one, and yet many -- This is not prophecy, but description (Ralph Ellison).[166]

Rather than providing a facile resolution of the problems I have discussed, I hope to provoke legal scholars and political scientists to engage in vigorous debate about the institutional requisites of equal representation and how they are connected to the normative concerns of politics. This debate should examine the behavioral and structural characteristics of local election systems, the political processes leading up to elections, and the quality of the representative processes that result from elections. While approaches to remedy vote dilution must figure strongly in this debate, the elusive voyage toward equal representation cannot be completed without a third reconstruction, one that actively explores the normative concerns of minority empowerment in a representative democracy.

Although my list is representative rather than exhaustive, I will end by mentioning three concerns that should figure in this debate.[167] The first is that the measurable guidepost of "minority electoral success" should not be read to frustrate the Voting Rights Act's more complicated path toward "equal opportunity to participate in the political process." One troublesome implication of the Supreme Court's Gingles ruling was its contention that to justify a remedy, the minority group challenging the election system must be "sufficiently large and geographically compact to constitute a majority in a single-member district."[168] Although understandable in its factual context -- a challenge to a multimember district system -- this requirement would undermine the voting rights of small or diffuse minorities if turned into a per se rule. Moreover, in some communities, the standard single-member district remedy may ultimately force minorities to choose between the

---

[163] This perspective might be termed "normative pluralism." See, e.g., Kathleen M. Sullivan, "Rainbow Republicanism," Yale Law Journal 97 (1988), p. 1714.
[164] Mobile v. Bolden 446 U.S. at 141, J. Marshall, dissenting.
[165] Douglas Rae, Equalities (Cambridge, MA, 1981), p. 19.
[166] Ralph Ellison, Invisible Man (New York, 1952), p. 499.
[167] Another difficult issue is how to identify minority-preferred candidates in Section 2 analysis. To insist that such candidates belong to the minority group might entrench polarized voting patterns even further. However, in communities where minorities have encountered obstacles to running candidates of their own, they may face elections in which none of the candidates running embody their preferences. For a sensitive discussion of this issue, see Note, "Defining the Minority-Preferred Candidate Under Section 2," Yale Law Journal 99 (1990), p. 1651.
[168] Thornburg v. Gingles 478 U.S. at 50.

objectives of residential integration and political empowerment.[169] As Pamela Karlan has noted, minorities may be segregated from the political process even if they are integrated into the political subdivision.[170]

The "intensely local" approach of the Voting Rights Act provides the flexibility for courts to construct special remedies meeting the representational needs of small or diffuse minorities a meaningful voice in representative government. If analyzing local politics reveals some possibility for effective coalition-building, courts might consider creating a "strong plurality" district with minority and nonminority populations of similar size.[171] Where polarized voting is more entrenched, it may be necessary to employ some alternative voting structure to take the interests of small or diffuse minorities into account.[172]

Perhaps the most promising of these alternatives, "cumulative voting," would modify at-large elections so that voters can cast all (or some) of their total votes for a single candidate. This approach, which has been employed with some success in a few jurisdictions, allows minorities to register intense preferences and may assist in their coalition-building efforts.[173] While this approach would not overcome all the social choice problems associated with registering preferences, it has the potential advantage of increasing the diversity of deliberation within representative institutions. However, more comparative study of this and other "alternative" districting systems needs to be done, exploring how they affect both the equality and quality of representation in political institutions.[174]

My second concern is to call for a stronger dialogue between political scientists and lawyers on the ways in which various approaches to districting and elections affect the equity and effectiveness of the political process. This dialogue should be "carried out in connection with democratic theory" and should "take into account the specific historical and socio-political situation under which an election system has to operate."[175]

Thus far, most successful minority vote dilution rulings have resulted in replacing at-large election districts with single-member plurality districts. Although students of policy-making have sometimes welcomed such changes, noting the historical affinity between single-member plurality districts and accommodationist

---

[169] Note, "The Single-Transferable Vote: Achieving the Goals of Section 2 without Sacrificing the Integration Ideal," Yale Law & Policy Review 9 (1991), p. 406.
[170] Karlan, "Maps and Misreadings," op.cit., p. 181.
[171] See Abrams, "Raising Politics Up," op.cit., p. 523.
[172] Karlan, "Maps and Misreadings," op.cit., pp. 223-236. See also Edward Still, "Alternatives to Single-Member Districts," in Davidson, ed., Minority Vote Dilution, op.cit., pp. 253-258.
[173] See Delbert Taebel, Richard L. Engstrom, and Richard L. Cole, "Alternative Election Systems as Remedies for Minority Vote Dilution," Hamline Journal of Public Law and Policy 11 (1990), pp. 24-29; Judith Reed, "Of Boroughs and Bullwinkles: The Limitations of Single-Member Districts in a Multiracial Context," Fordham Urban Law Journal 19 (1992), pp. 776-779.
[174] Cf. Dixon, Democratic Representation, op.cit., p. 525 (arguing that unlike pure proportional representation, cumulative and limited voting "do not impede effective leadership or weaken the two-party system").
[175] Dieter Nohlen, "Two Incompatible Principles of Representation," in Lijphart and Grofman, eds., Choosing an Election System, op.cit., p. 89.

two-party government, students of comparative election systems have sometimes found it puzzling that courts would seek to redress discrimination against groups within the framework of single-member districts, rather than moving toward some direct form of proportional representation.[176]

Because direct forms of proportional representation allow for "voluntary" constituencies in the place of discrete districts, they carry the advantage of eliminating any need for vote dilution remedies to focus on the single factor of minority affiliation. In so doing, they may be more sensitive to the growing differentiation of political attitudes within minority communities.[177] However, they may also produce the disadvantages often associated with voluntary-constituency systems, such as encouraging fragmented, multiparty government and minimizing "the integrative process of compromise and adjustment at the citizen level."[178] Unfortunately, much discussion for and against proportional representation has suffered from polemicism; these advocates have tended to exaggerate the relative merits of proportionality or plurality while slighting the wide variety of institutional arrangements that are possible within these general categories.[179] Rather than resorting to generalizations, participants in discussions about vote dilution have much to learn from the growing body of political science literature relating particular types of districting or election arrangements to effective group participation of groups in parties, elections, and representative bodies. The discussion must eventually move "beyond voting rights per se" to an assessment of the institutional arrangements that best encourage the normative goals of representative democracy.[180]

My final concern is probably the most difficult one: Discussions of voting rights should seriously consider the problems that social and economic inequalities pose for the effective exercise of equal representation. Modern vote dilution doctrine allows for a sensitive assessment of the continuing effects of discrimination in such fields as education and employment, and of the responsiveness of a government to minorities' needs. Unfortunately, while reform of voting systems can have some constructive effect, equal representation as an ideal cannot be fully institutionalized without significant improvement in minorities' socioeconomic conditions and in their perceptions of government.[181]

In light of these connections, recent evidence suggesting a widening gap

---

[176] See, e.g., Taagepera and Shugart, op.cit., p. 233.

[177] See, e.g., Martin Kilson, "Problems of Black Politics," Dissent (Fall 1989), p. 536.

[178] Dixon, Democratic Representation, op.cit., pp. 56-57. Compare Maurice Duverger, "Which is the Best Electoral System?" in Lijphart and Grofman, eds., Choosing an Electoral System, op.cit., p. 31 (arguing that proportional representation only threatens stability when the executive depends on a legislative vote of confidence in a parliamentary system).

[179] See Richard Rose, "Electoral Systems: A Question of Degree or Principle?" in Lijphart and Grofman, eds., Choosing an Electoral System, op.cit., p. 73.

[180] See, e.g., Bruce Cain, "Voting Rights and Democratic Theory," in Grofman and Davidson, eds., Controversies in Minority Voting, op.cit., p. 48.

[181] See Milton D. Morris, "Black Electoral Participation and the Distribution of Public Benefits," in Davidson, ed., Minority Vote Dilution, op.cit., p. 284.

between rich and poor[182] and a strong association between race and poverty[183] suggest that much remains to be done. The connection between socioeconomic and political equality raises concerns that are at the heart of modern discussions of pluralist politics in the United States. In Charles Lindblom's memorable phrase, "money not only talks in politics; it whispers conspiratorially and, at the other extreme, sometimes shouts so loud that no other messages can be heard."[184]

While voting rights law can contribute significantly to the practical implementation of equal representation, it would be naive to expect courts to achieve singlehandedly the sorts of political changes that would be needed to overcome socioeconomic barriers to equal representation.[185] Nor does it seem likely that courts in specific vote dilution cases would be well-equipped to implement comprehensive remedies to the problems that have tied race to poverty. But elected officials should not use these impracticalities as an excuse to adopt the complacent perspective that equal representation can be achieved without attention to these problems. Unless these concerns are addressed, neither the open society of pluralist theory nor the civic virtue of republican theory can live up to its promises.

Understood as a matter of reconstituting politics rather than simply a matter of measuring preferences, judicial protection against vote dilution may be considered a necessary, though not a sufficient, way to move political institutions toward equal and effective representation. Although there is no procedurally neutral way to conceive of a system that counts everyone equally, a normatively desirable goal of representative democracy is to shape the polity in a manner that makes everyone count. Perhaps this will prove to be an impossible journey, but the legitimacy of our representative institutions depends upon our continued willingness to search.

---

[182] Leo Rennert, "Poorer and Poorer," Oakland Tribune (September 4, 1992), p. A-1; Lester Thurow, "A Surge in Inequality," Scientific American (May 1987), p. 30.
[183] See Andrew Hacker, Two Nations (New York, 1992), pp. 93-106; David Swinton, "The Economic Status of African-Americans: 'Permanent' Poverty and Inequality," in National Urban League, The State of Black America (New York, 1991), p. 25; Loic J. D. Wacquant, "The Ghetto, The State, and the New Capitalist Economy," Dissent (Fall 1989), p. 508.
[184] Charles Lindblom, Politics and Markets (New York, 1977), op.cit., p. 123.
[185] See Paul Brest, "Further Beyond the Republican Revival: Toward Radical Republicanism," Yale Law Journal 97 (1988), p. 1626.

CHAPTER SEVEN

THE ROLE OF GOVERNANCE IN ECONOMIC DEVELOPMENT[1]

RAYMOND F. HOPKINS

Introduction: Linkages

"No taxation without representation" was a popular motto expressing public dissatisfaction prior to the American Revolution. Popular government has long been associated with economic health, while governments that appear oppressive, exploitive or unresponsive are frequently linked to economic turbulence or failure. From the observations of political philosophers since Aristotle to the evidence from events in East Europe, the former Soviet Union and Africa, this point seems well grounded.[2]

Indeed, the rapid changes in Eastern Europe and Africa since 1988 raise anew the more specific question about how the character and performance of a country's state organization affects the process of economic development. "Democratization" has been seen by many East European leaders, for example, as a prerequisite for ending the economic stagnation experienced under a communist, command-style rule. Somewhat analagously, in Africa in the 1980s, the negative impact of state policies that stifled initiative and extracted resources without providing public goods has become a central issue. The World Bank, for example, in a recent report, *From Crisis to Sustainable Growth: A Long-Term Perspective Study* (1989) has summarized considerable literature pinpointing aspects of state behavior in SubSaharan Africa believed to have been counterproductive to the efforts of African peoples and external donors to stimulate economic growth.

---

[1] An earlier version of this essay was prepared for the Task Force on Development Assistance and Cooperation. See G. Edward Schuh, et.al., International cooperation for sustainable economic growth: The U.S. interest and proposals for revitalization (Washington: Report of a task Force on Development Assistance and Economiv Growth, commissioned by the Board for International Food and Agricultural Development).

[2] Aristotle, for example, noted the enhanced industriousness of a society whose state followed democratic principles (see Aristotle, Politics) and Samuel Huntington argues in chapter 1 that strong political institutions, able to absorb -- thus not coercively regressing -- a population's urge to participate, are needed to shape political life as a solution to the turbulence and instability which otherwise accompanies economic transformation, Political Order in chanigng Societies (New Haven: Yale University Press,1968). Karl Deutsch argues that legitimacy and efficiency are improved by the responsiveness of a government based on correction feedback that occurs when a government's nerves are open to criticism, The Nerves of Government: Models of Political Communication and Control (New York: The Free Press, 1963; 2nd edition, 1966, with new introduction, ' The study of political communication and control, 1962-1966,' pp. vii-xxiii).

States and markets are not simply alternative or competing methods for allocating scarce resources. They also represent fundamental elements of human activity, each requiring the other and each able to stimulate or undermine the ability of the other to achieve collective human benefits. It is in the organization and interrelationship of these that welfare, development and equity emerge.[3]

Thus the key issue for understanding the role of governance in economic development is the recognition that a responsible government, long a concern of Charles E. Gilbert, plays an indispensable role in creating, sustaining and correcting markets. The role may facilitate or hinder the work of markets to diffuse technology, reward initiative, and distribute goods. While markets work at all levels of society, since World War II their effects have been especially strong in deepening international divisions of labor. Hence, the implications of governance address not only household and national performance, but also global trade and development. This explains some of the interest of industrial states in promoting improved governance in countries around the world.

The purpose of this paper will be to propose and discuss a set of characteristics of governance -- applicable quite universally -- that are conducive to successful economic development. These qualities are especially germane in cases where efforts to reform policy or change national economic and political strategies are underway.

Their relevance, however, is general and reflect a concern that the state act "responsibly". Often, in nation-states grappling with change, from former communist regimes to disillusioned third world socialist countries, the role of foreign assistance can be catalytic. By the beginning of the 1990s most donor country and multilateral agencies concerned with promoting economic development had begun to consider more explicitly and empirically the extent to which aid allocations to promote economic development could and should take into account and even shape the political environment of recipients.

Many citizens of democratic states support attaching "political conditionality" to aid. From the US to the Nordic states, from Australia to Japan, donors have seen a virtue in fostering values similar to their own in other states.[4] Political considerations for foreign aid have long been manifest in more overt diplomatic uses, e.g. efforts to cement alliances and build support for, among other things, the maintenance of foreign military bases and defense arrangements. In contrast, multilateral institutions such as the World Bank are prohibited by their mandate from interfering in the internal affairs and politics of member governments to whom they provide development loans. Indeed, a basic principle of the system of nation states is respect for the sovereignty of states. From this are derived rules against intervention in the domestic affairs of recognized legitimate states.[5] Nevertheless, increasingly the bilateral and multilateral agencies that provide aid to less developed countries -- often countries with large impoverished populations -- are now considering how features of governmental performance assist or vitiate project and program assistance. They care because they recognize the value in taking into account the importance of such characteristics in calculations about what allocations of foreign assistance will have positive results.

---

[3] Charles E. Lindblom, Politics and Markets (New York: Basic Books, 1977).
[4] Larry Diamond, "Promoting Democracy," Foreign Policy, No. 87 (Summer 1992), pp. 25-46.
[5] Stephen Krasner, "Sovereignty: An Institutional Perspective," Comparative Political Studies, Vol. 21, No. 1 (April 1988), pp. 66-94.

Four general qualities of government

Four general qualities of government promote economic development. These are: (1) openness, (2) institutionalized, legitimate rule of law, (3) respect for human dignity and (4) civic-mindedness. These four capture, I believe, a number of attributes that have been proposed as important as conditions for economic growth.

These qualities are often associated with "democratic" government. Analysts concerned with "development," however, appropriately focus more on the quality of governance than the character of the regime. In part, this is because of the mixed consequences of increased participation on stability and productivity.[6] Multi-party politics and political pluralism may encourage interest groups based on narrow economic advantage. Without checks upon them, these can harm development. Competitive qualities, therefore, should not explicitly be included in governance attributes designed to be directly supportive of development. They may be dangerous to development, at least in certain contexts even if increased political competition enhances indirectly economic competitiveness and efficiency and reinforces norms of responsibile governance that are directly helpful to a market-growth economy. Rational choice political economists and critics of the impact of special interests on American politics have long identified the danger of factions. Empowering special economic or sub-national interests may well occur when a political formula is adopted that encourages the use of power to perpetuate special economic advantages. This often leads to unproductive stalemates.[7]

Openness refers to transparency in public life. Thus expenditures by government, the decisions and workings of government officials, except for highly sensitive judicial and military areas, are open to public scrutiny. In addition openness suggests that freedom of press and expression along with the right to assemble and discuss either the elements of religion or political belief must be tolerated. Tolerance for dissent, for debate, and for non-violent expression of opposition is an important value enabling institutions to foster creativity, self-generative reform, and corrective feedback from mistaken policies and outdated ideas. "Speaking truth to power" is essential if a state is to perform its classically mandated functions in society such as promoting the common welfare, defending the borders of the country and correcting market failures. Moreover, openness can be a self-sustaining trait in the sense that it provides an avenue for frustration to be ventilated and dissipated. Hence, it promotes legitimacy and the encouragement of voice rather than the more economically costly alternatives for a population, namely loyal foot-dragging, exit or revolution[8]. Its dangers occur principally in deeply

---

[6] Samuel Huntington, Political Order in Changing Societies (New Haven: Yale University Press, 1968).

[7] This danger has been noted by James Madison in his familiar Federalist Paper No. 10 (1787). In more recent times the danger of the minority powerfully distorting economic growth (and for Africa, the most cited work) is argued by Robert Bates, Markets and States in Tropical Africa (Berkeley: University of California Press, 1981); Mancur Olson, The Rise and Decline of Nations (New Haven: Yale University Press, 1982); and Theodore Lowi, Interest Group Liberalism (Norton: 1967). The rational choice perspective and limit are discussed in Grindle (1989).

[8] James Scott's work Weapons of the Weak (New Haven: Yale University Press, 1986) that suggests how peasants may be unable to exit physically, as refugees from Eastern Europe frequently have, as have the educated who leap from Africa and other parts of the third world. Peasants, nevertheless, "exit" psychologically and economically, he argues, by foot-dragging and

divided societies -- ones perhaps inevitably headed for separation as in the case of post-1947 India, now broken into India, Pakistan and Bangladesh.[9] Interestingly enough, the quality of openness has also been recognized as important in superior performance among economic institutions, e.g. corporations. Thus studies at business schools have suggested that organizations that were more open and had less heirarchical structures were more adaptive and able to innovate and succeed in response to the rapidly changing and highly technical environment of today's world.[10]

A rule of law, the second governance quality, is universally mentioned as a condition for economic development. Laws are needed to guarantee contractual rights among parties, and to ensure predictability and the protection of the individual against larger, potentially predatory, institutions including the state. Often, however, rule of law is narrowly associated with the establishment and systematic operation of a court system. Totalitarian societies, of course, can achieve a perverted version of this governance quality. Edicts of a tyrant, even in states too weak to achieve totalitarian control, have been set forth as being lawful.

Clearly rule of law must mean something more than the mere presence of officials following some due process in arriving at decisions which are then authoritatively executed. Two qualities are crucial for the rule of law to achieve its positive benefits for economic development. First, it must be institutionalized. That is, people must believe that the laws are to be respected and that the promulgation of law, that is its "rule," arises from and is subject to scrutiny and criticism. Openness helps guarantee this, coupled with an inculcation of respect for the law. An institutionalized rule of law is one that reaches down to various economic stratas of society and encompasses various ethnic and racial groups that may exist within a pluralistic state. An institutionalized rule of law is one that is consistent in its application and anchored in the common and deeply shared expectations of both those who are specialized in law enforcement -- police, courts and administrators -- as well as the population over whom the rule of law is applied.

Second, the rule of law must be legitimate. Often institutionalized and legitimate rules of law reinforce each other. Nevertheless, legitimate rule of law refers to its non-exploitive and non-coercive character with respect to the opinions and culture over which it is exercised. In colonial states, for example, the rule of law imposed by the British, French and others was effective and sufficiently institutionalized to guarantee reasonably high probabilities of enforcement, at least among those sectors of the society over which day-to-day control was exercised -- generally the "modern" sector -- but was surely not accepted as legitimate by most of the population. Indeed just as "taxation without representation" was an instance of a rule of law that was not perceived as legitimate, so also, throughout many developing countries, rules enforced by the formal, often inherited process of justice do not create an atmosphere of voluntary compliance. Hence they do not nurture confidence and predictability among a populace, fundamental factors to the encouragement of economic risk-taking, the nurturance of economic institutions and enhanced productivity.

---

noncompliance that undermines objectives of the state and protects themselves from economically exploitative regulation.

[9] See Albert Hirshman's classic work on *Exit, Voice and Loyalty: Responses to Decline in Firms, Organizations and States* (Cambridge : Harvard University Press, 1971).
[10] Philip Slater and Warren G. Bennis, "Democracy is Inevitable," in *Harvard Business Review*, Vol. 68, No. 5 (September-October 1990), pp. 167-176.

On the one hand, therefore, an institutionalized but illegitimate rule of law might characterize strongly authoritarian states in which capriciousness by rulers and exploitation would stifle economic productivity. On the other hand, the extreme of a legitimate but uninstitutionalized rule of law would create conditions of "the wild west." In the latter case each individual would take care of her needs of security and enforce upon others her own understanding of justice, often justice meted out swiftly. Such conditions tend to degenerate so that law is neither institutionalized nor legitimate (except for the individual enforcers' preferences). The existence of a state structure over such a situation camouflages subterfuge under which particular individuals can use their putative positions and uniforms to extract resources in the form of rents from other citizens.

Indeed, the rent-seeking state has a deformed form of justice and its rule of law becomes more a pretext for extortion. Interestingly enough, this mafia-like quality of government, found in the petty but systematic corruption of states such as Zaire, Mexico, and even the Soviet Union, indicates that both weak and strong states are prone to systems of justice in which the rule of law fails to achieve an institutionalized and legitimate role in meting out fair and predictable outcomes for society. Under such conditions officials are seldom held accountable for their actions and graft, corruption and rent-seeking are encouraged.

Respect for human dignity is not mutually exclusive from the first two qualities mentioned. If anything, it is an extension. Where government fosters respect of each citizen, toleration increases and the assuredness with which one may obtain or practice openness is increased. Furthermore, rule of law is likely to demand certain "due processes" in which each individual's human dignity is respected. In societies where one ethnic group sees another without such human dignity, even sometimes as "less than human" or, more typically, where racial lines lead to invidious stereotyping, prospects for violence increase and respect for rule of law and toleration of dissent are threatened. Opposition is often seen as threatening because mutually exclusive identity structures fail to incorporate other portions of the society as being equally deserving and equally dignified. In a society where peasants, for example, are regarded as backward or mindless, it is unlikely that the agricultural economy will flourish. Allocations in these conditions often favor less productive rural landowners or industrial sectors.[11]

A view that human dignity is respected among the populace of the state, or indeed the entire world, expands the protections of individuals, one against the other, and at the same time enhances their empowerment to pursue wealth and other values as a right. Governance can foster this through its basic constitutional orientation and by implementing policies in a fashion that indicate implicitly as well as explicitly such a recognition. Invidious distinctions between races or members and non-members of the ruling party are examples of governance which has failed to nurture the capabilities and productive energies of its populace. Racial and ethnic intolerance frequently vitiates economic entrepreneurship and coping strategies. In the more mundane cases, economic resources become allocated on a basis of regional or tribal preferences, where exploitation by a "new ruling class," whether under apartheid or Marxism, acts as a drag on the spirit and respect of a citizenry.

---

[11] Alain de Janvry, The Agrarian Question and Reformism in Latin America (Baltimore: Johns Hopkins University Press, 1981); and Just Faaland and Jack Parkinson, "The Nature of the State and the Role of Government in Agricultural Development," in C. Peter Timmer, ed., Agriculture and the State: Growth, Employment and Poverty in Developing Countries (Ithaca: Cornell University Press, 1991).

At the extreme, such intolerance leads to ethnic violence and the fragmentation of the state.

The failure to nurture tolerance, mutual identity, and respect of others, both in public policies and through educational institutions, can bear fruit decades later as racial and ethnic conflicts destroy public resources and erode the framework within which markets can operate. The deterioration of conditions in Sudan, Ethiopia and Somalia are examples of this. The conflict in Mynnar (Burma) between the Burmese and Hill People similarly are part of an erosion that is closely associated with economic deterioration. Ethnic unrest in Sri Lanka, the states of the former Soviet Union and Eastern European countries, including Yugoslavia, suggest similar threats to economic progress as energies are vitiated on misplaced on unproductive targets of frustration. Of course, exploitation is real. Witness South Africa.

A government that nurtures respect for its fellow citizens and a common identity among them, and that demands each person be accorded human dignity, is not created artificially or in a short period. It is, nevertheless, a role the state needs to undertake as its very constitutive element and to carry out in a way that is effective, i.e. encourages the learning and inculcation of this value. Its achievement requires that people be treated equally before systems of justice, that they be given equal access to services of the state, whether the post office, health clinic or educational facility, that they be referred to not artificially, in terms created by the state, e.g. as "comrade," but rather as they invite others to refer to themselves and that they be free to form voluntary affiliations in civic society.[12]

Finally civic-mindedness, the fourth governance criteria proposed, is a demand upon the self to obey the state, and to voluntarily participate in civic activities. A classic study thirty years ago found that the "civic" attitudes among citizens was a strong indicator of loyalty to the state and of the institutionalization of demands for tolerance and fair play among other members of the population.[13] Civic-mindedness may be fostered by democratic formulae, which exalt participation and competition. Among a people long exposed to authoritarian structures in educational and workplace situations, a sense of participation and obligation to speak out or provide correction to failures of rule of law is unlikely to occur. Building pride in a national self-referent expands the capacity of the state to operate effectively. Doing so without checks on the state's policies, however, as often occurs in the heady days following a revolution or the successful end of colonial rule, may lead to distortive and excessive interventions by the state. In such times states operate as if they were hospitals -- designed to provide intensive care to their patients -- and not as institutions nurturing collective pride and voluntary self-reliant civic associations.

Foreign investment may also be eschewed uncritically when national self-confidence is low. The dangers of excessive government fostered by nationalism and national pride are clear. Nevertheless, civic-mindedness is necessary, indeed critical, for a state to expand its capacity to tax effectively and to redistribute capital through investments in public works and other collective goods such as research,

---

[12] Robert Putnam (in chapter eight of this volume), for example, offers persuasive evidence that people who come together voluntarily to pursue mutual interests, as in Italians joining choral societies, provide a basis for expectations among the populace of an Italian state that is an impressively accurate predictor of good governmental performance, often decades later, even more a force apparantly than economic performance in promoting effective governance.

[13] Gabriel Almond and Sidney Verba, The Civic Culture (Princeton: Princeton University Press, 1963).

education, health systems and the apparatus to insure reliable domestic law and adequate external defense. Such state contributions are much more easily sustained when people respect the state and take pride in it. Civic-mindedness can be helped by external donors, but only as long as foreign aid is not seen as illegitimate or contaminating.

Among the World Bank's basic data on countries, Switzerland ranks highest in gross national product per capita.[14] With two national languages, and a third language widely used in southern cantons (Italian), one could imagine rampant civil strife among language and regional groupings in this small country. The fact that women received the right to vote only in 1973 might further suggest a lack of participation and failure to extend the definition of citizen to the entire population. An examination of the distortions created by the intervention of the state in agriculture, perhaps the most highly subsidized agricultural system in the world, might further lead an observer to expect this country to fail to meet some of the criteria for positive elements of governance promoting economic development.

Clearly this is not the case. Voting participation in Switzerland is low often because consensus is high. Habits of participation among women, while recent in formal terms, show progressive trends. Voting is by and large highest among the younger generation who have acquired a heightened sense of civic identity and internalize more a demand upon themselves to participate in elections. Furthermore, the Swiss have had a sense of common national pride for a long and emotionally deep period. Such pride has overridden other potentially divisive elements of the society. Aside from business and banking affairs, the work of the government has been manifestly transparent, as have the public elements of social and economic life. Rule of law has been an exemplary feature of the society. It has been a symbol of fairness and respect for all. Indeed it serves as a nurturing ground for meeting the needs of the world's state system. The headquarters of the League of Nations was located here and currently its buildings, the Palace of Nations, houses much of the United Nations. With Switzerland's long service to international causes, including the League of Red Cross Societies, the notion of respect for human dignity is an honored tradition. Finally, civic-mindedness, that is pride in the physical appearance of one's country and in the responsibility of each citizen to look after the laws and to maintain their private and public places, is well established. Swiss civic-mindedness reflects the pride of the individual in the state and the dedication to its success as a corporate body, while at the same time demanding a strong role for the private sector and for regulation rather than exploitation of markets.

Agriculture, development and governance[15]

Thanks to the large role played by agriculture in developing countries, how governance affects agriculture is crucial to economic development. Especially in states with GNP per capita below $600, the agricultural sector is usually the largest source of employment and food the largest household expenditure. It is appropriate, therefore, to give special attention to ways in which governance affects the

---

[14] World Bank, World Development Report, 1992: Development and the Environment (Washington, D.C.: World Bank, 1992).
[15] I want to acknowledge the influence and help of Peter Timmer, Walter Falcon, and others who attended the Marbach Conference on "The Role of Agriculture in Economic Development," September 1989, in Oeningen, Germany.

performance of national food and agricultural systems.

State policy intervention in agriculture has a long tradition. Economic historian Peter Lindert presents evidence to show a changing role for agricultural policies in the course of economic growth.[16] In early modern European and contemporary developing countries, most often agriculture experienced net taxation; in modern industrial states, in contrast, governments generally subsidize agriculture. This pattern does not arise, Lindert finds, from economic rationality (usually) but from political and economic forces ascendent at a particular time in a nation's history.

A traditional political economy analysis, in fact, readily explains this evolution of agricultural policy from exploitation to subsidization. The dynamics are more complex, however. Thus, theories of pure rational choice are inadequate, at least as elaborated by some economists, i.e. the view that policy outcomes are essentially the result of success by a self-interested pursuit by the strongest, most organized social groups.[17] Over time, for example, we can see how the purposes that powerful forces sought from state action have often been divergent from consequences.[18] Often there are perverse and unintended consequences of state action for agriculture. In addition, causality is interactive. Hence, the very evolution of the state itself is closely linked to the development of agriculture and the effects that agricultural policies have upon it. Hence, there is a dynamic. Governance and agricultural performance in a society act over historical periods as endogenous but independent variables in a country's history, operating in a non-recursive fashion -- a point implicit in most analyses of economic historians and social scientists.[19]

Anthropologists, furthermore, have closely linked the expansion of governing institutions -- from those of minimalist governments to complex, modern state systems -- with changes in agricultural production. The need to regulate market activity and resolve land disputes for settled agriculturalists, for instance, is postulated as the basis for the rise of African feudal-type systems.[20] Likewise, the centralization of state power and national policies in the modern era is linked to changes in agriculture.[21] Indeed, state financing for agricultural modernization and

---

[16] Peter Lindert, "Economic Influences on the History of Agricultural Policy," in C. Peter Timmer, ed., Agriculture and the State: Growth, Employment and Poverty in Developing Countries (Ithaca: Cornell University Press, 1991).

[17] E.g. Mancur Olson, The Rise and Decline of Nations -- Economic Growth, Stagflation and Social Rigidities (New Haven: Yale University Press, 1982).

[18] Charles Tilly, ed., The Formation of National States in Western Europe (Princeton: Princeton University Press, 1975); Andrew Coulson, Tanzania: A Political Economy (Oxford: Oxford University Press, 1982).

[19] Barrington Moore, Jr., Social Origins of Dictatorship and Democracy: Lord and Peasant in the Making of the Modern World (Boston: Beacon Press, 1967); Alexander Gerschenkron, Economic Backwardness in Historical Perspective: A Book of Essays (Cambridge: Belknap Press of Harvard University Press, 1962).

[20] See M. Fortes and E. E. Evans-Pritchard, eds., African Political Systems (London: Oxford University Press, 1940); and Lucy Mair, Primitive Government (Baltimore: Penguin, 1962), pp. 29-31.

[21] See Geoffrey Barraclough, The Crucible of Europe (Berkeley: University of California Press, 1976); and William Cochran, The Development of American Agriculture: A Historical Analysis (Minneapolis: University of Minnesota Press, 1979).

the expansion of markets, some argue, played the critical role in the modernization of Europe and the expansion of the European state System.[22]

Agricultural transformation, not surprisingly, is also seen as essential for successful economic development in late-developing countries, such as Turkey, and very late developers, such as SubSaharan African countries.[23] Thus agricultural transformation may be regarded as central to economic development. In addition it plays a critical role in enhancing or undermining state authority.[24] Given this centrality, a key question arises. How can differences in governance shape state intervention in agriculture in ways that enhance economic development?

Purposes and consequences of agricultural policies

In different historical and agronomic situations, states formulate different agricultural policies. They differ because they seek different goals and choose varying instruments of policy. It is difficult, of course, to be certain about the real purposes of states, as opposed to the merely stated ones. Furthermore, while formal, stated policies are generally accessible to historic or economic interpretation drawing upon explicit legal actions and recorded state expenditures, the actual implementation of policies and the utilization of state funds may vary considerably from those formally stated. This is particularly true in societies in which state capacity is weak, that is a "soft" state exists, to use Myrdal's term.[25] Throughout contemporary SubSaharan Africa, for instance, where countries have a dismal record in agricultural performance in the 1970s and 1980s, policies for regulating markets, subsidizing agricultural inputs, fixing prices, and even creating nutritional safety nets expose a wide gap between official policy and actual performance. What allows this to happen over an extended period? First, the absence of openness and legitimate rule of law in many states has prevented protests and corrective feed-back to expose this disjunction between stated goals and actual consequences for producers. Second, failures in agriculture can undermine the civic-mindedness of farmers marginalized or exploited by policies that backfire.

The effectiveness of policy instruments may thus be highly limited in periods of nascent state formation. Although rural populations often lack organization and appear vulnerable to the interests of the powerful, they nonetheless may pose a

---

[22] Immanuel Wallerstein, The Modern World System: Capitalist Agriculture and the Origins of the European World Economy in the Sixteenth Century (New York: Academic Press, 1974); Tilly, 1975; and Michael Tracy, Agriculture in Western Europe: Crisis and Adaptation since 1880 (London: Jonathan Cape, 1982, 2nd edition).

[23] See A. Adnan Akay, From Landlordism to Capitalism in Turkish Agriculture, Working Paper #12 (Milton Keynes, U.K.: The Open University, 1988); John W. Mellor, Christopher L. Delgado and Malcolm J. Blackie, eds., Accelerating Food Production in sub-Saharan Africa (Baltimore: Johns Hopkins University Press, 1987).

[24] Bruce Johnston and Peter Kilby, Agriculture and Structural Transformation (New York: Oxford University Press, 1975); Raymond F. Hopkins, "Food Security, Policy Options and the Evolution of State Responsibility," in F. Lamond Tullis and W. Ladd Hollis, eds., Food, the State, and International Political Economy (Lincoln: University of Nebraska Press, 1986), pp. 3-36, and "Political Calculations in Food Subsidies," in Per Pinstrup Andersen, ed., Food Subsidies in Developing Countries (Baltimore: Johns Hopkins University Press, 1988), pp. 107-126.

[25] Gunnar Myrdal, Asian Drama: An Inquiry into the Poverty of Nations (New York: Pantheon Books, 1968).

formidable obstacle to state manipulation. This seem equally true in Africa in the late twentieth century or in Europe in the eighteenth and nineteenth centuries.[26] The disjunction between "good" intentions of policy and perverse consequences can be attenuated when the rural sector has the benefit of an open society, when they are accorded respect and when law guarantees them equal rights, then policies that hurt the rural sector and small producers and represent opportunities for official rent-seeking will be less sustainable.

The historically dynamic process of the role of the state in agriculture moves from purposes to policy choices to implementation and, finally, to consequences. This dynamic is pervasive in the history of relations between the state and producers, merchants, and consumers. On the one hand, cases exist in which the state has used its resources to promote efficient agriculture, for example, through provision of collective goods, with results that are positive for both economic and non-economic values.[27] Several Asian states are such cases. On the other hand, states with weak structures and the absence of responsible governance can exploit agriculture, thus undermining growth opportunities and alienating segments of society.[28]

A focus on consequences, therefore, rather than policy stipulations is important both for development and especially for the agricultural sector. An institutionalized, legitimate rule of law is conducive to this consequential approach to agricultural development.[29] However, the emergence of higher economic productivity in some states, thanks to industrialization, has led to the diffusion of demands for a broader, welfare role for states, a role that exceeds ability.

Human dignity as a quality of governance has a connection also. Such value requirements limit rights to regulate markets solely in the interest of efficiency and social profitability (if they ever could); they also must redistribute social values to insure some degree of equity or justice.[30] In the last several centuries, responsibility for administering to the needs of weak and vulnerable people has shifted from the

---

[26] See Faaland and Parkinson, in Timmer, 1991; James C. Scott, Weapons of the Weak (New Haven: Yale University Press, 1985); Goren Hyden, Ujamaa (Berkeley: University of California Press, 1980); and Harvey Glickman, ed., The Crisis and Challenge of African Development (New York: Greenwood Press, 1988).

[27] For purposes here, the outcomes of state agricultural transactions are referred to both in terms of benefirs that are directly economic -- in the sense that they yield monetized effects whose net benefits and costs can theoretically be assessed using standard economic accounting methodologies -- and in terms of non-economic benefits, which include important aspects of human behavior, such as loyalty to the government, voluntary compliance with policy, national self-esteem and rectitude, and other values. These are not monetized directly. Even shadow prices for such values would be hard to calculate since their manifestations in society often occur in step-level events. Changes in such values, however, are conceptually discrete movements. For example, government legitimacy can vary by degrees, but changes in government legitimacy outside revolutionary situations are not readily measurable.

[28] Alberto Valdes, "Export-led Growth: What Role for Agriculture?" in C. Peter Timmer, ed., Agriculture and the State: Growth, Employment and Poverty in Developing Countries (Ithaca: Cornell University Press, 1991), pp. 1-28.

[29] Bruce F. Johnston and Peter Kilby, Agricultural and Structural Transformation: Economic Strategies in Late Developing Countries (New York: Oxford University Press, 1975), p. 474.

[30] See Arthur Okun, Equality and Efficiency: The Big Trade Off (Washington: The Brookings Institution, 1975).

private to the public sector. Thus, the welfare state, with its plethora of programs that provide citizens minimum guarantees of goods and services, has emerged as a manifest result of this shift. Further it is a concrete expression of material justice that respects individual human dignity (a "liberal" value to be sure). Thus in the modern, "well-governed" state, economic development naturally provides citizens with minimum guarantees of goods and services. As there is an expansion of the capacity of the state to do this, a result of natural shift in the size and capacity of the economy, it can do this better. It is not necessarily, therefore, a change in the desiderata of responsible governance.

Food price policy in developing countries has been particularly affected by this shift. To guarantee access to basic foodstuffs and augment the household income of those extremely poor, many states have adopted such measures as fixed prices or subsidy policies. Ethical considerations, arising from the very fabric of society itself, lead to this redistribution on behalf of the poor.[31] Most recently, governmental concern for dignity of all, including the poor, has manifested itself (even in very poor states) in such initiatives as the UNICEF proposal for "adjustment with a human face" and the World Bank's effort to achieve "food security" in Africa. Such policies are not without economic costs, however; the frequent trade-offs between equity and efficiency, between short- and long-term consequences, and between economic and non-economic values, become especially poignant in cases where government capacity is already constrained by slow rates of economic development.

Political economy considerations in the evolution of agricultural policy

Economists frequently criticize government policy that distorts markets. They argue that such interventions lead to non-Pareto optimal outcomes, reduce efficiency, slow the expansion of the production frontier, promote disincentives, and protect the unduly privileged. Such criticisms arise not only from neoclassical assumptions from which most economists approach social analysis but also from a genuine concern to seek better social welfare outcomes from government intervention. Market failures, exploitative government behavior, and policies encouraging stagnation rather than economic growth seem pathological from this perspective. To account for such policy failures, economists frequently blame "politics."

Recently, analyses of "political economy" have sought to interpret the development and change of policy in various historical contexts.[32] At least three alternative "ideal types" exist in political economy writings. Let me outline these to suggest how different roles for the state can affect the pattern of governance and economic development especially in the agriculture sector.

State as Arena. In the first ideal type, political economy sees the state as an arena for competing interest groups. Call this Model I. It is the most prevalent analytical model for describing causes of government action. Powerful interests, often urban based, as in a white collar salariat class, or grounded in powerful

---

[31] Robert Chambers, Rural Development: Putting the Last First (London: Longman, 1983); Jean Dreze, and Amartya Sen, Hunger and Public Action (New York: Oxford University Press, 1989).
[32] E.g. Martin Staniland, What is Political Economy? (New Haven: Yale University Press, 1985); and Robert Bates, Beyond the Miracle of the Market (New York: Cambridge University Press, 1989).

landowners have partial or complete control over the instruments of the state and use them to advance their own interests.[33] For these powerful groups, the only trade-off is between short- and long-term gain; they otherwise promote their group's rational choice strategies for state action, which will only coincidentally promote the interests of the society as a whole.

State as Actor. A second vision of the state used by political economists is a model of the state as an actor in its own right. The clan of tribal societies, the royal families of the feudal ages, and the modern bureaucratic state with its cadres of officials are examples of the personal state. Here the rational calculator of costs and benefits is based on maximizing state power and the income of its officials. Such calculations are, of course, constrained by the pliability of the state's subjects and the technology the state can use to enforce its will. The basic calculus, however, derives from the interests of those running the state itself, whether royalty, a privileged class, or an entrenched bureaucracy.

Examples of the state as self-interested actor range from the reign of France's Louis XIV with his diffidence towards those outside his state ("l'Etat c'est moi!") to the kleptocracy of Zaire. Activities of rent-seeking states have been caustically described by citizenries of countries ranging across the ideological spectrum. The Soviet Union, under *Glasnost*, has printed numerous complaints about management both in agriculture and in officialdom generally. Such popular complaints about state-controlled exploitation are widely reported in the literature on dependency in Latin America and Africa; attitudes with the same valence are voiced more gently in criticisms of the "heavy hand" of government expressed by the American farm population.[34]

State as Developer. In the third "ideal" model of a state's role in society described by political economists, the state is focused on building social capacity. Weak states seen through this model seek power but not as an end in itself, as in the case of Model II. Rather, here the state attempts to build support and discover policies that will best serve purposes required for survival of national sovereignty.[35] According to this ideal-type model, the key distinction among states and their policies arises from the state's capacity -- as ranked on a continuum from a weak (or soft) state to a strong (or hard) one. For the state to be an agent of development (and other human goals) it cannot be ephemeral and elusive; it must be tough and effective. The writ of state authority itself is the issue in question.[36] Often a weak state's capacity extends no further than the capital city or the personal friendships of top leaders. To act as a "builder," a state's "strength," therefore, determines the degree to which it can be effective. Excessive intervention, exceeding capacity, undermines economic strength and eventually political control. Figure 1 summarizes these three ideal type models of the role of the state in policy making.

---

[33] For a discussion of urban bias, see Michael Lipton, Why the Poor Stay Poor: A Study of Urban Bias in World Development (London: Temple Smith, 1977).

[34] Williard W. Cochran, The Development of American Agriculture: A Historical Analysis (Minneapolis: University of Minnesota Press,1979).

[35] Stephen Krasner, "Sovereignty: An Institutional Perspective," Comparative Political Studies (April 1988), pp. 66-94.

[36] See Samuel P. Huntington, Political Order in Changing Societies (New Haven: Yale University Press, 1968).

FIGURE I: Three "Ideal Types" of State/Society Relations

MODEL I: STATE AS ARENA

Groups form outside government, based on rational interest calculations, and seek to influence policy.

Variant A:
Competitive, pluralist system: multiple groups, changing alliances, and failures of public interest. Failures arise from divisible benefits that provide incentives to some groups (e.g. farm organizations) to pressure for policy preference, while more diffuse, larger groups (consumers) are less active due to the problems that collective benefits offer no selective incentives to mobilize.

Variant B:
Non-competitive, class-dominated situation in which a group, largely external to state officials (e.g., bourgeoisie, salariat, ethnic groups, etc.), dictate policies that systematically disadvantage one or several other groups. Little or no advantage accrues to public officials.

MODEL II: STATE AS ACTOR

State officials act to maximize their values (wealth, power, safety, affection, etc.).
    If the state has a high discount value, its leadership usually self-destructs. Its features are rent-seeking, bureaucratic self-protection, and extortion by individuals. The state is seen by itself and others as competing with society to maintain the privileges of the state office holders. If the state has a low discount rate, leaders may move toward a broader incorporation of popular interests with state interest -- a possible transformation, especially in "weak" states, toward a Model III type.

MODEL III: STATE AS DEVELOPER

The goal of strengthening nation-state desiderata of security, growth, and welfare are maximized.
    Weak states, typical among LDCs, give high priority to inculcating habits of compliance and improving the probability of enforcement. Security, particularly domestic, is a central issue. As the state as agent becomes stronger, its capacity and interest in serving national goals moves it to allocate more resources or allow more risk in policies aimed at economic growth and, eventually, welfare. Weak states that prematurely give high priority to economic growth and welfare frequently fail.

In examining the extent any given state's governance reflects each of these three "ideal" types, a distinction between formal, "de jure" but ineffective states and stronger "de facto" states is particularly apt. A number of writers have alluded to the inability of states, especially in Africa, to adopt policies that genuinely regulate the economy -- that demonstrate capacity beyond control over imports and exports. Even in the trade control realm, smuggling can be a major element allowing agriculture to escape state regulation.[37] It is important to recognize that even in countries where states represent powerful forces of society, such as the United States, or of a powerful organization in society, such as the Communist Party in the former Soviet Union, state policy is not solely in control. Other factors, particularly implementation problems and reactions of individual producers or consumers, frequently lead to policy outcomes quite different from the consequences expected or predicted by sophisticated analysis. In these conditions, actions by the state to intervene in agriculture, whether to support producers or consumers, or to stimulate and to redistribute wealth, may also represent a series of trials and errors in policy formation.

State intervention in agriculture and opportunities to enhance governance

The history of agricultural policy in various countries allows us to analyze how the ideal type distinctions above help us account for the evolution of policies, either across cases or over particular time periods in a country. Further, we can examine the purposes served by state intervention and how different ideal approximations and locations on capacity, hierarchy and openness may affect agriculture policy. States as actors for themselves (Model II), for example, are aggrandizing in character but frequently have short-term successes and long-term failures. Perhaps the Philippines under Marcos fits this pattern. A state acting as an arena for competing groups (Ideal Model I) may become captured by narrow interests, whether of powerful landlords or military officers, as in Argentina, which may lead to important policy distortions and to lost opportunities for the economy as well as disaffection of the population.[38] Where organized agriculture and a political elite overlap, as in Kenya and the Ivory Coast, policies favorable to agriculture (if not rural society in general) are also possible. The third vision, the state as would-be entrepreneur, may best account for states that intervene in society primarily to bring order and some semblance of control over agriculture; unfortunately this purpose in weak states may be highly transient and hard to implement; Tanzania is such a case. Since the state is not deeply institutionalized -- its leadership and/or circumstances change fairly quickly -- such a state might also be opportunistic.

Consider further that the state's search for optimizing behavior takes place under high uncertainty. Ironically, because weak states are not anchored in tradition or legal formalities, they may be more erratic in the policies they follow, but they are also more influenced by policy advice given by economists. Policies of developing countries, especially those in Africa, frequently fit this model. The advice of agricultural policy analysts to advance development might be most critical in weak states; it has the greatest opportunities to restructure agriculture, particularly after a

---

[37] See Hyden, 1980; Michael Bratton, "Beyond the State," World Politics, vol. 41, no. 3 (April 1989), pp. 407-430.
[38] Samuel P. Huntington, Political Order in Changing Societies (New Haven: Yale University Press, 1968).

revolution or foreign conquest -- for example, consider the effects of land reforms in Japan, Taiwan, or China.

Six purposes specific to agriculture seem to explain historical evolution in agricultural policy and relate to openings during which shifts toward enhanced governance can occur. Government intervention has nearly always involved some mixture of these purposes (outlined as broad goals). The six purposes of the state in asserting governance in agriculture are outlined below. Consequences of policy to achieve such purposes have also shaped the future capacity of the state for undertaking policies more broadly (i.e. in all sectors of the society). Short-sighted, unsuccessful interventions can harm both the state and agriculture. The success of the economic transformation of agriculture and the development of national loyalties and institutionalization of desirable features of governance, e.g. ones conducive to economic development, are all deeply interrelated as multiple consequences of evolving policy, in this instance in the agricultural sector.

(1) Extract Resources from Agriculture. The first purpose, classic for self-serving or rent-seeking states (Model II), is to extract resources from the agricultural sector for the purpose of state maintenance, including guaranteeing a high standard of living among official or royal classes. Since such extraction from the production or exchange of agricultural products serves only the purpose of redistributing wealth to office holders and central state authorities, it represents the purest case of exploitation. Such action is the functional equivalent of mafioso-style extortion in the private sector. The government's treatment of French peasants prior to the 1789 revolution is a classic instance of such a purpose dominating state policy. Zaire in the 1970s is another instance.[39] In Model III, extracting resources from agriculture may be linked by expenditure policies to more altruistic intentions and even consequences.

(2) Expansion of the State. The state intervenes to expand its connections throughout society. The expansion of the state, for good or ill, requires replacing local fiefdoms and baronies with the imprint of central authority. States thus devise policies that require low investment in personnel and seek to represent central authority as a positive force in the life of the peasantry.[40] Capitalist agriculture, for example, required centralized authority over local manor systems or tribal economies; the substitution of state regulations for such systems made possible the encouragement of capitalist practices. The state acted to assert its authority, however, rather than to base its policies on a theory of economic development. This assertion of authority itself was most often the core purpose for such action.[41]

(3) Protect Agriculture as a Resource. At times the state has intervened to put agriculture on a competitive basis with other economic sectors. By nature, agriculture is a risky business. Climatic forces make crop yields uncertain. Protection of land tenure rights and fair marketing arrangements for the often poor and disorganized farmers depends on laws and government. Producers who

---

[39] Scott, 1985; Thomas Callaghy, The State-Society Struggle: Zaire in Comparative Perspective (New York: Columbia University Press, 1984).

[40] Harold J. Laski, The Rise of European Liberations (London: Unsrin Books, 1938); Barrington Moore, Jr., Social Origins of Dictatorship and Democracy (Boston: Beacon Press, 1967); Michael Bratton, "Beyond the State: Civil Society and Associational Life in Africa," World Politics 41, no. 3 (April 1989), pp. 407-587.

[41] Charles Tilly, ed., The Formation of National States in Western Europe (Princeton: Princeton University Press, 1975).

provide the physical labor in agriculture, as distinguished from large landowners and managers, frequently have little power over the affairs of a state. Such numerous but disorganized elements of society lack the free time or direct rewards to organize and pay the cost of collective bargaining with the state.[42] The state aiming at development, however, can serve to secure socially efficient collective benefits for such important productive groups, which the "free rider" problem in politics would otherwise cause to be neglected.

(4) Promote Economic Development. The state undertakes various measures to stimulate economic development, such as investment in agricultural research, encouragement of new technology, or greater guarantees of profitability to producers taking risks or investing more of their own labor. This role of the state is the classic one assumed by most economists (given the normative assumptions within which most of their work is cast). With this purpose in mind, analysts carefully try to assess the optimal benefit-cost ratios of various government investments to maximize efficiency among producers, lower marketing costs, and alleviate uneconomical fluctuations in demand and unemployment among the poor. Open, strong and participatory states are likely to evolve policies that balance market efficiency with state exchange guarantees and investments. This is a result of the information feed-back and decision flexibility of such states.

(5) Improve Welfare of the Poor. Often cited as a goal of government policy is the promotion of equity and the meeting of human needs. Subsidies targeted to the hungry poor, absorption of the adjustment costs for those moving out of agriculture, and other state-funded compensatory actions may not have positive rates of return on investment, but are justified by basic ethical considerations and, secondarily, perhaps by the goal of state survival as a national, social instrument (see the purpose of political stability below). Such interventions to assist the poor might be a drag rather than a spur to general economic development. Egypt and Sri Lanka, for example, have been cited as cases where the burden of food subsidies, equaling 10 to 20 percent of total government revenues in the 1970s, was, in terms of economic growth, a long-term negative factor. While industrialized states, such as the United States, Europe, and other OECD countries may well afford "welfare state" policies that include targeted food guarantees through programs such as food stamps, institutional feeding, and direct distribution, their costs as a portion of the government's budget are modest. Such redistribution, however, weighs heavily on states with lower incomes, less efficient economies, and with a large portion of the population employed in agriculture.[43] Some effort, however modest, may be important to signal a respect for human dignity and maintain respect or legitimacy for the state. Hence, the next point.

(6) Promote Political Stability. Even from a quite strict economic perspective, political stability, however difficult to estimate, is worth some economic benefit. Maintenance of political authority reflects, in part, the political ties, both personal and ideological, between state leadership and the rural sector of the economy. Thomas Jefferson regarded the agricultural ethic as the basis of American

---

[42] Robert Dahl, Modern Political Analysis (Englewood Cliffs, NJ: Prentice-Hall, 1963), pp. 55-71; Mancur Olson, The Logic of Collective Action (Cambridge: Harvard University Press, 1965); Charles E.Lindblom, Politics and Markets (New York Basic Books, 1977).

[43] Per Pinstrup-Andersen, ed., Food Subsidies in Developing Countries (Baltimore: Johns Hopkins University Press, 1988).

democracy -- an argument that has supporters even two centuries later.[44] Analogously, agriculture as an embodiment of state virtue has flourished under Felix Houphouet-Boigny, of Cote d'Ivoire. Houphouet proclaims himself the country's "number one peasant." Emotional ties, therefore, can bind agriculture and the state in ways that sustain national character, project cultural values, and bolster political stability. These cultural forces can emotionally distort the "rational choice" template often placed upon government intervention.[45]

In summary, the state intervenes in agriculture usually to accomplish one or several of these six purposes. In Model I the state as an arena for powerful "private" forces establishes public policy aimed at advancing their interests. Generally, agricultural interests "lose" priority to industrialization but "win" among advanced industrial states, as in Europe, Japan and the U.S. In Model II the state is a maximizer on behalf of itself as an actor -- that is, it maximizes the private interests of officialdom. Agricultural interests invariably lose. In Model III the state is also an actor, but one motivated by sovereignty goals and limited by missing information, uncertain popular loyalties, and ineffectual instruments. Agriculture has its best chance to have supportive policies pursued by the state during industrialization; Korea is arguably an example. The three models are not mutually exclusive; they do, however, organize distinctive analytical elements to explain the actions of a state. In any actual case, some mixture of all three models is likely. In most cases, however, one or another model will prove more illuminating and predictive of state action than others.

Strategies that support economic-promoting governance

Sections III and IV, focusing on the state in agriculture, laid out some general ways that governance factors affect societal performance and agricultural development. Let us return, in conclusion, to the qualities of the state outlined in section II, i.e. openness, rule of law, human dignity and civic-mindedness. These qualities, while not unrelated to democracy, are not simply the equivalent of democracy. In most cases these qualities will be enhanced by democratic features such as participatory institutions, decentralization, and certain democratic techniques (e.g. elections, multi-party system, and checks and balances between the different branches of government). The qualities I proposed, however, can exist at least somewhat independently of national democratic institutions. They reside most fundamentally as part of and in relation to a broader fabric of society. The three ideal-type models proposed in section III reflect this point. Short-term mechanical fixes, such as new "constitutions," or elections, are less salient for sustaining stable governance, therefore, than maintaining a culture of governance properties throughout organizations in civil society. At independence, for example, African states almost universally adopted democratic forms of government, only to see these institutions transformed into one-party states or military dictatorships within a decade. Latin American countries are famous for the number of constitutions which

---

[44] Donald F. Hadwiger and Ross Talbot, "The United States: A Unique Development Model," in Raymond F. Hopkins, Donald J. Puchala and Ross B. Talbot, eds., Food, Politics, and Agricultural Development (Boulder: Westview Press, 1979); Grant McConnell, The Decline of Agrarian Democracy (Berkeley: University of California Press, 1952).

[45] See Merilee Grindle and John Thomas, "Policy Makers, Policy Choices and Policy Outcomes," Policy Science, vol. 22 (1989), pp. 213-248; and David Potter, People of Plenty (Chicago: University of Chicago Press, 1954).

they have adopted over the years, few of which represented the underlying or real constitutions, that is the authoritative expectations of the population with respect to order and justice. A similar disjuncture existed in the Soviet Union and East Europe.

In examining the role of governance in economic development, therefore, it is important not to look at the formal institutions which one might recommend to a country as a part of an economic assistance package. Democracy may be good, but it is not a panacea. Furthermore, its artificial insertion may only lead to cynicism and an innoculation against the virtues that democracy can bring.

The second facet of the four qualities outlined in section II is their enabling capacity for the state. They often promise to strengthen state capabilities and vice versa. Weak states are incapable of regulating and sustaining markets. They frequently fail to resolve inequities and distortions that markets can allow. Monopolistic trading may be outlawed by the state, but state monopolies often behave as badly or worse than private monopolies (especially regulated ones) while state controls to protect parastatal monopolies encourage illegal parallel markets that bring risk premium income to the least deserving. Hence weak states that attempt strong policy intervention frequently inculcate contempt not respect for human dignity and nourish a culture of personal-mindedness not civic-mindedness. Furthermore, autocratic states exacerbate these tendencies and undermine respect for human dignity as coercive force becomes the increasingly used method of law enforcement. Thus these four underlying, basically cultural qualities are keys to good governance.

A major factor in determining what state action is likely to advance best these described qualities of governance is the size, strength and territorial extension of the government. We can see the expansion of governance institutions, from those of minimalist governing institutions to complex modern state systems -- have occurred in strong correlation with changes in the economy. The shift from an agricultural to an industrial society, from rural to urban life, have all allowed state apparati to expand in scope. Indeed such state expansion was necessary and inevitable, I argued earlier, in order to govern the more complex, industrial and world-wide economic activities that have ensued. State financing for economic development, particularly for agricultural modernization in developing countries, and the expansion of markets which requires transportation infrastructure, rules of marketing and the enforcement of transparency or openness in exchange, played a critical role in the modernization of Europe.[46]

Economic development, therefore, cannot do without the state nor the important functions that government plays. However, a state in which governance is dominated by special interests, which interferes and disrupts markets and which nurtures incivility and eventually violence among its population, leads a country towards economic ruin rather than productivity. The economic crises of Africa in the 1970s and 80s, many of which are clearly associated with the failures of governance, provide the most poignant and empirical evidence of this proposition.[47] To be effective, governments must be supported by the attitudes and cultural

---

[46] Charles Tilly, ed., The Formation of National States in Western Europe (Princeton: Princeton University Press, 1975); Michael Tracy, Agriculture in Western Europe: Crisis and Adaptation Since 1880, 2d ed. (London: Jonathan Cape, 1982).

[47] Richard Sandbrook, The Politics of Africa's Economic Stagnation (New York: Cambridge University Press, 1985); World Bank, From Crisis to Sustainable Growth: A Long-Term Perspective Study (Washington: World Bank, 1989).

attributes described in section II above and must, in response to them, do more than regulate markets in the interest of efficiency and social profitability. Governments must redistribute social values to assure some degree of equity and justice in the society. Such government action is crucial to the outward appearance of recognizing the human dignity of all citizens and for promoting the legitimacy and institutionalization of a rule of law.

Assessments of economic development and evaluation of aid projects frequently fail to take into account the externalities of a project or program upon such qualities of governance. Normal rates of return calculation cannot capture the kind of benefits to good governance or responsible government which attending to the principles of openness, rule of law, respect for human dignity and civic-mindedness require. Moreover, these qualities which have a less "western" aspect to them are, I submit, more likely to be adaptable to a variety of societies, including those in which formal institutions of elections, competitive political parties and narrow pluralist interests (often lobbying or pressuring government) are not accepted as part of the definition of civic virtue. Consider that authoritarian structures such as the Catholic Church have promoted in Latin America a doctrine of human dignity that demands rules of law and progressive redistribution. The king in Thailand similarly provides cultural and practical support for at least some of these qualities. Such cases and others offer a strong argument for pressing for these deeper cultural elements in governance, ones which pervade all social institutions --the family, the school, the workplace and the religious bodies. Their attainment can provide a framework within which responsible government and good governance can evolve and in which the functions of the state will be channeled to facilitate greater productivity by these qualities of good governance.

CHAPTER EIGHT

MEASURING THE EFFECTS OF INSTITUTIONAL REFORM:
THE CASE OF ITALIAN REGIONAL GOVERNMENT*

ROBERT D. PUTNAM

For the first century of its existence the Italian state represented an historical paradox and a political-administrative nightmare: one of the most geographically and socially variegated lands in the modern world was ruled through one of the most highly centralized systems of government. Since 1970, however, Italy has been engaged in a remarkable institutional experiment, involving the creation of potentially powerful, directly elected regional governments. This essay assesses the first two decades of this reform, using evidence from this natural experiment to explore the consequences of institutional reform.

In an era of heightened hopes for democratization in other parts of the globe, lessons from the Italian experience are especially relevant, for at issue is how changes in formal institutions induce changes in political behavior.[1] One conundrum facing would-be reformers in former authoritarian states is whether rewriting the rules of the game will produce the intended effects -- or any effects at all -- in how it is actually played. The Italian regional experience can help us come to grips with this important issue, for the experiment inaugurated in 1970 remains, as Sidney Tarrow observed, "one of the few recent attempts to create new representative institutions in the nation-states of the West."[2]

The new institutionalism argues that politics is structured by institutions. James March and Johan Olsen summarize this theory about the effects of institutions:

> The organization of political life makes a difference, and institutions affect the flow of history. . . . Actions taken within and by political institutions change the distribution of political interests, resources, and rules by creating new actors and identities, by providing actors with criteria of success and failure, by constructing rules for appropriate behavior, and by endowing some individuals, rather than others, with authority and other types of resources. Institutions affect the ways in which individuals and groups

---

* This essay is drawn from Robert D. Putnam, <u>Making Democracy Work: Civic Traditions in Modern Italy</u> (Princeton: Princeton University Press, 1993). I wish to acknowledge the essential contributions of my collaborators on this larger project, Professors Robert Leonardi and Raffaella Y. Nanetti.
[1] For the classic discussion of institutionalization and political development, see Samuel P. Huntington, <u>Political Order in Changing Societies</u> (New Haven: Yale University Press, 1968).
[2] Sidney Tarrow, "Local constraints on Regional Reform: a Comparison of Italy and France," <u>Comparitive Politics</u>, v.7, p. 36 (October, 1974).

become activated within and outside established institutions, the level of trust among citizens and leaders, the common aspirations of political community, the shared language, understanding, and norms of the community, and the meaning of concepts like democracy, justice, liberty, and equality.[3]

If institutional reforms can have such profound effects, that is good news for reformers.

Two centuries of constitution-writing around the world warn us, however, that designers of new institutions are often writing on water. Institutional reform does not always alter fundamental patterns of politics. As Deschanel characterized politics and government in the French Fourth Republic: "the republic on top and the empire underneath."[4] "Old wine in new bottles" was a common expectation when the Italian regions were established, for Italians had had much experience with institutional change that changed nothing.[5] That institutional reforms alter behavior is an hypothesis, not an axiom. Theorists of institutions have lacked controlled settings in which to assess empirically the effects of changing the rules.

Against this backdrop, the Italian regional experiment takes on special interest. This essay asks how the new institutions were created, how they evolved during their first two decades, and what impact they have had on practical politics and government. Did this institutional reform actually reshape the identities of political actors, redistribute political resources, and inculcate new norms, as institutionalists predict? How were the customary practices of Italian governance shifted by these new institutions -- indeed, *were* they altered in any noticeable way?

Before describing the progress of Italy's regional reform, a word or two about our research project will be useful. The bases for our study were laid by a 1970 survey of 20-25 newly elected councilors in each of five diverse regions, ranging from wealthy Lombardia in the North to impoverished Basilicata and Puglia in the South, and from Emilia-Romagna, the buckle of the Communist-controlled Red Belt, to Lazio, dominated by its hydrocephalic capital of Rome. In July, 1976, we reinterviewed these same people, as well as an additional sample of councilors elected for the first time in 1975. (At the same time, we added Veneto, heartland of traditional Catholicism, to the study, so that our sample of six regions represented the full range of the political, economic, social, and cultural diversity of the Italian peninsula. See Figure 1 for an overview of our regional study.) In 1981-82 and again in 1989 we conducted third and fourth waves of interviews with several hundred of our original respondents and their successors.

In addition to this panel survey of regional politicians, in 1976, in 1981-82, and in 1989 we interviewed samples of approximately twenty community leaders in each region -- journalists, businessmen, bankers, trade unionists, farm leaders, mayors, and regional administrators -- and in 1983 we carried out a nationwide mail survey of such community leaders in each of the country's twenty regions. In addition, in 1972, 1977, 1981, 1982, 1987, and 1988, we carried out nationwide surveys on regional affairs with ordinary voters. In several rounds of field research, we have gathered and analyzed extensive documentary and statistical evidence on the

---

[3] James G. March and Johan P. Olsen, Rediscovering Institutions: The Organizational Basis of Politics (New York: Free Press, 1989), pp. 159, 164.

[4] Cited in Harry Eckstein, "Political Culture and Change," American Political Science Review, vol. 84 (1990), p. 254.

[5] Percy A. Allum and G. Amyot, "Regionalism in Italy: Old Wine in New Bottles?," Parliamentary Affairs, vol. 24 (Winter 1970/71), pp. 53-78.

regions' organization, budgeting, legislation, and administrative operations, as well as case studies of territorial and socioeconomic planning in each region. Finally, we have collected quantitative evidence on the institutional performance of all twenty regions, adding breadth and comparative perspective to the depth of our knowledge of the six "core" regions in our study. In previous reports from this project we have described the national political process that led to the creation of the regions[6], we have analyzed patterns of attitude stability and change over the regions' first six years[7], and we have sought to explain regional differences in institutional success.[8] Our primary focus in the present essay is diachronic: How have patterns of politics and governance in the Italian regions changed over the years since 1970?

---

[6] Robert Leonardi, Raffaella Nanetti, and Robert D. Putnam, "Revolution as a Political Process: The Case of Italy," Publius (Winter 1981), pp. 95-117.

[7] Robert D. Putnam, Robert Leonardi, and Raffaella Nanetti, "Attitude Stability among Italian Elites," American Journal of Political Science, v. 23 (August 1979), pp. 463-494.

[8] Robert D. Putnam, Robert Leonardi, Raffaella Nanetti, and Franco Pavoncello, "Explaining Institutional Success: The Case of Italian Regional Government," American Political Science Review, v. 77 (March 1983), pp. 55-74; Robert D. Putnam, with Robert Leonardi and Raffaella Nanetti, "Institutional Performance and Political Culture: Some Puzzles about the Power of the Past," Governance, vol. 1, no. 3 (July 1988), pp. 221-242; and Putnam, Making Democracy Work (Princeton: Princeton University Press, 1993).

Figure 1: Italian Regional Study, 1970 - 1989

Creating the regional government

Strong regional and local identities are part of history's bequest to Italy. Regional entities -- geographically defined, politically independent, economically differentiated, and generally dominated by a strong city -- have been prominent threads in the tapestry of Italian history for more than a millennium.[9] Indeed, when the Italian state was proclaimed in 1860, linguistic variegation was so pronounced that no more than 10 percent of all "Italians" (and perhaps as few as 2.5 percent) spoke the national language.[10] For the Piedmontese monarchists who unified Italy, regional differentiation was the principal obstacle to national development. *Fatta l'Italia, dobbiamo fare gli italiani* was their slogan: "Having made Italy, we must now make Italians."

The makers of modern Italy, like most of their counterparts in the emerging states of today's Third World, insisted that decentralization was incompatible with prosperity and political progress. The highly centralized Franco-Napoleonic model was the latest word in administrative science. Strong central authority was, they concluded, the necessary remedy for the weak integration of the new nation state.[11] Top local officials were appointed by the national government in Rome. Local political deadlock (or even local dissent from national policy) could lead to years of rule by a commissioner appointed by the national government.[12] Strong prefects, modeled on the French system, controlled the personnel and policies of local governments, approving all local ordinances, budgets, and contracts, often in the minutest detail.[13] Most areas of public policy, from agriculture to education to urban planning, were administered by field offices of the Roman bureaucracy.

In practice, the rigor of this extreme administrative centralization was somewhat moderated by characteristic Italian political accommodations. To maintain their fragile political support in the nascent parliament, Italy's leaders developed the practice of *trasformismo*, in which patronage deals were struck with local notables. Vertical networks of patron-client ties became a means of allocating public works and softening administrative centralization. Political channels to the center were more important than administrative channels, but in either case the link to the center

---

[9] Emiliana Noether, in Luigi De Rosa and Ennio Di Nolfo, eds., Regionalismo e centralizzazione nella storia di Italia e Stati Uniti (Florence: Olschki, 1986), p. 34.

[10] Giulio Lepschy, "How Popular is Italian?" in Zygmunt G. Baranski and Robert Lumley, eds., Culture and Conflict in Postwar Italy: Essays on Mass and Popular Culture (London: Macmillan, 1990), p. 66.

[11] See Carlo Ghisalberti, "Accentramento e decentramento in Italia," in De Rosa and Di Nolfo, eds., Regionalismo e centralizzazione. The decision of Italy's unifiers to reject regionalism in place of centralism continues to be debated by Italian historians. For a thoughtful argument that the sociocultural backwardness of the South made it unprepared for local autonomy, see Carlo Tullio-Altan, La nostra Italia: Arretratezza socioculturale, clientelism, trasformismo e rebellismo dall'Unita' ad oggi (Milan: Feltrinelli, 1986), pp. 50-52.

[12] Martin Clark, Modern Italy 1871-1982 (New York: Longman, 1984), p. 58; Robert C. Fried, Planning the Eternal City: Roman Politics and Planning since World War II (New Haven: Yale University Press, 1973), pp. 168-69; Raphael Zariski, Italy: The Politics of Uneven Development (Hinsdale, Illinois: Dryden Press, 1972), pp. 121-122.

[13] Percy A. Allum, Italy: Republic without Government? (New York: Norton, 1973), pp. 221-223; Robert C. Fried, The Italian Prefects (New Haven: Yale University Press, 1963).

remained crucial.[14] For local policy makers under the monarchy, under Fascism, and for more than two decades under the post-Fascist Republic, all roads led to Rome.

Only after World War II, with the advent of democratic politics and growing grassroots revulsion against extreme centralization, did regionalist sentiment begin to re-emerge. Newly powerful political parties, both the Christian Democrats on the center-right and the Socialists and Communists on the left, had historically opposed the national government and thus generally had argued for greater decentralization. Under their aegis, the new Constitution of 1948 provided for directly elected regional governments.[15]

This constitutional mandate was carried out almost immediately in five "special" regions, located along the national borders and on the islands of Sicily and Sardinia, areas threatened by separatism and ethnic problems.[16] Creation of the remaining, "ordinary" regions, containing 85 percent of Italy's population, required enabling legislation, however, and was delayed by intense political resistance. The central administration was naturally reluctant to divest itself of any significant authority. More important, the Christian Democrats, now dominant at the national level, feared with good reason that several of the regions in the Red Belt of north-central Italy would be controlled by the Communists. For more than twenty years the constitutional provision for regional governments remained a dead letter, and central control remained the rule.

By the middle of the 1960s, however, much had begun to change. In the background was the astounding pace of social and economic transformation in postwar Italy. During the two decades from 1950 to 1970, the economy grew faster than ever before in Italian history and faster than virtually any other Western economy. Millions of Italians migrated from the impoverished South to the industrial North.[17] Agriculture's share of the workforce plummeted from 42 percent to 17 percent in half the time that similar changes had taken elsewhere in Western economic history. Diets improved; illiteracy and infant mortality were cut by two thirds; bicycles were replaced by Vespas, and then Vespas by Fiats. Millions of

---

[14] For a similar analysis of center-periphery relations in Italy at the beginning of the 1970s, as the regional reform was getting underway, see Sidney Tarrow, Between Center and Periphery: Grassroots Politicians in Italy and France (New Haven: Yale University Press, 1977).

[15] For more detailed accounts of the regional reform movement, see Robert Leonardi, Raffaella Y. Nanetti, and Robert D. Putnam, "Devolution as a Political Process: The Case of Italy;" Robert Leonardi, Raffaella Y. Nanetti, and Robert D. Putnam, "Italy -- Territorial Politics in the Post-War Years: The Case of Regional Reform," in R. A. W. Rhodes and Vincent Wright, eds., Tensions in the Territorial Politics of Western Europe (London: Frank Cass & Company, 1987), pp. 88-107; Peter Gourevitch, "Reforming the Napoleonic State: The Creation of Regional Governments in France and Italy," in Sidney Tarrow, Peter J. Katzenstein and Luigi Graziano, eds., Territorial Politics in Industrial Nations (New York: Praeger, 1978), pp. 28-63; and Tarrow, "Local Constraints on Regional Reform," Comparative Politics, Vol. 7 (October 1974), pp. 1-36.

[16] Regional governments were established by 1949 in Sicily, Sardinia, Valle d'Aosta, and Trentino-Alto Adige. Creation of the fifth special region, Friuli-Venezia Giulia, complicated by the Trieste dispute with Yugoslavia, was postponed until 1964.

[17] More than seven percent of the entire population of southern Italy moved to the North in just five years, 1958-1963. See Paul Ginsborg, "Family, Culture and Politics in Contemporary Italy," in Zygmunt G. Baranski and Robert Lumley, eds., Culture and Conflict in Postwar Italy: Essays on Mass and Popular Culture (London: Macmillan, 1990), p. 33, and Paul Ginsborg, A History of Contemporary Italy: Society and Politics 1943-1988 (London: Penguin Books, 1990), pp. 218-220.

Italians changed jobs, homes, and life-styles. Italy, and most of her regions and citizens, experienced one of the most concentrated periods of social change ever recorded.

Politics and government lagged far behind these social and economic changes. Nevertheless, the increasingly frustrating sclerosis of Italian central administration, an emergent interest in regional planning, and a leftward drift in national politics combined to raise once again the issue of regional governments. In February 1968, after a record-breaking filibuster by hostile conservatives, parliament passed a law providing electoral machinery for the ordinary regions. Two years later a bill ordering regional finances was approved, allowing the first regional councils (numbering thirty to eighty members, depending on the region's population) to be elected in June 1970. In the ensuing months each council, following the conventions of the Italian party-dominated parliamentary system, elected a regional president and cabinet (*giunta*) and wrote a regional "statute," spelling out organization, procedures, and areas of regional jurisdiction, subject to the provisions of the Constitution and national enabling legislation.

A wide variety of objectives had been enunciated by proponents of the new institutions. Populists claimed that regional government would raise levels of *democracy*, by fostering citizen participation and responsiveness to local needs. Moderates argued that decentralization would increase *administrative efficiency*. Southerners believed that regional government could speed *social and economic development*, reducing regional inequalities. *Regional autonomy* appealed to whichever group happened to be the "outs" in national politics -- Communists at mid-century, like Catholics several decades earlier. Progressive technocrats argued that the regions were necessary for rational *socioeconomic planning* and could lead to a "*new way of doing politics*," more pragmatic than the traditional, ideological Italian political style.

Proponents of regionalism believed in the power of institutional change to reshape politics. They interpreted the destiny of the new governments in almost messianic terms, believing that "the creation of politically autonomous regional governments would be responsible for a radical social and political renewal of the country."[18] Our first wave of interviews with the newly elected councilors in 1970 found them full of hope and enthusiasm. Optimistic about the reform's future, they saw the regions as posing a potent challenge to the central authorities. These were years of idealism and euphoria among Italian regionalists.

But the struggle to assure the new regions adequate funding and authority was only beginning. Two more years were required for the central government to issue decrees transferring powers, funds, and personnel to the regions, so that the new governments effectively did not open for business until April 1, 1972. Worse yet, at the regional level the 1972 decrees were widely condemned as wholly inadequate by representatives of almost all parties and by the attentive public, as well as by regional officials themselves. During these early years, an alliance of conservative national politicians, an entrenched national bureaucracy, and a tradition-minded judiciary combined to impose numerous legal, administrative, and fiscal restraints on the regions. Euphoria turned to dismay and anger, as the regionalists realized that real devolution would require a political struggle with the center.

Led by the independent-minded regional governments of Lombardia (controlled by progressive Christian Democrats) and Emilia-Romagna (controlled by the Communists), and encouraged by a leftward tide in national politics in 1974-75,

---

[18] Percy A. Allum, Italy: Republic without Government? (New York: W.W. Norton, 1973), p. 236.

the regionalist forces renewed their attack. A sympathetic press helped rally grassroots support from regional interest groups and public opinion. Regional governments of various stripes -- North and South, red and white -- joined forces in the so-called "regionalist front." This coalition was strengthened by support from new national organs that had been established as part of the original reform -- the Ministry for the Regions and the Interparliamentary Committee for the Regions. Institutional change was creating its own momentum.

In July, 1975, just after a powerful swing to the left in the second round of regional elections, the regionalists succeeded in pushing through parliament Law 382, authorizing the decentralization of important new functions to the regions. Preparation of the decrees implementing Law 382 would occupy two more years of intense and often acrimonious negotiation among the national government, the regional authorities, and the parliamentary committee of the regions, as well as all the major political parties. Our 1976 wave of interviews found our respondents much less confident about the ability of the regions to assert their autonomy. They reported more conflict between center and periphery, and more central control, than they had foreseen six years earlier. Their previous optimism about the new institution's capacity to address urgent social and economic problems was now more restrained, and they were quick to point the finger of blame at foot-dragging in Rome.

As is true of intergovernmental relations everywhere, this center-periphery game was played simultaneously in two distinct, but related forms, which we term "one-on-one" and "all-on-one." In the one-on-one version, the individual region tried to escape or mitigate central controls over specific decisions. In the all-on-one version, the regional governments as a group struggled to shift the rules of the one-on-one games, in order to increase their bargaining resources. In these early years, the one-on-one battles were mostly lopsided victories for the central authorities. All sides agreed that relations between center and periphery during these years were formalistic, antagonistic, and unproductive.

But while the one-on-one battles favored the center, the all-on-one battle reached a climax more favorable for the regions. In a lengthy series of summit meetings among representatives of the major parties in June-July 1977, agreement was reached on a packet of regulations (the so-called 616 decrees) that dismantled and transferred to the regions 20,000 offices from the national bureaucracy, including substantial portions of several ministries, such as the Ministry of Agriculture, as well as hundreds of semipublic social agencies. Comprehensive legislative authority in several important fields, including social services and territorial planning, was delegated to the regions. Fiscal provisions of the 616 decrees gave the regions responsibility for approximately one quarter of the entire national budget, with some estimates running as high as one third. Meanwhile, independent reforms had begun to transfer to the regions virtually full responsibility for the national hospital and health care systems. By 1989, this sector alone accounted for more than half of total regional spending (and like health policy everywhere, well more than half the administrative headaches).

This regionalist victory came partly for national political reasons, for the 616 decrees represented a concession by the Christian Democratic (DC) Prime Minister Giulio Andreotti to maintain Communist (PCI) support for his government. But equally important, the existence of directly elected regional governments had created strong pressures and political incentives for more effective decentralization. The winning regionalist front drew on forces that had been unleashed by the initial reform, and in some cases had actually been created by that reform.

Devolution is inevitably a bargaining process, not simply a juridical act. The legal and constitutional framework, the administrative framework (controls, delegated powers, personnel patterns, and so on), and finances are both key resources in today's game and outcomes of earlier games. As seen by regional leaders, the central authorities' main bargaining chips were control of funds and control over the delegation of formal authority -- the pocketbook and the rulebook. Leaders of the richer, more ambitious regions of the North were more concerned about the rulebook, while the South was more conscious of the pocketbook.

In the face of central recalcitrance fortified by central control over laws, rules, and money, the regions turned to less formal political resources. They relied heavily on interregional solidarity and on grassroots support from regional and local interest groups, the press, and public opinion. (Southerners depended more on "vertical" strategies, such as private petitions to sympathetic national patrons, while Northerners were readier to resort to "horizontal" collective action by a broad, regionalist front.) By the mid-1970s voters and community leaders, both North and South, had become strong supporters of the principle of regional reform, even when they were critical of the actual operations of their own regional government. The political momentum for devolution had become self-sustaining.

The 616 decrees reflected the regions' victory in the crucial struggle to establish their formal authority. The less dramatic, but more demanding, struggle to deploy the new powers and spend the new money still lay ahead. The regions' all-on-one victory was sufficiently sweeping that they could no longer so plausibly blame the central authorities for their own shortcomings. With the benefit of hindsight, one regional leader told us in 1981, "They threw us into the water, hoping that we could swim." A senior figure in the Roman bureaucracy used a more cynical, but perhaps more accurate image: "With the 1977 decrees we finally gave the regions enough rope to hang themselves."

The new division of authority between the center and the regions was still far from federal. Most regional funds came from the center, and the central authorities retained a veto over regional legislation. But the regions were more powerful than local government had ever been in unified Italy. The legislative authority of the regions now encompassed such areas as health, housing, urban planning, agriculture, public works, and some aspects of education. In addition, the regional statutes successfully claimed jurisdiction over territorial, economic, and structural planning. The far-flung activities of the *Cassa per il Mezzogiorno* [Fund for the South], responsible for massive public investments in the South, were subjected to increased control by representatives of the regional governments.

> Henceforth the regions, or the municipalities under regional supervision, could found and staff their own specialist agencies for welfare, run their own subsidy schemes for farmers and artisans, and organize their own cooperatives and nursery schools. They could draw up regional development and land use plans; they could take over the Chambers of Commerce. . . . Perhaps most startling of all was the handing over of the vital task of 'safeguarding public morals' -- i.e. the power to issue licenses to restaurant-owners, shopkeepers, taxi-drivers, gun-owners and the like. These were real powers of patronage and policing. Here, at last, was a revolution in government.[19]

Responsibility for many aspects of government that touch the lives of ordinary Italians -- many of the essential functions that successive national

---

[19] Martin Clark, Modern Italy: 1871-1982 (New York: Longman, 1984), pp. 391-392.

governments had failed to perform -- passed into the hands of the regions.

A practical measure of the importance of the regional governments was the resources they now controlled. Tens of thousands of administrative posts were created to serve the new governments, and during the waves of decentralization in the early 1970s, thousands of employees were transferred from the central bureaucracy to the regions. By April, 1981, the fifteen ordinary regions accounted for 46,274 administrative personnel, a figure that had grown by 76 percent in the preceding five years. (The five special regions employed another 29,383 persons.)[20]

Total funds available to the regions grew exponentially during the 1970s and 1980s, rising from roughly $1 billion in 1973 to roughly $9 billion in 1976, roughly $22 billion in 1979, and more than $65 billion in 1989, the lion's share of this coming from the central government in the form of general-purpose and special-purpose transfers.[21] (The profile of regional spending in 1989 is summarized in Table 1.) By the beginning of the 1990s nearly one tenth of Italy's gross domestic product was flowing through the regional governments, only slightly below the figure for American states. For organizations that existed only on paper barely fifteen years earlier, the regions had come to control extremely large sums of money. Indeed, during most of the 1970s and 1980s unspent appropriations carried over from one fiscal year to the next ballooned nearly everywhere, as the resources flowing to the regions exceeded their unfledged administrative capacity.

---

[20] Censis Ricerca, XV rapporto/1981 sulla situazione social del paese (Roma: Franco Angeli, 1981), p. 503. By 1991 the total number of regional bureaucrats had reached 90,000; Il Messaggero (Rome), August 10, 1991, p. 12.

[21] Ottavo Rapporto sullo Stato dei poteri locali/1991 (Rome: Sistema Permanente di Servizi, 1991), pp. 231-240. Despite demands from regions for greater taxing authority, income raised directly by the regions (as distinct from funds devolved by the state) fell from 4.3 percent in 1980 to 1.8 percent in 1989. This inconsistency between centralized taxing authority and decentralized spending authority remains a serious obstacle to regional autonomy and accountability. As we shall see in Table 7, most Italians support regional demands for greater financial autonomy, and by 1991 further reform proposals of this sort were under active consideration. See Il Messaggero (Rome), August 10, 1991, p. 12.

Table 1: Italian Regional Spending (by sector), 1989

	Current Account (£ billion)	Capital Account (£ billion)	Total (£ billion)	Total ($ million)	Total (%)
health	48779.2	2269.7	51048.9	37,208	56.3
agriculture	2004.3	4895.7	6900.0	5,029	7.6
transportation	4561.7	1646.9	6208.6	4,525	6.8
general administration	4874.6	1059.0	5933.6	4,325	6.5
housing/public works	121.7	5149.4	5271.1	3,842	5.8
education	2232.4	385.4	2617.8	1,908	2.9
environment	340.6	1863.7	2204.3	1,607	2.4
social assistance	1364.4	539.0	1903.4	1,387	2.1
industry/artisanry	282.6	1513.9	1796.5	1,309	2.0
commerce/tourism	447.5	896.4	1343.9	980	1.5
culture	429.4	386.0	815.4	594	0.9
debt service	0	622.7	622.7	454	0.7
other	1711.2	2262.9	3974.1	2,897	4.4
total spending	67149.6	23490.7	90640.3	66,064	100.0

Apart from establishing the organization and procedures of the new institution, the major focus of regional legislation during the early years was distributing funds -- loans for agricultural cooperatives, scholarships for needy students, aid for the handicapped, subsidies for interurban buses, subventions for La Scala, and so on. Seeking public support, but lacking the necessary administrative infrastructure and often even the legal authority for carrying out substantial social reforms, most regions occupied themselves with distributive politics, often in the highly disaggregated form that Italians call *leggine* [little laws] and *interventi a pioggia* [projects "showered" indiscriminately over the region].

On the other hand, some regions did introduce substantive reforms in such areas as urban planning, environmental protection, and Italy's chaotic health and social services. In certain "new" areas of public policy, such as energy and the environment, a number of regions moved into the void left by the ponderous Roman ministries, which had been slow to adapt to changing public demands and social needs. Whether the regions' legislative reach exceeded their administrative grasp is an important issue to which we shall return. But for better or for worse, much of Italian domestic policy was now regionalized. Regional government had become, in Max Weber's evocative phrase, "a strong and slow boring of hard boards."[22]

The regional political elite: "A new way of doing politics"

The rules of the game of government in Italy were altered in the two decades after 1970. What effect, we must now ask, did these institutional changes have on the way politics was actually played and Italians were actually governed?

Montesquieu observed that at the birth of new polities, leaders mold institutions, whereas afterwards institutions mold leaders. Interaction between institutional change and the political elite is an important part of the story of the Italian regional experiment.

During the debate before the regions were established, some critics had prophesied that the councils would be packed by the parties with "falling stars", that is, superannuated party hacks. A few utopian regionalists, on the other hand, had predicted the emergence from the regional grass-roots of a new group of novice citizen-politicians. In the event, neither expectation was justified. From the very beginning, the new councils have been composed of well-trained, upwardly mobile, ambitious, and highly professional politicians.[23]

About 45 years old at the time of his election, the average councilor has had nearly a quarter century of prior involvement in party affairs. Councilors are on average a few years younger and less experienced than members of the national parliament, although in other respects the councilors' profile is closer to that of a national deputy than to that of a city councilor. In fact, at least 20 percent of all regional councilors between 1970 and 1985 (and more than a third of all those who had held a regional leadership post) left for seats in the national parliament.[24] On the

---

[22] Max Weber, "Politics as a Vocation," in H.H. Gerth and C. Wright Mills, eds. and trans., From Max Weber: Essays in Sociology (New York: Oxford University Press, 1958), p. 128.

[23] This chapter's description of the changing regional political elite is based on our surveys of regional councilors in six diverse regions in 1970, 1976, 1981-82, and 1989.

[24] Marcello Fedele, Autonomia Politica Regionale e Sistema dei Partiti (Milano: Giuffrè, 1988), pp. 18, 42. Fedele's sample of regions is identical to ours, except that he includes Toscana instead of Basilicata, while his sample of parties includes only the DC, the PCI, and the PSI, whereas ours also includes the minor parties.

Italian political ladder, the job of regional councilor has become an important step, marking broadly the passage from the domain of the part-time amateur to the domain of the professional politician.

The new regional political elite is mostly comprised of self-made men. (Fewer than 5 percent of the regional councilors are women; whatever its accessibility along other important dimensions, the regional council, like Italian politics more generally, remains a male-dominated world.) The councilors' social origins are more modest than those of national deputies, but much higher than the levels found among city councilors. With one exception, the regional legislators have firm roots in the towns and villages of their respective regions.[25] Roughly 35-40 percent of the regional councilors are sons of workers, artisans, or farmers, but only 15-20 percent of the councilors themselves have ever engaged in these professions. More than half of the fathers of the councilors did not go beyond elementary school, and only about 10-15 percent of the fathers attended university. Among the councilors themselves, however, the overwhelming majority (77 percent in 1989) attended university, a figure that is close to the average for the national parliament and roughly double the average for Italian city councilors.

The regional councilors are seasoned politicians with long experience in local government and party affairs. Over three quarters have held prior elective office, and more than four fifths have held a major leadership post in their political party. The city council remains an important springboard toward the regional council, for two thirds of all regional councilors have served previously in city government. Over the first two decades of the regional government, the region itself gradually replaced the province (the administrative unit between the region and the local government) as a crucial step in the Italian political hierarchy. Between 1970 and 1989 the number of former provincial office holders among regional councilors declined from 45 percent to 20 percent, and the number of past or present provincial party leaders fell from 82 percent to 65 percent. By contrast, the number of councilors who have held (or now hold) a major post in their regional party organization rose from 26 percent in 1970 to 59 percent in 1989. This trend in career paths reflects the steady (though still incomplete) "regionalization" of the Italian party organizations, and offers initial evidence for the emergence of a distinctive regional political *cursus honorem*.

The regional councilor has gradually come to see his role as a full-time job, one indicator of increased institutionalization.[26] The number of councilors who continue to pursue some other occupation in addition to their post in regional government fell from 69 percent in 1970 to 45 percent in 1989. The regional council

---

[25] The significant exception is Lazio (the region centered on Rome), roughly half of whose councilors have been raised in other regions, mainly in the South. This incidence of newcomers on the Lazio council reflects the rapid and sustained influx of Southern immigrants into Rome over the last four decades.

[26] Declining turnover is sometimes taken to be an indicator of legislative institutionalization, but it does not fit the Italian regional case so neatly. Turnover was relatively low for the founding generation of councilors; two-thirds of those elected in 1970 were re-elected in 1975, a rather high level of stability compared to subnational legislatures elsewhere. Turnover modestly increased to roughly 50 percent in subsequent legislatures, however, so that average tenure on the regional council has stabilized at slightly less than two five-year terms.

has become a recognized arena for professional politicians.[27] The first test for any new political institution is that it must engage the aspirations and harness the ambitions of serious politicos. The Italian regional governments have passed this important hurdle.

Even more important, the regional government has transformed elite political culture. *The most striking metamorphosis in regional politics to appear in our repeated talks with both councilors and community leaders between 1970 and 1989 is a remarkable ideological depolarization, coupled with a strong trend toward a more pragmatic approach to public affairs.*

The ideological depolarization is attributable primarily to a rightward convergence of views on a whole series of controversial issues, sparked by a powerful trend toward moderation among Communist and other leftist politicians. The proportion of leftists (PCI, PSI, and other minor left-wing groups) who agreed, for example, that "capitalism represents a threat to Italy" fell sharply and steadily from 97 percent in 1970 to 76 percent in 1976, 54 percent in 1981-82, and finally 28 percent in 1989.[28] On this and a wide range of similar questions, on the other hand, Christian Democrats and politicians from other center-right parties displayed a much more modest and uneven conservative trend. The proportion of centrists and rightists who concur, for instance, that "unions have too much power in Italy" fluctuated from 67 percent in 1970 to 74 percent in 1976, 86 percent in 1981-82, and back to 65 percent in 1989. As a result, the gap between the parties of the left and right narrowed substantially between 1970 and 1989.

The net effect of these changes is summarized in Figure 2, which pictures the distribution of our politicians on a composite *Left-Right Issues Index*, based on questions about capitalism, union power, the distribution of income, divorce, and public sector strikes. (The components of the *Left-Right Issues Index* are listed in Table 2.) In 1970 the views of these politicians were distributed in a classic polarized bimodal fashion, skewed to the far left. Six years later the distribution remained bimodal, but the distance between the modes had narrowed. By 1981-82 the center of gravity had moved further to the right, so that the distribution, though no longer so polarized, was still quite wide. By 1989, the pendulum had swung back toward the center, so that the distribution was archetypically "normal," with the mode at the center of the distribution, and the left-right spread much narrower than two decades earlier.[29]

---

[27] For a discussion of institutionalization in the American Congress that touches on many of the issues raised here see, Nelson W. Polsby, "The Institutionalization of the U.S. House of Representatives", <u>American Political Science Review</u>, vol. 62 (March 1968), pp. 144-168.

[28] Much of this change occurred even before the advent of Thatcher and Reagan, and it was completed before the collapse of Communism in Eastern Europe.

[29] These results are fully confirmed by questions that invited councilors to place each political party on a 100-point left-right scale. Between 1970 and 1989, the average placements of left-wing parties shifted rightwards, and the average placement of right-wing parties shifted leftward, while centrist parties oscillated in a narrow range around the middle of the scale, so that altogether the parties steadily converged toward the center of the political spectrum.

Table 2: Components of Left-Right Issues Index

In the distribution of income the workers are really in an unfavorable position. (agree)

The unions have too much power in Italy. (disagree)

The institution of divorce in Italy is a sign of progress. (agree)

In the public services (for example, gas, transport) the right to strike should be limited. (disagree)

Capitalism represents a threat to Italy. (agree)

Respondents "agreed completely," "more or less agreed," "more or less disagreed," or "disagreed completely" with each item. The *Index* is additive across all five items.

136   RESPONSIBLE GOVERNANCE: THE GLOBAL CHALLENGE

Figure 2: Left-Right Depolarization, 1970-1989

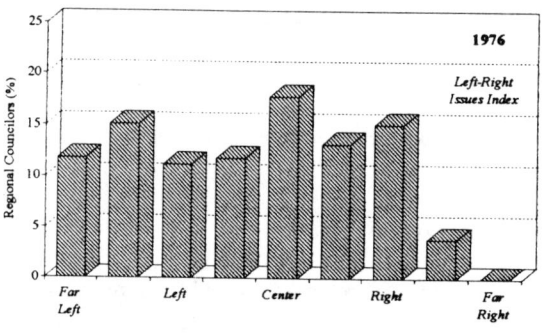

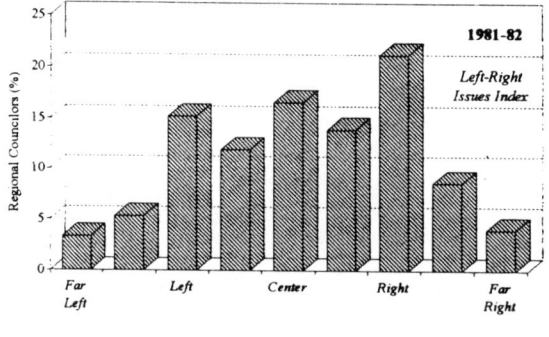

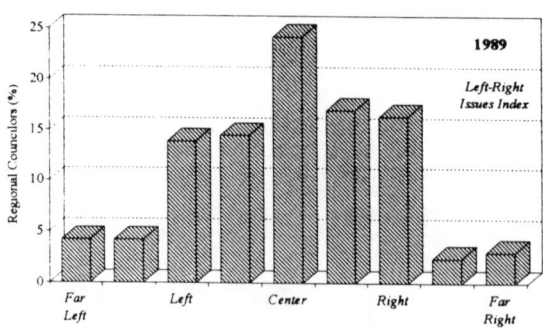

Table 3 presents the same evidence in a slightly different format, showing a sharp decline in the proportion of councilors who espoused extreme positions on either the far left or the far right of the *Left-Right Issues Index*; the share of extremists in this sense plummeted from fully 42 percent in 1970 to barely 14 percent in 1989. The first two decades of the new institution witnessed a steady, powerful centripetal tendency in regional politics.

Table 3: Depolarization of Regional Councilors, 1970-1989

	1970	1976	1981-82	1989
Extremist	42	31	21	14
Moderate	58	69	79	86
	100%	100%	100%	100%
(N)	(72)	(154)	(151)	(166)

Extremism and moderation are measured by scores on the *Left-Right Issues Index*. Scores in the four "outer" categories of Figure 2 (two at the far left and two at the far right) are coded "extremist," while scores in the five middle categories are coded "moderate." The *Index* and cutting points are constant across all four waves of interviews.

As ideological distances narrowed, tolerance across party lines blossomed. In each survey we asked each politician to indicate his sympathy or antipathy toward the various political parties by rating them on a "feeling thermometer" from 0 (complete antipathy) to 100 (complete sympathy). Figure 3 charts the changing sympathy scores assigned to each party by opposing politicians. The results show a strong trend toward greater mutual acceptance among virtually all parties. The average sympathy expressed for the Italian Communist party by non-Communists rose from 26 in 1970 to 44 in 1989, for example, while the average sympathy toward Christian Democrats among councilors of all other parties rose from 28 in 1970 to 39 in 1989. Only the neo-Fascist Italian Social Movement (and to a lesser extent, the far left Proletarian Democracy) remained ostracized by the rest of the political elite, and even this repulsion was less wholehearted by the end of the 1980s than earlier in the 1970s.

Virtually all of these scores remain in the lower half of the sympathy-antipathy scale, for politicians in a competitive system could hardly be expected to express deep affection for their opponents. Sympathy toward opposing parties (even toward the relatively well-received Italian Socialist Party) seems bounded by a ceiling of 50-50 neutrality. Nevertheless, during the first two decades of the regional experiment the high-voltage tensions that had traditionally characterized Italian party politics gradually dissipated, to be replaced by budding mutual respect.

Figure 3: Sympathy towards Political Opponents among Regional Councilors, 1970-1989

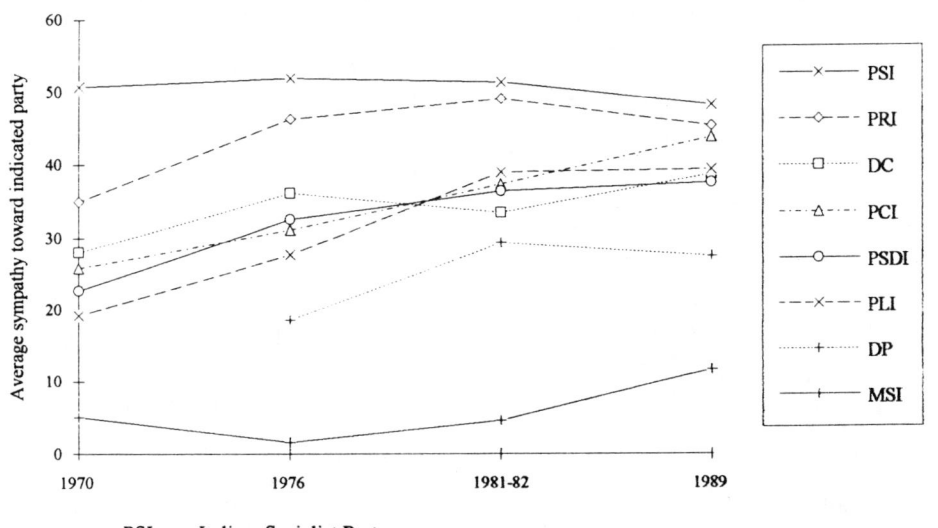

PSI: Italian Socialist Party
PRI: Italian Republican Party
DC: Christian Democracy
PCI: Italian Communist Party
PSDI: Italian Social Democratic Party
PLI: Italian Liberal Party
DP: Proletarian Democracy
MSI: Italian Social Movement

The mellowing of partisanship within the regional political elite did not merely mirror broader changes in Italian society. Our parallel surveys of the mass public show that during the late 1970s, while interparty relations within the regional political elite were warming, partisan hostility was actually on the increase among ordinary Italian voters. In the 1980s partisanship at the mass level began to recede, a timing consistent with an interpretation that depolarization in Italian politics has been "elite-led," although further research would be necessary to confirm that hypothesis in detail. Be that as it may, at the founding of the regional governments, newly-elected councilors from different parties were more hostile to one another than were their respective constituents. Two decades later, this pattern had been completely reversed, so that interparty relations were significantly more open and tolerant among regional politicians than among partisan voters.

One important consequence of these trends for regional policy making is that the process of reaching accommodation on practical issues is no longer so inhibited by partisan hostility. This conclusion is fortified by evidence that the ideological style of politics has steadily faded over these two decades. Regional politicians no longer see their world in stark blacks and whites, but in more nuanced (and more negotiable) shades of gray.

Table 4 summarizes how the political culture of the regional councilors was recast between 1970 and 1989. The proportion of councilors who agreed that "in contemporary social and economic affairs it is essential that technical considerations should have more weight than political ones" surged up from 28 percent in 1970 to 63 percent in 1989. The proportion suspecting that "to compromise with ones political opponents is dangerous because it usually leads to the betrayal of ones own side" plummeted from 50 percent in 1970 to 29 percent in 1989. Those who counseled moderation, concurring that "generally in political controversies one should avoid extreme positions because the proper solution usually lies in the middle" rose from 57 percent in 1970 to 70 percent in 1989. The proportion endorsing the view that "in the final analysis loyalty to ones fellow citizens is more important than loyalty to ones party" soared from 68 percent in 1970 to 94 percent in 1989. The idea of putting civic loyalty ahead of party loyalty was transformed over these years from a debatable proposition into a platitude. Closer examination of the year-by-year changes in Table 4 suggests that most of this metamorphosis in elite political culture had been accomplished by the beginning of the 1980s.

Table 4: Trends in Elite Political Culture, 1970-1989

Percentage of councilors who agreed that:	1970	1976	1981-82	1989
In contemporary social and economic affairs it is essential that technical considerations should have more weight than political ones.	28	43	64	63
To compromise with ones political opponents is dangerous because it usually leads to the betrayal of ones own side.	50	35	34	29
Generally in political controversies one should avoid extreme positions because the proper solution usually lies in the middle.	57	72	70	70
In the final analysis loyalty to ones fellow citizens is more important than loyalty to ones party.	68	72	84	94
(Approximate N)	(77)	(158)	(154)	(171)

After little more than a decade of the chastening and mellowing effects of involvement in regional government, ideological intransigence was being supplanted by an appreciation of the virtues of compromise and technical expertise. Asked to rate their own region on a five-point scale from "ideological" to "pragmatic," the proportion of councilors who described their region as distinctively ideological fell from 26 percent in 1970 to 21 percent in 1976, 14 percent in 1981-82, and a mere 10 percent in 1989. Pragmatism was no longer an epithet, but a way of doing business.

Comparison of the open-ended interviews with councilors in 1970, 1976, and 1981-82 reveals some interesting changes in the way these policy makers analyze specific regional issues, such as social services or economic development.[30] By comparison with our opening round of conversations, councilors in the later periods framed their analyses less in terms of ultimate goals and more in terms of practical means. Councilors came to interpret their role less as being "responsive to" and more as being "responsible for," less as eloquent tribunes for popular causes and more as competent trustees of the public interest. After a decade of regional government, regional leaders had become less theoretical and utopian and less concerned with defending the interests of particular regional groups at the expense of others. Practical questions of administration, legislation, and financing became more salient. Councilors now spoke more of efficient service delivery and of investment in roads and vocational education, and less of "capitalism" or "socialism," "liberty" or "exploitation."

These trends were doubtless related to the leaders' sense of institutional priorities. In talking about the most important issues facing the regional government and about their hopes for the future, councilors in the 1980s gave less attention to justice, equality, and social reform than they had in 1970. They now focused more on administrative, political, and procedural reforms. Legislative autonomy and administrative efficiency (or, more often, administrative inefficiency) bulked much larger in their discussions of regional government, whereas concern for the "radical social renewal" of the messianic early years had faded.

When they entered the council chambers for the first time, the new legislators had brought with them a conception of politics and social relations as essentially zero-sum, revolving about conflicts that were ultimately irreconcilable. This outlook, rooted in the social and ideological struggles of the Italian past, predisposed the councilors to stridency and hobbled practical collaboration. These perspectives on social and political conflict were singularly transformed during the first decade of the regional experiment. Figure 4 shows that during this period the councilors' emphasis on irreconcilable conflict ebbed, while their emphasis on consensus steadily heightened.

---

[30] The analysis summarized in this paragraph is based on quantitative coding of "political style" like that described in Robert D. Putnam, <u>The Beliefs of Politicians: Ideology, Conflict, and Democracy in Britain and Italy</u> (New Haven: Yale University Press, 1973), pp. 34-41. The 1989 surveys were restricted to closed-ended questions that did not allow for extended discussions of policy issues.

Figure 4: Trends in Councilors' Views of Conflict, 1970 - 1989

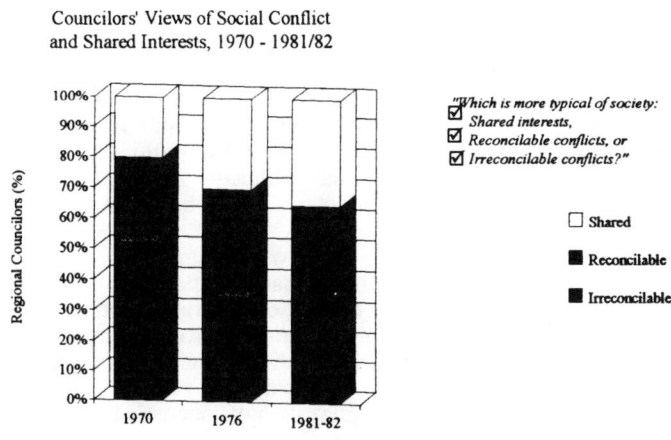

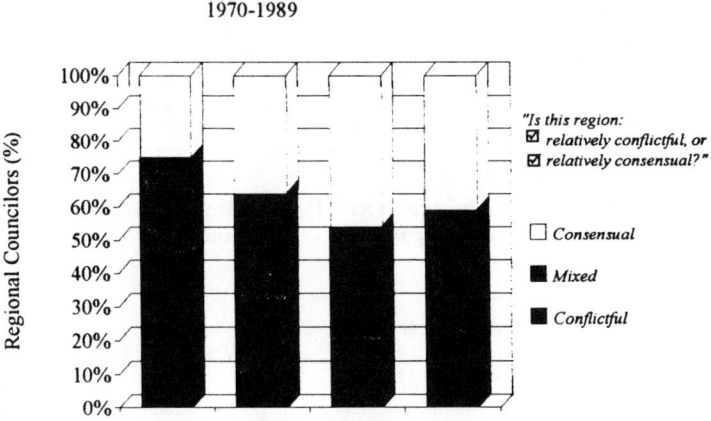

Politics in the regional arena is generally temperate. Most councilors throughout these twenty years have said that they can trust their colleagues, even their political adversaries. Roughly two thirds insist that ideological opponents can reach agreement on practical problems of the region. Three quarters say that council activities are marked more by collaboration than by conflict, a judgment shared by the overwhelming majority of community leaders with whom we have spoken.

These reports certainly do not mean that everyone agrees on all issues. Disagreement over specific policy matters actually increased after 1977, when the transfer of authority and resources from the central government gave regional leaders for the first time real choices, and thus real issues to disagree about. Controversy has not disappeared from regional politics, nor is conflict itself incompatible with good government. Nevertheless, contrary to the traditions of Italian politics, the regional councils are increasingly characterized by "open" rather than "closed" partisanship. The pluralism of party politics in the regions is not the "polarized pluralism" long ascribed to Italian national politics.[31] Regional leaders have learned to disagree without being disagreeable, and they have learned to respect their opponents.

The accumulation of evidence is overwhelming: The first two decades of the regional experiment witnessed a dramatic change in political climate and culture, a trend away from ideological conflict toward collaboration, from extremism toward moderation, from dogmatism toward tolerance, from abstract doctrine toward practical management, from interest articulation toward interest aggregation, from radical social reform toward "good government."

Some regionalists mourn "the relaxation of idealistic tensions," and we have a certain sympathy for their plaint. Trends away from idealism and toward mere "competence" might lead in time to an arid, uninspiring, and unresponsive technocracy.[32] In the Italian context, however, we believe that the trends we have described mark an important stage in transforming Italian politics. For better or for worse, the "idealistic tensions" were relaxed, as the new regional leaders got on with the task of building the new institution.

How did it happen that the political culture of regional elites changed so strikingly over these two decades? Accounting for these trends in the aggregate outlook of successive regional councils is far from simple. Among several alternatives, three hypotheses are prominent.[33]

· *Electoral replacement*. Perhaps the more firebrand members of the initial councils failed to win re-election and were replaced by

---

[31] Giovanni Sartori, "European Political Parties: The Case of Polarized Pluralism," in Joseph LaPalombara and Myron Weiner, eds., Political Parties and Political Development (Princeton: Princeton University Press, 1966), pp. 137-176.

[32] For a discussion of this "problem" in conjunction with postwar changes in West European party systems see Otto Kirchheimer, "The Transformation of the Western European Party Systems," in LaPalombara and Weiner, eds., Political Parties and Political Development, pp. 177-200.

[33] An exhaustive list of possible explanations would distinguish various subtypes and hybrids, such as life cycle change combined with selective retirement. (Attributing moderation simply to aging politicos, for example, would not do the trick since the average age of successive councils did not change.) To distinguish among these complex alternatives would require more elaborate analyses and more robust data than ours. The three theories discussed in the text are the most plausible and parsimonious.

- moderates, more to the liking of voters or of party nominators outside the regional government itself. If so, minds were not changing, although the composition of the councils was. We can test this hypothesis by comparing councilors newly elected in 1975 and 1980 with those who departed in those years.

- *National politics.* Perhaps the changes we detected among regional councilors reflected a depolarization in national politics. Perhaps Italian politicians generally -- not merely those directly involved in regional government -- became more centrist and pragmatic during the 1970s and 1980s. As we have already noted, this interpretation is called into question by evidence that party polarization among ordinary Italians persisted and even intensified throughout much of this period. We lack directly comparable evidence on the changing outlooks of national politicians, but we can shed further light on this hypothesis by comparing the views of councilors newly elected in 1975 and 1980 with the initial views of their counterparts five years earlier. Were successive waves of entrants more moderate, suggesting that the nationwide pool of candidates from which they were drawn was becoming more moderate?

- *Institutional socialization.* Perhaps involvement in regional government itself converted its protagonists from ideological dogmatism to a more consensual pragmatism. Alone among these three alternative interpretations, this one implies that the institutional reform itself was consequential for regional politics, providing a venue within which political leaders could come to terms with one another and with the practical problems of their region. The most relevant evidence for this hypothesis comes from a direct comparison of the views of holdover councilors in 1975 and 1980 with *their own* views five years earlier.

Our panel surveys, in which we interviewed many of the same individuals in 1970 and 1976, and again in 1981-82, cast light on these alternative interpretations, although we cannot resolve the issue definitively.[34] Our study, however elaborate, was not a fully controlled scientific experiment. Although we can make a "before-after" comparison of councilors once elected, we have no straightforward control group of politicos outside the regional institution. Nevertheless, our evidence supports the following conclusions.[35]

- *Electoral replacement* made virtually no contribution to the growing moderation of the regional councils. Newly elected councilors were generally no more moderate than the outgoing councilors whom they replaced; indeed, the newcomers were sometimes *less* moderate than their predecessors. Replacement

---

[34] Since our 1989 survey was not a panel -- that is, we did not reinterview respondents from our 1981-82 survey -- we cannot carry this detailed analysis of change through the 1980s, but evidence presented earlier shows that the most dramatic changes occurred during the 1970s.

[35] Statistical analysis of social change is notoriously labyrinthine; the relevant statistical evidence appears in Putnam, Making Democracy Work, Appendix B.

- *Nationwide trends*, though sometimes difficult to distinguish from institution-specific trends, appear to have made a modest contribution to the story. Successive waves of newcomers to the council were more centrist than their predecessors *had initially been*, but less centrist than those predecessors *had by now become*. Although national effects were not important between 1970 and 1976, our evidence suggests that in the following five years nationwide depolarization accelerated and became a more significant influence on regional politics.

- *Institutional socialization*, that is, conversion of individual incumbents, was powerful and explains much of the trend toward moderation. These institutional effects were strongest during the early years of the reform, as the new regional leaders first got to know one another and their shared problems. The same councilors who espoused ideological extremism and intense partisanship when first elected exhibited more moderate views five or ten years later. The growing moderation from one council to the next was concentrated precisely among the holdover incumbents. Members of the founding generation who ultimately survived into the third legislative period (roughly one third of the original cohort) had been among the most extremist and dogmatic when they first entered the council, but by the time of our third wave of interviews, they had become among the most temperate and tolerant. The most obdurate partisans initially were also those who stayed on the council longest, and as they became more deeply engaged in the life of the institution, they succumbed to its moderating effects.

The most reasonable conclusion from these sometimes fragile data is that the new regional institution fostered a tolerant, collaborative pragmatism among its members. In Italy in the 1970s and 1980s political change occurred both inside and outside the regional council chambers, but change was more rapid and far-reaching inside than outside, particularly during the early years. Italian politics had traditionally been characterized by ideological dogmatism and closed partisanship.[36] The hands-on, face-to-face political realities of the regional governments, warts and all, helped change that. Years spent grappling together with the difficult challenges of forging a new organization taught the regional councilors the virtues of patience and practicality and reasonableness. Just as its advocates had hoped, the regional reform nurtured "a new way of doing politics."

---

[36] See Joseph LaPalombara, "Italy: Fragmentation, Isolation, and Alienation," in Lucian W. Pye and Sidney Verba, eds., Political Culture and Political Development (Princeton: Princeton University Press, 1965), pp. 282-329, and Robert D. Putnam, The Beliefs of Politicians: Ideology, Conflict, and Democracy in Britain and Italy (New Haven: Yale University Press, 1973).

The deepening of regional autonomy

"The autonomy of political institutions is measured by the extent to which they have their own interests and values distinguishable from those of other social forces."[37] Are the Italian regional governments becoming institutionalized in this sense: Is there a trend toward an authentically *regional* political system, with an identity distinct from local and national social and political forces? Did the changed rules shift the real balances of power and interest in Italian politics and government?

The question is apt because the regions were born trapped between powerful national and local forces. As we have seen, the regions were in part a by-product of national party politics, and regional politics continues to be influenced by the national political climate. On the other flank, the first generation of regional councilors were firmly rooted in local politics. In those early years nominations for the regional council were mostly controlled by local party organizations, and the councilors' most important political connections were local. In the beginning the regions were essentially a *national* creation led by *local* politicians. If the regional government was to become an inspired and powerful institution, rather than merely another formalistic addition to Italy's catalog of moribund public agencies, it would have to outgrow its origins. Its new leaders would have to gain greater independence from their erstwhile local and national patrons.

Our investigation suggests that regional institutional autonomy and identity have flowered, particularly after 1976. For example, in each survey we invited councilors and community leaders to rate the influence of a long list of actors, from local notables to national ministers, from agricultural organizations to labor unions, from business to the Church, and from the president of the region to local bureaucrats. One trend is unmistakable: The ascendancy of regional executives. The president of the region, members of the regional cabinet, regional party leaders, and regional administrators all moved up in the rankings between 1970 and 1989. By contrast, virtually all outside groups lost clout, whatever their political stripe: agriculture, unions, business, the press, the Church, national parliamentarians, and local party officials. These successive soundings chart a major shift toward the predominance of regional officials, increasingly autonomous from (though not unaffected by) outside forces, in precisely Huntington's sense. Within the limits of representative democracy, the leaders of the new institution came to be more and more in charge of their own destiny.[38]

Changes in patterns of power within the political parties confirm the institutionalization of regional politics. We regularly asked councilors about the influence of national, regional, and local party leaders in three specific arenas: nominations for the council, negotiations for the formation of the regional cabinet, and decisions about legislation before the council. In every arena and virtually every region the power of regional leaders rose steadily from 1970 to 1989, while the power of national and local leaders declined. (See Figure 5.)

The once-unchallenged monopoly of local party bosses over nominations to the council skidded, while the power of regional party officials to name candidates rose, although even in 1989 local officials retained a significant voice. Although

---

[37] Samuel P. Huntington, Political Order in Changing Societies, p. 20.
[38] Even in Calabria, by all accounts the least successful of all the regions, James Walston, The Mafia and Clientelism: Roads to Rome in post-war Calabria (New York: Routledge, 1988), pp. 79, 127, argues that the advent of the regional government has meant a significant decline in the importance of deputies, ministers, and the prefect, and a rise in the power of regional officials.

national leaders were rarely involved in nominations, they often sought to influence coalition-making. In Sardinia, for example, the national DC held up the formation of a regional cabinet for many months, fearing that an alliance with the PCI (favored by the region's Christian Democrats) would undercut the national party's strategy. However, as Figure 5 reveals, regional autonomy in this domain, too, has surged upward over the last two decades. Finally, regional authority over legislative programs has become unquestioned. In this sector the most notable change in recent years has been a growing independence of the councilors themselves from regional party leaders outside the council. This trend reinforces our theme of growing authenticity of the regional institution.

Figure 5: *Influence of Party Leaders in Three Arenas, 1970-1989*

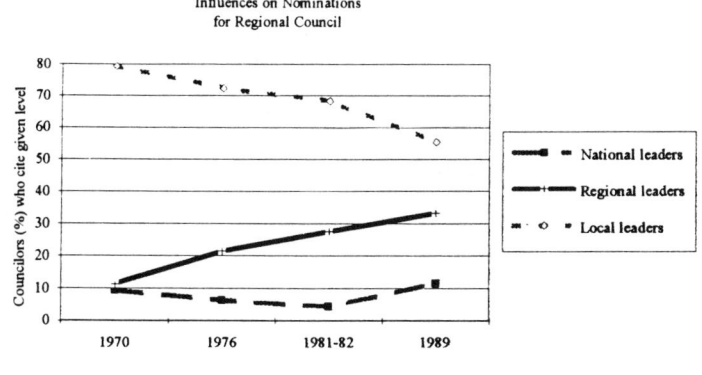

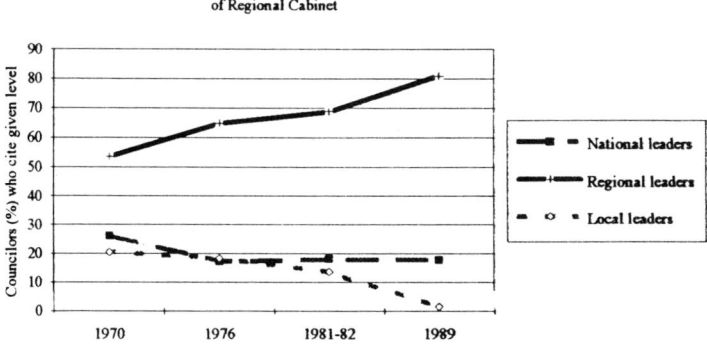

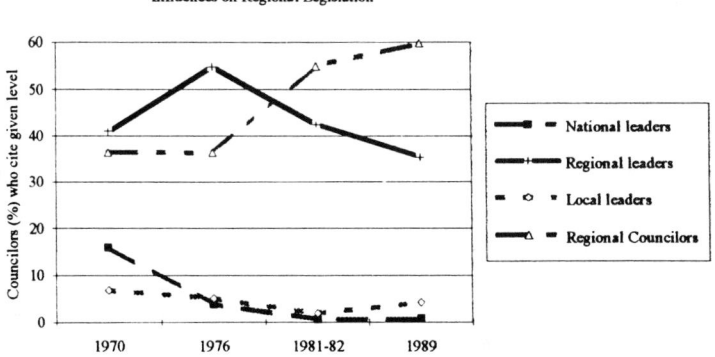

As a concomitant of this growing regional power and autonomy, regional politicians have become more reluctant to toe the national party line when that line conflicts with regional needs. Our *Index of Support for National Party Discipline*, summarized in Figure 6, shows how, particularly after 1976, the balance of opinion swung sharply toward support for more independence from national party dictates. In the early 1970s supporters of national party discipline outnumbered critics by more than two to one, whereas by 1989 critics outnumbered supporters by more than four to one. These changing attitudes appear to be reflected in behavior, as well. Marcello Fedele reports that the fraction of all *regional* government coalitions that shifted in the aftermath of *national* cabinet crises steadily declined between 1970 and 1990. One consequence is that the average durability of regional governments rose from 525 days in 1970-75 to more than 700 days in 1985-90, as compared with an average of only 250 days for national cabinets during this period.[39] In this domain, too, regional autonomy has grown.

---

[39] The fraction of regional government coalitions that dissolved within six months of a national political crisis declined from 37 percent in 1970-1975 to 8 percent in 1985-1990. Marcello Fedele, "I processi politico-istituzionali nei sistemi regionali," a research report to the Parliamentary Committee for Regional Questions, Dossier n. 416, X Legislature (Rome: Camera dei Deputati, 1990). We are grateful to Nando Tasciotti for bringing this report to our attention.

Figure 6: Declining Support for National Party Discipline, 1970 - 1989

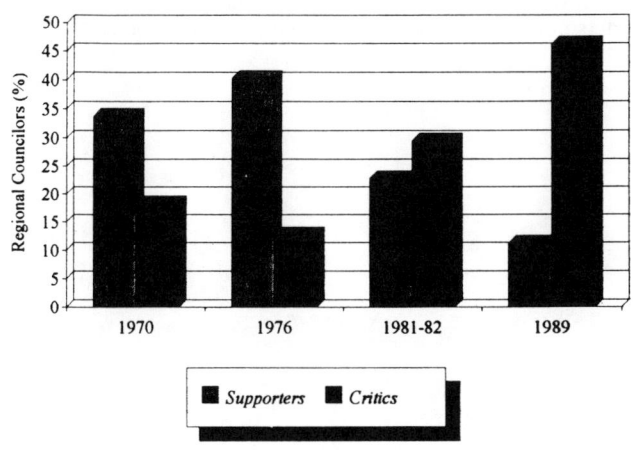

Supporters and Critics
of National Party Discipline, 1970-1989

Index of Support for National Party Discipline

1. The regional political struggle ought to be seen above all as part of the national political struggle. (agree)

2. It is not necessary that a party's strategy be the same in every region. (disagree)

3. When one joins a political party, one must give up a certain measure of one's independence. (agree)

4. In the final analysis loyalty to one's fellow citizens is more important that faithfulness to one's party. (disagree)

   Respondents were asked whether they "agree completely," "more or less agree," "more or less disagree," or "disagree completely" with each item. The Index is additive across all four items.

The emergence of an autonomous regional political system is reflected in the workaday contacts of regional councilors. Once a primarily local figure who happened to hold a regional post, the councilor has become a genuinely regional figure, though like any elective politician, he retains a local political base. As Figure 7 shows, in 1970 the average councilor met more often with representatives of local groups than with representatives of regional groups and more often with local administrators than with regional administrators. By the 1980s those patterns were reversed, sharply so in the case of contacts with administrative officials. Implicit in these charts is the emergence of an autonomous regional political system, with real decisions at stake (as represented in the contacts between councilors and regional administrators) and with real efforts to influence those decisions (as represented in the contacts between councilors and regional interest groups).

Figure 7: Regional and Local Contacts of Regional Councilors, 1970-1989

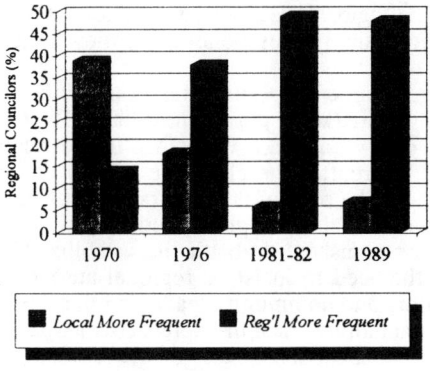

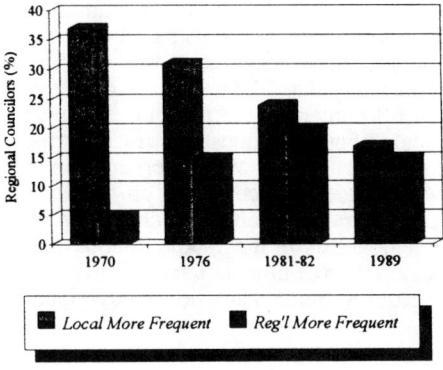

Consistent with this growing autonomy are councilors' reports about the changing influences on electoral behavior. In 1970 traditional party ties and national party programs were said to determine regional elections, while regional candidates themselves were deemed strictly secondary. In the ensuing years, however, individual candidates rose in perceived importance, and the significance of party identification and national platforms waned. Between 1970 and 1989 the proportion of councilors who attributed major importance to party identification as a factor in voters' decisions fell from 72 percent to 48 percent, while the proportion stressing national party programs fell from 55 percent to 24 percent. The proportion who rated the individual candidate as a major factor jumped from 38 percent to 57 percent, taking over the top slot.[40] We have no direct evidence on voters' motives, to be sure, but in the world of practical politics, perceptions have an importance of their own. Councilors see regional elections less and less as mere midterm referenda on national politics. Increasingly they believe that they hold their political fate in their own hands.

In strictly intergovernmental politics, relations between the regions and the central authorities improved markedly during the 1980s. The 616 decrees enacted in 1977 represented, as we saw earlier, a watershed in the relationship between the state and the regions. Thereafter the climactic battles of the crisis of regional empowerment receded into the past. The great crusade of the 1970s to define the proper boundary between central and regional authority was followed in the 1980s by less rancorous border skirmishes. As battle lines stabilized between the centralist and regionalist fronts, the need to insist on regional autonomy was no longer so pressing. Both councilors and community leaders in the 1980s reported smoother relations with the central authorities than their predecessors had described in the mid-1970s. Conversely, the practical deficiencies of the regions became more apparent to their protagonists, as we shall see in detail later. In the aftermath of the 616 decrees, regional officials could no longer plausibly blame all their failings on excessive central control.

One consequence of these changes was that animosity toward the central authorities declined both among councilors and among community leaders. Between 1976 and 1989 the proportion of councilors, for example, who agreed that "the central government must rigorously exercise its rights of control over the activities of the regions" rose from 39 percent to 58 percent, while the proportion of community leaders who argued emphatically that "the institution of the prefect can and must be abolished" slipped from 60 percent to 32 percent. Combined in a single "Anti-Central Government" Scale, these two questions trace a striking trend in councilor attitudes, as illustrated in Figure 8. While fervent centralists remained a tiny minority over these two decades (concentrated on the far right), the number of fervent opponents of the central government declined by more than half, and the proportion of moderate regionalists in the middle doubled. The tensions associated with the birth of the regional governments have progressively dissipated, and the regional elite are less fearful for regional autonomy now than they were two decades ago.

---

[40] Councilors attributed minimal importance in voters' decisions to national, regional, and local party leaders and to regional and local party platforms.

INSTITUTIONAL CHANGE IN ITALY: THE FIRST TWO DECADES   155

Figure 8: Regional Councilors' Attitudes toward Central Government, 1970-1989

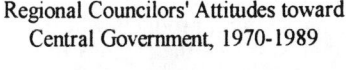

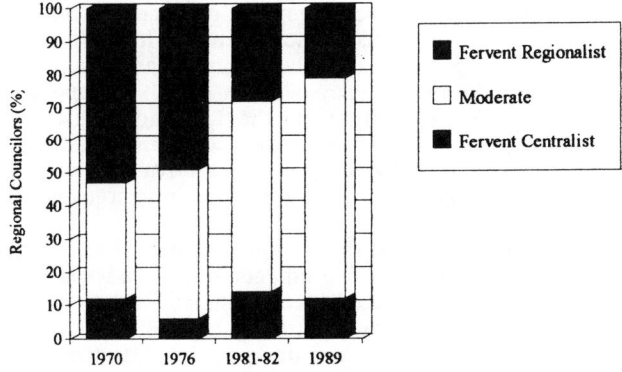

Index of Opposition to Central Government Controls

1. The institution of the prefect can and must be abolished. (agree)

2. The central government must rigorously exercise its rights of control over the activities of the regions. (disagree)

   Respondents were asked whether they "agree completely," "more or less agree," "more or less disagree," or "disagree completely" with each item. The Index is additive across both items.

Both at the center and in the periphery, to be sure, one still hears frequent complaints about infringements on the respective turfs of the national and regional governments. Such charges mark the normal controversies endemic to any genuinely decentralized system of government. National officials, concerned about mounting budget deficits that they attribute to the regions' irresponsible inefficiency -- "representation without taxation" -- call for substantial cuts in regional funding. Regional officials retort that the lion's share of the funds they receive from the national government is too closely tied to particular programs, even to the point of identifying the species of agricultural products whose production can be subsidized. The national ministries, they say, see the regions too often as mere field offices of central administration.[41]

To Americans accustomed to governors' complaints about federal grants-in-aid and federal controls, these laments of Italian regional officials have a familiar ring. Similarly, members of the Italian parliament reportedly see regional officials as rivals for control of the patronage that is such an important political resource in much of Italy. Even deputies of the Left, ideologically committed to political decentralization, work behind the scenes in parliament, it is said, to restrict the discretion of regional government. Such rivalry between federal legislators and state and local officials is, of course, familiar in intergovernmental politics from Chicago to Bavaria.

Meanwhile, as the regions began to exercise their newfound powers of supervision over local governments, tussles between regional and local government began to take the place of the older simplicities of center-periphery conflict. In the intergovernmental triangle among central, regional, and local officials, new alignments and complicated three-cornered strategies began to evolve.[42] To the consternation of some Italian jurists, the Italian system moved in the direction of the marble cake model of intergovernmental relations, rather than the neater layer cake model.[43]

Instead of a simple contest over central and regional jurisdiction, most issues now evoke a multi-cornered struggle, including local governments, party officials at various levels, and even private agencies.[44] Rather than a clear division of responsibilities allocated to one and only one level, many programs in such fields as agriculture, housing, and health services are in effect shared among the national, regional, and local levels. Politicians and administrators from all three levels consult informally and negotiate with one another, often rancorously, even when one level

---

[41] The research center of the Conference of Regional Presidents (*Cinsedo*) has estimated that 82 percent of the resources available to the "ordinary" regions (though only 36 percent of the resources of the "special" regions) are bound by decisions taken by Rome. See Il Messaggero (Rome), August 10, 1991, p. 12.

[42] Raphael Zariski, "Approaches to the Problem of Local Autonomy: The Lessons of Italian Regional Devolution," West European Politics, vol. 8 (July 1985), 64-81; Bruno Dente, "Intergovernmental relations as central control policies: the case of Italian local finance," Government and Policy, vol. 3 (1985), 383-402.

[43] Morton Grodzins, in Daniel Elazar, ed., The American System: A New View of Government in the United States (Chicago: Rand McNally and Co., 1966), p. 8-9, 14, introduced this metaphor to describe intergovernmental relations in the United States.

[44] See Zariski, "Approaches to the Problem of Local Autonomy," and Nicola Bellini, "The management of the economy in Emilia-Romagna: the PCI and the regional experience," in Robert Leonardi and Raffaella Y. Nanetti, eds., The Regions and European Integration: The case of Emilia-Romagna (New York: Pinter, 1990), p. 121.

has primary legal authority for decision-making. By the early 1980s nearly one hundred joint committees had been established to coordinate regional and national policies in particular sectors.

Conversely, the regions sought to increase their leverage in Rome on issues which are not formally within their jurisdiction, such as national economic policy and even international trade. Each region opened an office in Rome to represent its interests and to lobby the national government. In 1981 the chief executives of all the regions formed a permanent Conference of Presidents to provide a forum for expressing their views to the central government. By 1983 this group had established institutional ties with the national Council of Ministers, with the aim of improving top-level coordination between the central and regional authorities. As the European Community moved toward greater integration in 1992, the regions also sought direct influence on decisions in Brussels.

It would be premature at best to proclaim an "era of good feelings" between the regional and national governments, for as James Madison pointed out to his countrymen at the birth of the American federal system, shared powers mean permanent controversy. Nor has the Italian system of government become fully federal, for the constitutional and political status of the Italian regions is less autonomous than, for example, the American states or the German *Länder*. The distinction between centralized and federal systems is a continuum, however, not a dichotomy.[45] Over the last two decades Italy has moved significantly toward the decentralized end of that dimension, not only in formal terms, but also in terms of practical politics and policy making.

Regional leaders exercised more independent influence at the end of this period than their predecessors had at the beginning. Although the new structures did not determine informal power relations in any simple sense, changes in the formal structures gradually remolded informal relations. The logic of decentralization has become self-sustaining. Over the last two decades the region has become an authentic, autonomous, and increasingly distinctive arena in Italian politics.

Putting down roots: the region and its constituents

"The protest marches now all go to the regional headquarters instead of the prefecture," lamented one southern prefect privately. In Basilicata, one of the most backward regions of Italy, in a single day in November 1980 -- as it happened, only two days before the regional government would be forced to confront the devastation of a major earthquake -- the press carried reports about a regional tourist development on the Ionian sea, a protest by handicapped citizens against regional inaction, claims for regional aid to the investors in a bankrupt industrial development, demands for regional assistance to laid-off workers in a steel plant and a local supermarket, a report on a newly opened regionally-funded home for the aged, and criticism about the role of the region in a proposed petrochemical project. The protest marchers' changing destination subtly symbolizes the growing

---

[45] The recent literature on decentralization and center-periphery relations in Western states is vast. For useful compendia of comparative studies, see Tarrow, Katzenstein and Graziano, eds., Territorial Politics in Industrial Nations; L. J. Sharpe, ed., Decentralist Trends in Western Democracies (Beverly Hills: Sage Publications, 1979); Yves Mény and Vincent Wright, eds., Centre-Periphery Relations in Western Europe (London: Allen & Unwin, 1985); Rhodes and Wright, eds., Tensions in the Territorial Politics of Western Europe; and Edward C. Page and Michael J. Goldsmith, eds., Central and Local Government Relations: A Comparative Analysis of West European Unitary States (Beverly Hills: Sage Publications, 1987).

significance of the regional government in Italian governance.

As early as 1976, community leaders across Italy, such as mayors, labor leaders, bankers, industrialists, merchants, agricultural representatives, and journalists were actively engaged with the new governments. Nearly half the community leaders with whom we spoke met regularly with regional cabinet members, councilors, and administrators. These community and organizational leaders had more frequent contact with regional officials than with the equivalent figures either in local government or in the field offices of central government. (One impact of the regionalization of Italian government is that many national organizations, including the trade union federations and business and agricultural organizations, as well as political parties, have also been reorganized along regional lines in recent years.) By the 1980s most community leaders in our surveys (roughly 60 percent) reckoned that the regional government had a "very" or "rather" significant impact in their field, while fewer than one in ten claimed that the region had had no impact at all. Although (as we shall shortly see in detail) these community leaders were often critical of the new institution, roughly two thirds judged that its impact in their own field was fundamentally positive. Within less than a decade, the new governments had begun to put down roots.

Up to this point our description of the Italian regional experiment has emphasized trends consistent with the hopes of the proponents of the experiment. However, nearly all sides in the regionalist debate agree that the actual administrative performance of most of the new governments has been problematical. Public management in many regions has been a Kafkaesque combination of lethargy and chaos.

Throughout the late 1970s and the 1980s, a sense of frustrated hopes, fruitless plans, missed opportunities, and wasted hours pervaded many regional offices, especially in the South but not only there. Gloom about the gap between the regionalists' high aspirations and their limited practical achievements began to spread. By 1976, 42 percent of the councilors and 67 percent of the community leaders approved the region's official policies in the areas of most concern to them, but only 24 percent of the councilors and 35 percent of the community leaders approved the implementation of those policies. Although regional planning had been a high priority of most regional governments, two thirds of the councilors themselves in 1976 rated their region's efforts as unsuccessful, fully one half as "very" unsuccessful. The most common criticism was a lack of administrative follow-through on the regional governments' promising ideals.

Community leaders amplified these criticisms, focusing on the administrative failings of regional government. Throughout the 1980s, more than half of the community leaders we interviewed (55 percent in 1982 and 60 percent in 1989) agreed that "the administration in this region is decidedly inefficient."[46] Regionalization of the national health system, the largest sector transferred to regional jurisdiction in the reforms of the mid-1970s, was regarded by many as an administrative fiasco. In interviews with both community leaders and ordinary citizens, only a third agreed that "the regionalization of the health services has produced positive results," and barely 5-10 percent accepted this upbeat assessment without qualification.

---

[46] Intriguingly, ordinary voters are somewhat less critical of the regions on this score; only 40-45 percent of them agreed with this proposition in our surveys of 1982, 1987, and 1988.

Table 5 spells out the community leaders' complaints.[47] Bureaucratic procedures (patterned too often on practices of the central administration) are maddeningly slow and inefficient, cramped by controls designed to assure procedural regularity, not real effectiveness. Regional administrators are often unmotivated, unprofessional, inefficient, and unqualified. Agencies of the regional government act in mutual ignorance, without coordination with one another or with other levels of government. Projects proposed by regional officials too often seem impractical and unfeasible. Business and labor leaders are united in the view that no one at the regional government is able to discuss regional development plans intelligently. Worst of all, it takes forever to get an answer -- any answer -- from the region. Regional officials, the community leaders acknowledge, are eager to get their input, and the basic policy directions are often admirable. But implementing those shared objectives has proved beyond the capacity of too many regional agencies.[48] All in all, these community leaders say, the regional governments *sanno ascoltare, ma non sanno fare* -- "they know how to *listen*, but they do not know how to *act*."

---

[47] Table 5 is based on our 1982 nationwide survey of community leaders. Virtually identical results were obtained in our 1989 survey of community leaders in selected regions.

[48] Damningly, these criticisms are voiced most strongly by just those sectors (industry, labor, agriculture, and commerce) most often in contact with the regional administration; local government officials are somewhat more tolerant of the region's administrative failings, probably because they appreciate the frustrations of public management in Italy.

Table 5: Community Leaders' Views of Regional Administration (1982)

"How satisfied are you with these six aspects of the activities of the regional government in this region?"

Aspects of regional government activities	*Percentage "rather" or "very" satisfied*
Openness to consultation with your organization	55
Programmatic choices	41
Qualifications and diligence of personnel	32
Coordination with local government	28
Feasibility of regional projects	23
Time required to process a case	15
(Approximate N)	(302)

Many of the regions' administrative difficulties derive from personnel problems. Throughout the 1980s nearly two-thirds of the community leaders we spoke with rejected the proposition that "the civil servants of this region are well-trained and conscientious." Fearing bureaucratic elephantiasis (and perhaps ambivalent about strengthening the regions), the national parliament had stipulated that the regional governments be staffed primarily by bureaucrats transferred from the national ministries and semipublic agencies, thus restricting the ability of the regional governments to select their own employees. Worse yet, the transfer system gave no incentive to the national agencies to provide the regions with the best-qualified staff, committed to the success of the regional reform. The system was virtually guaranteed to provide personnel ill-suited to administer the "radical social and political renewal" of which the regionalists had dreamed.

It is far from clear that the regions would have exercised any more discretion wisely. Clientelism and party affiliation, rather than expertise and experience, were the main criteria for recruitment where the decisions were left to the regional authorities. Regional politicians were ready to demand autonomy, but less ready to manage that autonomy when it was granted. In many regions parties saw the new governments as a lucrative new source of money and jobs. Particularly in the impoverished South, efficient administration is less productive in electoral terms than old-fashioned patronage. Too much money has been spent on doorkeepers, chauffeurs, and phantom jobs of various sorts. Neither the national transfer system nor the regional recruitment system has produced a cadre of officials eager and able to implement innovative regional policy.

Top regional executives often acknowledge the justice of these criticisms. Indeed, 88 percent of the senior regional administrators we interviewed in 1981-82 judged the quality and training of regional personnel to be an important obstacle to efficient administration in their region, and 81 percent expressed a similar view about coordination among the regional departments. Said one sadly, "In too many respects we have reproduced the defects of the Roman mentality."

Against this background of severe criticism, it is interesting that -- as Table 5 showed -- the community leaders are generally pleased with the accessibility of the regional administration, an important factor that sharply differentiates the regions from the national administration. Regional and local organizations have been able to get regional government officials to listen to their complaints and suggestions. In our four waves of interviews with community leaders, three out of four leaders consistently have agreed that "contacts with the national administration are more frustrating than those with the regional administration." Despite their complaints about the region, Rome is much worse.[49]

One important reason for the greater accessibility of the regional administrators, of course, is propinquity: the regional capital is simply easier to get to than Rome. But administrative culture may be as important as geography, for regional bureaucrats appear to be more democratic in outlook than their national counterparts. Research in 1971 on the national bureaucratic elite found that "the typical member of the Italian administrative elite [is] the very essence of a classical bureaucrat -- legalist, illiberal, elitist, hostile to the usages and practices of pluralist

---

[49] Detailed analysis shows that in nearly every sector, spokesmen for smaller groups -- smaller towns, smaller farmers, smaller businesses, and so on -- are more favorable to the regional reform than spokesmen for larger groups. The smaller interest groups seem to be particularly sensitive to the advantages of dealing with the region, as compared with distant Roman bureaucracies.

politics, fundamentally undemocratic."[50] Among the regional administrators we interviewed just five years later, however, we found much more openness to democratic politics. As Table 6 shows, top regional administrators seem more comfortable with democratic government than was the norm in the national bureaucracy from which many of them have come.

Table 6: Democratic Attitudes among National and Regional Administrators (1971-1976)

	National Administrators	*Regional Administrators*
Percentage who agreed that:		
Few people know what is in their real interest in the long run.	75	39
In a world as complicated as the modern one, it doesn't make sense to speak of increased control by ordinary citizens over governmental affairs.	63	23
The freedom of political propaganda is not an absolute freedom, and the state should carefully regulate its use.	57	14

---

[50] Robert D. Putnam, "The Political Attitudes of Senior Civil Servants in Western Europe: A Preliminary Report," British Journal of Political Science, 3 (1973), p. 278.

In sum, on the "input" side of government the regions represent a substantial improvement over the central authorities, but on the "output" side regional administration leaves a great deal to be desired. Regional leaders may have learned a "new way of doing politics," but most of them have yet to discover an efficacious "new way of managing." Interestingly, regional officials themselves are at least as critical of regional shortcomings as are community leaders outside the government.

The verdict rendered on the regional reform by the Italian electorate is muffled by ignorance. Public awareness of the new regional institution spread slowly in the first years. In 1972, when the regions still existed mainly on paper, a nationwide survey found that two-thirds of the electorate had heard little or nothing about their own regional government, including 43 percent who had heard nothing at all. The salience of the new institution rose during the mid-1970s, as the great debates about the new regional government rose on the national agenda, and information about it filtered into the less politically conscious strata of the population. Thereafter, a certain plateau in public awareness was reached, although attention to the regional governments faded somewhat in the South, where (as we shall see) the new institutions were slower to make their mark.[51] By the end of the 1980s, two thirds of southern voters and three quarters of northern voters had heard at least something about their regional government. Regional governments lack the immediacy of contact with the daily lives of citizens that characterizes local government, and they lack the kind of media attention that is devoted to national affairs. Like American states, the regions are probably fated to remain less visible to the public than the levels of government above and below them.[52]

In absolute terms Italians are far from satisfied with the performance of their regional governments. By the beginning of the 1980s, only one third of Italians were reasonably enthusiastic supporters of the region, saying they were "very" or "rather" satisfied with the activities of the regional government; one half were disgruntled, declaring themselves "little" satisfied; and one in six was outraged, that is, "not at all" satisfied. These figures were virtually identical for both community leaders and ordinary voters. Most agreed with the mayor who told us in 1976, "The general lines of the region are fine, but the operative reality is not."

Both voters and leaders are less critical of the regional governments when they consider the alternative of centralized government. For many years Italians have had very little confidence in their public institutions. This alienation deepened just as the new institutions were being founded at the beginning of the 1970s. Indeed, the very disenchantment of Italians with the central administration may have inflated expectations of the new regional governments. In any event, despite their unhappiness with the results of the regional reform, both voters and community leaders have been consistently less critical of the performance of the new regional governments than of the national government. In 1981-82, for example, 34 percent of all Italians were at least "rather" satisfied with their regional government, as compared to only 15 percent for the national government; the comparable figures for community leaders were 29 percent for the regional government and 8 percent for the national government. In a head-to-head comparison, supporters of the regional governments outnumbered those who had more faith in the national government by eight to one. Community leaders who preferred to work with regional officials

---

[51] Ironically, awareness of the regional government was most scant in the two "special" southern regions, the oldest of all the regions; in 1982 fully half the citizens of Sicily and Sardinia claimed to have heard nothing at all about their own regional governments, by then more than 35 years old.
[52] M. Kent Jennings and Harmon Zeigler, "The Salience of American State Politics," <u>American Political Science Review</u>, v. 64 (1970), 523-35.

outnumbered those who favored national administrators by three or four to one. In a climate of general repudiation of public institutions, the regional government, though barely a decade old, was already more respected than the national government.

However vigorously Italians criticize the failures of their regional governments, they favor broader regional jurisdiction and autonomy instead of central authority. Table 7 presents illustrative evidence from our 1982 surveys.[53] Most Italians want to keep law and order in the hands of the central government, but roughly half would transfer greater powers to the regions in sectors now dominated by the state, such as education and industrial development, and roughly two thirds favor regional pre-eminence in such fields as health, agriculture, and the environment. Four out of five Italians support the demands of regional officials for greater financial autonomy from the state. Among community leaders, the pro-regional majorities on these questions are even more lopsided. Despite Italians' criticisms of the regional governments, they want the regions to be stronger, not weaker.[54]

---

[53] Responses to the questions presented in Table 7 were quite stable throughout our surveys in the 1980s.

[54] Since we shall later present much evidence of justified southern unhappiness over the current failings of their regional governments, it is important to emphasize that support for greater regional autonomy on the questions represented in Table 7 is almost as strong among southerners as among northerners.

Table 7: Attitudes of Italian Voters and Community Leaders toward Regional Autonomy (1982)

"Here is a list of things with which the State and the Region can be concerned. In each of these sectors is it preferable that the State or the Region have more power?"

Percentage who want to give more power to the **Region.**

Sector of policy	Voters	Community Leaders
Environment	72	85
Agriculture	70	84
Health	63	70
Industrial development	50	69
Education	47	46
Police	24	13
(Approximate N)	(1585)	(295)

Percentage who **agree**

	Voters	Community Leaders
"The regions should have more financial autonomy from the State."	78	81
(N)	(1376)	(305)

Table 8: Public Satisfaction with Regional Government, 1977-1988

"How satisfied are you with the activities of the regional government here?"

	1977	1981	1982	1987	1988
Very satisfied	3	2	2	2	3
Rather satisfied	30	33	32	38	42
Little satisfied	43	44	42	42	39
Not at all satisfied	24	22	23	17	17
	100%	100%	100%	100%	100%
(N)	(1497)	(1936)	(1845)	(1923)	(1899)

Figure 9: Public Satisfaction with Northern and Southern Regional Governments, 1977-1988

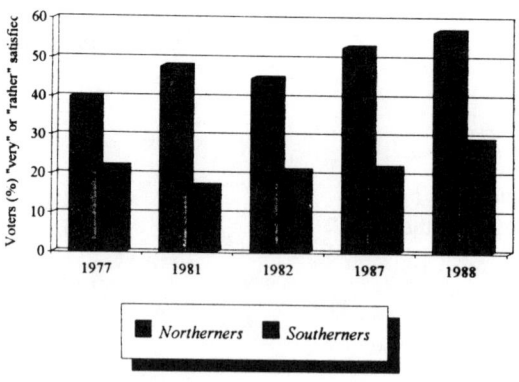

Public Satisfaction with Regional Governments, 1977 - 1988

Northerners ■ *Southerners*

Voter satisfaction with the performance of the regional government rose slowly but steadily throughout the 1980s, as Table 8 shows. Between 1977 and the end of 1988 the proportion of Italians at least "rather" satisfied increased from 33 percent to 45 percent. These national averages conceal important disparities across the regions. By the end of 1988, Figure 9 demonstrates, 57 percent of the northern electorate was reasonably satisfied with their regional government, as contrasted with only 29 percent of southern voters.[55] By the end of the 1980s, *nearly all* the northern regional governments (9 of 10) were satisfying most of their citizens, but *none* of the southern regions approached that goal.[56]

Figure 10, which compares voter satisfaction with national, regional, and local government, makes plain that from the point of view of most Italians, the three major levels of government form a ladder of increasing efficacy as one moves from the most distant and most distrusted level (national government) to the closest and most trusted (local government). In the North, however, voters see a stark difference between the central government, on the one hand, with which most of them are heartily dissatisfied, and regional and local government, on the other hand, with which most of them are reasonably content. By contrast, southerners are dissatisfied with all levels of government, and regional and local government are barely less censured than the central authorities.[57]

---

[55] "North" refers to all regions from Toscana, Umbria, and Marche northwards and "South" to all regions from Lazio and Abruzzi southwards.

[56] This generalization refers to respondents who declared themselves "very" or "rather" satisfied. Two of the twenty regions, Valle d'Aosta and Molise, are too small to appear in national mass samples, and are thus necessarily excluded from this analysis.

[57] Figure 9 is based on our 1988 survey, but the same pattern appears in all of our surveys.

168   RESPONSIBLE GOVERNANCE: THE GLOBAL CHALLENGE

Figure 10: Northern and Southern Satisfaction with National, Regional, and Local Government (1988)

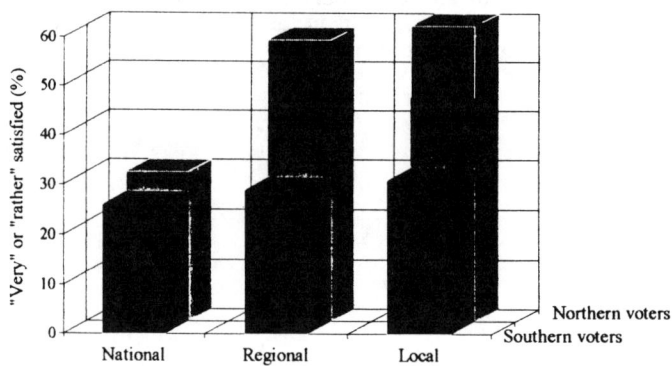

Queries about administrative inefficiency and legislative ineffectiveness highlight North-South differences. Throughout the 1980s, roughly 60 percent of southern voters agreed that "in this region the administration is definitely inefficient," as contrasted to roughly only 35 percent of northern voters. On the other hand, roughly 60 percent of northerners agreed that "all in all, the council in this region has functioned so far in a satisfactory manner," as compared to only 35 percent of southerners.

Whatever the shortcomings of the new regional administration, northern Italians prefer to be governed from closer to home. For many southerners, by contrast, being ruled from Bari or Reggio Calabria is not much better than being ruled from Rome, and for many the region has the additional disadvantage of unfamiliarity. "Better a known evil than a new one" is a view still occasionally heard in the South, but not in the North.

This strong North-South discrepancy in public satisfaction is consistent with other measures of the performance of the various regional governments.[58] On the other hand, Figure 9 also shows that by the end of 1988, in the South as in the North, the standing of regional governments in the eyes of their constituents was higher than ever before.

We can summarize much of the dynamics in regional government over the last two decades by directly comparing the changing views of regional councilors with those of their constituents, both community leaders and ordinary voters. (See Figure 11.) In the earliest years of the reform, the councilors, as the main protagonists of the new institution, were upbeat and ebullient. Between 1970 and 1989, however, this buoyant euphoria about their venture in institution-building was steadily replaced by a grimly realistic assessment of the practical challenges of making the new government work. Community leaders and voters, on the other hand, were initially much more skeptical, but their doubts have gradually been replaced by modest optimism.[59] By the end of the 1980s, as this chart shows, all strata in regional political life were converging toward moderate, but still hopeful realism.

After two decades of experience, the average Italian seems, in effect, to distinguish two different issues:

- Is his or her own regional government performing satisfactorily?

- Is the principle of the regional reform desirable?

Many Italians, particularly in the South, respond negatively to the first question, but affirmatively to the second. In that sense, we may term them "sympathetic critics." This distinction is politically significant, because while their criticism calls attention to the need for major improvements in the regional governments, their strong sympathy for the principle of regionalism underlines the need to reinforce the authority of those governments. Discontent with the practical performance of the regional government has not undermined popular support for a strong and autonomous regional institution. This paradoxical combination of sharp practical criticism and strong fundamental support is even more characteristic of the

---

[58] See Putnam, Making Democracy Work, chapters 3 and 4.
[59] We began posing these questions to community leaders in 1976, but we did not ask them of the mass public until 1981.

170   RESPONSIBLE GOVERNANCE: THE GLOBAL CHALLENGE

Figure 11: Optimism about Regional Government:
Councilors, Community Leaders, and Voters, 1970-1989

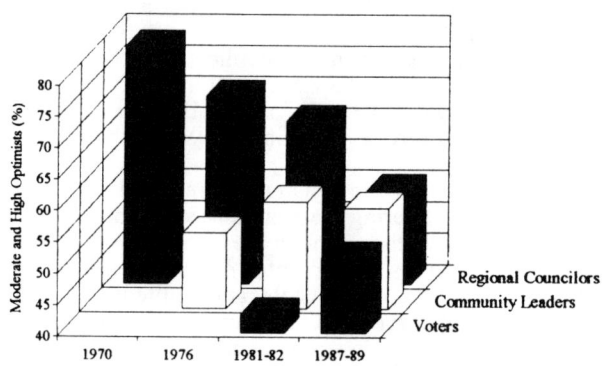

Index of Optimism about Regional Government

1. All in all, the council in this region has functioned satisfactorily so far. (agree)

2. Realistically speaking, in this region it is difficult to foresee great concrete accomplishments of the regional government. (disagree)

Respondents were asked whether they "agree completely," "more or less agree," "more or less disagree," or "disagree completely" with each item. The Index is additive across both items.

younger generation of voters, as well as of community leaders.[60] The vast majority (especially among the younger generation) wish to improve the regional institution, not to diminish or replace it.

What Italians want is not more limited regional government, but more effective regional government. No doubt an important part of the explanation is that most Italians are even more skeptical about the performance of the central authorities than they are about the regions. However, another part of the explanation may be that many citizens are still willing to give the benefit of the doubt to the new regional institution. The Italians' gradually increasing satisfaction with the regional governments, and their greater approval of regional than of national government, correspond to real differences in performance. Recall that regional governments are, for example, more than twice as stable as national governments, and that the stability of regional governments has steadily increased.[61]

Table 9 presents some additional evidence that synthesizes this conclusion. The basic question summarized here has been asked of Italians for nearly thirty years, beginning well before the advent of the ordinary regions.[62] Not surprisingly, in the earliest years a substantial portion of the public simply had no idea what to expect, and many others feared the worse. In the ensuing years, the ratio of favorable to unfavorable judgments rose steadily, so that by 1987 (the latest year for which comparable results are available), nearly two-and-a-half times as many Italian voters approve (41 percent) as disapprove (17 percent) the regional reform. Among community leaders, the balance of opinion is even more favorable to the regional reform, despite their severe criticism of the practical operations of the regional government. During the 1980s supporters of regionalism among community leaders outnumbered the critics by roughly six to one.[63] In light of southern grievance over the practical operations of the regional government, it is important to emphasize that southerners, like northerners, on balance endorse the regional reform.[64]

---

[60] Throughout our mass surveys, youth is never correlated with evaluations of the practical operations of the regional government, but is always a strong predictor of support for the principle of regional reform. In other words, younger Italians are more likely to be "sympathetic critics."

[61] See Fedele, "I processi politico-istituzionali nei sistemi regionali," and the data presented at p. 25 above.

[62] We are grateful to the DOXA survey organization for their collaboration with our research, including putting at our disposal data from their previous studies.

[63] To ensure comparability over time, the data on community leaders in Table 9 are limited to our six selected regions, but in 1982 and 1989, when we sampled other regions as well, the distribution of opinion in those six regions accurately reflects nationwide opinion.

[64] In 1987 southern voters said, by a ratio of 37 percent to 24 percent, that more good than bad had come from the regional reform; the equivalent ratio for northern voters was 45 percent to 11 percent. In 1989 southern community leaders, by a ratio of 54 percent to 15 percent, saw more good than bad in the regional reform; the equivalent ratio for northern community leaders was 68 percent to 3 percent. See also footnote 54 above.

Table 9: Evaluations of the Regional Reform, 1960-1987/89

"Do you think that from the creation of the regions has come [in 1960 and 1963: 'would come'] more good than harm or more harm than good?"

Mass Public	1960	1963	1976	1979	1981	1982	1987
More good than harm	19	31	38	31	31	31	41
Neither good nor harm	6	11	16	29	30	28	30
As much good as harm	4	6	7	8	13	11	7
More harm than good	20	22	21	14	18	21	17
Don't know	51	30	18	18	8	9	5
	100%	100%	100%	100%	100%	100%	100%
Support-criticism Index*	-1	9	17	17	13	10	24

Community Leaders	1981	1982	1989
More good than harm	65	59	62
Neither good nor harm	22	6	13
As much good as harm	6	18	17
More harm than good	7	17	8
	100%	100%	100%
Support-criticism Index*	58	42	54

*Support-criticism Index = (*More good than harm - more harm than good*).

Creating a new political institution is neither quick nor easy. Ultimately, success must be measured not in years, but in decades. It is instructive to pause for a brief comparison with the history of German attitudes toward the state governments (*Länder*) created in 1949. Asked in 1952 whether it would be a good idea or a bad idea for the *Länder* to be dissolved, critics in the German public outnumbered supporters, 49 percent to 21 percent. A 1960 poll found, for the first time, a slim majority (42 percent to 24 percent) opposing the abolition of the new institutions, and support remained at this lukewarm level for more than a decade. During the third decade after their creation, however, support for the *Länder* rose steadily, and by 1978 supporters had become vastly more numerous than critics (71 percent, compared to 10 percent).[65]

Figure 12 charts the gradual growth of support for strong subnational government in Germany, in comparison with similar trends during the early years of the Italian regions. This figure shows that the regions had won the support of a plurality of their constituents even earlier than the German *Länder*, and that thereafter public support for the regions drifted upwards relatively slowly. There is no assurance, of course, that public support for the Italian regions will accelerate in the years ahead, following the path blazed by the German *Länder*, nor that the Italian regions will prove as durable and effective as their more powerful German counterparts. But evidence from the German experiment in building subnational institutions reminds us that the popular legitimacy of new institutions, even successful ones, grows only gradually. This standard provides a realistic and sobering benchmark for evaluating changes in public attitudes to the Italian regional governments, as well as the new democratic institutions now being established elsewhere in the world.

---

[65] Elisabeth Noelle and Erich Peter Neumann, <u>Jahrbuch der Öffentlichen Meinung</u> (Allensbach: Institut für Demoskopie, 1967), p. 458; Elisabeth Noelle-Neumann, <u>The Germans: Public Opinion Polls, 1967-1980)</u> (Westport, Connecticut: Greenwood Press, 1981), p. 175; and unpublished German polling results supplied to us by DOXA (Milan). Arnold Brech, <u>Federalism and Regionalism in Germany</u> (New York: Oxford University Press, 1945), examines German federalism and regionalism from the era preceding German unification in the 1870s. For a comprehensive overview of German intergovernmental relations, see Joachim Jens Hesse, "The Federal Republic of Germany: From Co-operative Federalism to Joint Policy-Making," in Rhodes and Wright, eds., <u>Tensions in the Territorial Politics of Western Europe</u>, pp. 70-87.

174   RESPONSIBLE GOVERNANCE: THE GLOBAL CHALLENGE

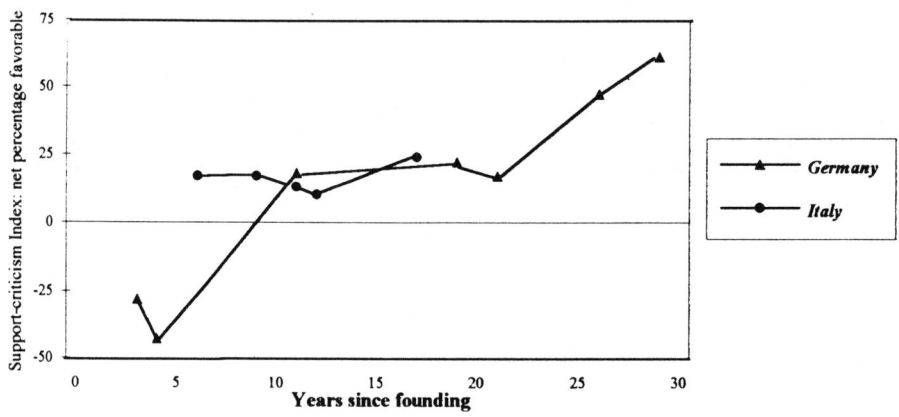

Figure 12: Support for Subnational Government:
Germany (1952-1978) and Italy (1976-1987)

Germany: "What would you say if the state governments were dissolved and there were only the federal government in Bonn? How do you feel about that suggestion?"

Support-criticism Index: Net percentage favorable to the states

Italy: "Do you think that from the creation of the regions has come more good than bad, or more bad than good?"

Support-criticism Index: Net percentage favorable to the regions

Conclusions

Examined week by week, or month by month, or sometimes even year by year, development in any human institution is hard to chart. The rhythms of institutional change are slow. Often several generations must pass through a new institution before its distinctive effects on culture and behavior become clear. Evanescent fads and the vagaries of individual participants obscure deeper trends. Occasionally in the early years of our regional research we thought we had discerned signs of some important development, only to have our expectations disrupted by new evidence from our next visit. Those who build new institutions and those who would evaluate them need patience -- this is one of the most important lessons of the Italian regional experiment.

The trends discussed in this essay, however, have been sustained through several decades of Italian political tumult. Our research methods allow us directly to compare today's attitudes and behavior with those of a decade or two ago, without relying on vague and fallible reminiscence. We can compare a leader's views on party discipline or capitalism or regional efficiency today with what he (or his predecessors) actually told us years ago, not merely with what people now recall about prevailing views then.

By these demanding evidential standards, the regional reform has significantly affected grassroots politics in Italy. As a result of this institutional change, Italian political leaders pursue different career paths, espouse different ideals, address social ills in different terms, struggle with different rivals, and collaborate with different partners. Italian citizens and community leaders depend on different agencies for government action. Often they receive improved service, though certainly not always, and when they don't, they address their complaints to different officials. Important things have changed because of the regional reform.

Twenty years into the regional experiment, subnational government is clearly more important on major issues of public policy in Italy in the 1990s than in 1970. The new institutions have taken root, gained autonomy, and (slowly) won constituent support. They have attracted an up-and-coming cadre of professional politicians. This institutional reform has had powerful consequences for the way Italian politics and government work. But what is the balance sheet for these new institutions in terms of the *quality* of politics and government?

On the positive side, the new institutions are closer to the people, as proponents had claimed they would be. The regional governments are more familiar with regional realities and more accessible to regional demands than the remote Roman ministries they replaced. They provide multiple laboratories for policy innovation. They help to nurture a moderate, pragmatic, tolerant style of policy-making and conflict-management -- "a new way of doing politics." They engage the interests of regional social groups and community leaders, and they are gradually earning cautious approval from their constituents.

Against these gains must be laid two important entries on the negative side of the ledger. First, the administrative efficiency that some regionalist reformers anticipated has not materialized. On the contrary, any fair-minded jury would convict many of the regions of maladministration. Second, and perhaps even more important for the future of Italian politics, the regional reform appears to be exacerbating, rather than mitigating, the historical disparities between North and South. The reform freed the more advanced regions from the stultifying grasp of Rome, while allowing the problems of the more backward regions to fester.

In assessing these two indictments, however, we must ask about actual alternatives, not unattainable ideals. After an hour of passionate and detailed criticism of his region by a southern mayor, we asked whether things were better under the centralized regime. Looking stunned at the naïveté of our question, he exclaimed, "For the love of God, no!"

By the beginning of the regions' third decade, a new season of revived regionalism seemed to be opening. Despite widespread disappointment that the regional governments had not lived up to the original hopes, renewed concern about the ineffectiveness of the central government led to widespread talk of further "regionalization" of the Italian state. In the wealthy northern regions, upstart regionalist "leagues," such as the *Lega Lombarda* and the *Lega Veneta*, made major inroads against the established parties in regional and local elections in 1990 and 1991, and these gains were consolidated in the national elections of 1992. The rise of the leagues was fueled by regional pride, anger against the inefficiencies of Rome, backlash against "handouts" to corrupt southerners, and veiled racism. The *Lega Lombarda*, which had called for "liberation of the Lombard nation," won more than 20 percent of votes in the richest, most populous region in the country. A dozen regional governments petitioned for a national referendum to transfer major additional powers to the regional level.

In 1991 the Constitutional Affairs Committee of the Chamber of Deputies approved virtually unanimously a constitutional amendment that would completely eliminate several major national ministries (including Education, Health, Agriculture, Social Affairs, and Urban Affairs, among others), transferring their responsibilities to the regions, and more than doubling the regions' share of the entire national budget to almost 70 percent.[66] In some respects, the ambitions were reminiscent of the mood at the birth of the regions in the 1970s. The history of governmental reform in Italy suggests caution in interpreting these developments, since the central authorities would strongly resist any further devolution of their powers, but regionalist pressures continued to mount, especially in the North. Another page was about to be turned in the story of Italian regional government. The evidence we have here reviewed from the first twenty-year chapter of the experiment vividly illuminates the power of institutional reform to transform the practice of politics and government.

---

[66] See Il Messaggero (Rome), August 10, 1991, p. 12; La Repubblica (Rome), November 20, 1991, p. 17; and Ottavo Rapporto sullo Stato dei poteri locali/1991, pp. 18-19.

CHAPTER NINE

ECONOMIC REFORM AND RESPONSIBLE GOVERNMENT IN AFRICA

JOHN W. HARBESON

The African continent in 1993 stood on the threshold of a possible political renaissance as profound as that which produced its independence from colonial rule in the 1960s. For more than a decade, international donors, with sometimes reluctant cooperation from African governments, have insisted upon policy reforms and a reduced scale of government to lift the continent out of its enduring economic and political malaise. In the 1990s, both African peoples and the donors have begun to perceive that political democratization is a necessary component of, and condition for, such a renaissance. Stimulated in part by the example and competition of the post-Cold War liberation of eastern Europe from Soviet domination, many African countries have begun to take important steps toward what they view as their own political liberalization, in the form of multiparty democracy.

The new emphasis on African political reform highlights a long underexamined and complex dimension of the development crisis: who bears what responsibility for transforming the contours of African economic and political life. Insofar as responsibility has figured in the debate between African countries and donors over how to lift the continent out of poverty, the issue has been the the relative contributions of the international economy's structure and performance, host country policies, and donor strategies to causing and perpetuating the crisis. Underlying the policy positions of African countries and African donors alike have been implicit but largely unexamined assumptions concerning how ideas, patterns, and distributions of political responsibility are to change with the restructuring of political and socio-economic institutions, policies, and roles.

The thesis of this chapter is that the success of policy and structural reforms in stimulating an African political and socio-economic renaissance depends directly upon the extent to which the implied restructurings of political responsibility are coherent, realistic, and accepted in the arenas of African politics. These issues are complicated by the variety and complexity of extant definitions of responsibility, so that the the assumed meanins of the term as well as well as the assignment and distribution operationally of political responsibility for reformed African polities and societies may also be at issue.[1] It follows that clarification as well as resolution of competing ideas of political responsibility may be critical to the success of African political and socio-economic reform initiatives.

This chapter offers a preliminary exploration of political responsibility issues

---

[1] One of the best examinations of alternative meanings of the term is still Charles E. Gilbert, "The Framework of Administrative Responsibility," 21 Journal of Politics 3 (1959), pp. 373-408.

embedded in analyses of, and prescriptions for the African development crisis. Against this background the chapter then explores issues of political responsibility in contemporary African democratization initiatives.

The nature of the development crisis

The tangible, empirical indicators of the on-going African development crisis are clear and relatively uncontroversial.[2] Most of sub-Saharan Africa has enjoyed political independence for thirty years or longer, at least in a juridical sense. Each of the fifty odd independent nation states was born amidst euphoric expectations at the moment that its appearance would contribute to a new era of African political imagination, innovation, and creativity. From the dark night of their colonial subjugation, they expected to evolve in the light of their new day approaches to government, tailored to their own distinctive circumstances, that would improve upon perceived shortcomings of European philosophical traditions. Moreover, within the scholarly community, particularly those joining it at about that time, there was a mixture of hope and anticipation that dialogue between newer African and older non-African civilizations would yield new insights into the human condition and its possibilities.

These heroic and hopeful political visions quickly receded to the vanishing point, casualties of seemingly intractable economic malaise and political decay. Per capita real income for sub-Saharan Africa was lower in 1990 than in 1965: average annual per capita income increased by only 0.3%, more than counterbalanced by double digit inflation. More troubling, during the 1980s, the first decade of international, strictly sanctioned economic reforms, the average annual growth of gross domestic product has been only 2.1%, below all other developing country regions and only half the rate of the previous decade. Meanwhile, the rate of annual population increase has accelerated from 2.7% prior to 1980 to 3.1% during the 1980s, signifying declining growth real per capita growth. Food production per capita declined during the 1980s, the only world region not registering improvement during that period. African calorie intake remained the lowest and least improved of any world region during the 1980s. Indicators of productivity and economic diversification have shown little improvement and in some cases regression. In the agricultural sector, accounting for about one-third of domestic product and supporting 70% or more of the work force, such productivity as has occured has resulted more from expanding cultivated area than from improved per hectare yields. Overcultivation, overgrazing and rapid deforestation have contributed greatly to undermining the environmental and ecological foundation of potential African economic progress.

Sub-Saharan Africa's achievements in cultivating its human resources have been more encouraging. There were only about half as many people per doctor and a third as many per nurse in 1984 as in 1990 and school enrollment percentages have improved dramatically at all levels since 1965. However, in both health and education sub-Saharan Africa's rate of progress has lagged well below that of other developing country regions, and there are some indications that rates of

---

[2] Some have argued that it is no longer appropriate to refer to the African development "crisis" because it has been so prolonged. I continue to argue that there can be, and are long term as well as short term crises.

improvement on these indicators began to stabilize or even decline.³ Finally, sub-Saharan Africa's international economic position vis-a-vis both the industrialized and other developing country regions has worsened or has not significantly improved on a variety of measures: export growth, terms of trade, balance of payments, and public debt as percentages of GNP and export income.

Economic stagnation has been accompanied by pervasive political decay: chronic political instability, abuses of power, and degrees of weakness threatening in some cases the very survival of the political order itself. The voluntary retirements of presidents Julius Nyerere of Tanzania and Leopold Senghor were exceptions confirming the rule of forcible overthrows of governments, often by cadres of military officers. State-centric development strategies and expansive public sectors tended strongly to achieve their dialectical antithesis: burgeoning informal sectors operating largely beyond the reach of formal state authority. Widespread, extensive participation by public officials in the informal sector during working hours has further hemorrhaged the energy and capacity of governments to govern. Thus weakened, African governments have lost much of whatever capacity they may once have possessed to restrain large scale abuses of power and self-aggrandizement by public officials, often thereby enlarging the scale of intra-societal conflicts, particularly those of an ethnic and regional nature. Such conflicts in some cases have broadened into full scale civil wars further tearing at the fabric of African polities. In the extreme, in the case of the Horn of Africa, the scale of political decay and conflict has threatened the very existence of the polity in Somalia and potentially in Sudan and Ethiopia.

From the inception of their campaigns early in the 1980s to impose reforms on African countries, the World Bank (IBRD) and the International Monetary Fund (IMF) have focused explicitly on public policies to revive African economies and liberation of the private sector from the clutches of overextended albeit weak and ineffective governments.⁴ The Bank and the Fund have conceded that multilateral and bilateral development agencies themselves bear some responsibility for having supported African government policy initiatives that ultimately have been deemed ineffective and inappropriate. They have conceded also that the vagaries of the international economy particularly in the 1970s impeded and frustrated African economic development. They have insisted, however, that the root causes of, and solutions to the African development crisis are the responsibility of African governments. They, and collaborating major bilateral donors, have heavily reinforced and focused that burden of responsibility by requiring African governments to adhere strictly to Bank/Fund policy reform guidelines as a condition for development assistance and budgetary support.

---

³ Data are drawn from the World Bank's World Development Report 1992 (New York: Oxford University Press, 1992), United Nations Development Programme and the World Bank, African Development Indicators (Washington, D.C.: World Bank, 1992), and World Bank, Sub-Saharan Africa: From Crisis to Sustainable Growth: A Long-Term Perspective Study (Washington, D.C.: World Bank, 1989).

⁴ The major World Bank reports articulating the joint Bank/Fund strategies for structural adjustment include Accelerated Development in Sub-Saharan Africa: An Agenda for Action (1981), Toward Sustained Development in Sub-Saharan Africa (1984), Financing Adjustment with Growth in Sub-Saharan Africa (1986-1990), and Sub-Saharan Africa: From Crisis to Sustainable Growth (1989).

The Bank and the Fund have been much clearer about what African governments are to do to discharge their responsibility for reforming their countries' economies than about how that responsibility is to be discharged. The scope of the "how" problem has expanded in proportion to the gradually expanded scope of the agendas the Bank and the Fund have imposed on the African governments. Initially the IMF and IBRD mandated reforms in four areas: (1) trade and exchange rate practices, (2) economic decision making, (3) organization and management, and (4) the scope of governmental activity.[5]

1. They directed African governments to devalue their currencies and to rely on such devaluations more than upon import restrictions to preserve scarce foreign exchange. They called upon African governments to abandon protection of fledgling industries, in order to promote import substitution, through selective lifting of import restrictions on capital equipment and raw materials.

The Bank and Fund directed African governments to abandon discrimination against the agricultural sector. This they had routinely done through overvaluation of exchange, stimulating artificial competition from imported agricultural products, and through artificially depressing farm gate grain prices in order to coddle politically volatile urban constituencies.[6] These demands of African countries implied larger objectives of economic democracy and integration. Fully 75% of the African workforce continues to derive livelihoods from rural employment, and the agricultural sector itself still accounts for a third or more of gross domestic product in most African countries. Moreover, artificially low farm gate prices drove rural producers out of government-managed grain markets in droves into the informal economy and/or subsistence production. Urban dwellers, despite their subsidized food prices, found themselves driven to participate in the informal economy as both producers and consumers.

2. The Bank and the Fund faulted African governments' direct, full service participation in economic development activities from planning to implementation. A government's comparative advantage, they contended, lay in priority setting and cost-benefit analysis of potential development projects rather than in "doing development" themselves in which they were allegedly inherently less effective than private entrepreneurs. This pattern of decision making, the Bank and the Fund contended, had resulted in suboptimal project selection, misallocation of scarce resources, and inefficient project implementation, thereby diminishing the governmental legitimacy and strength. In organizational terms this inappropriate decision-making was reflected in the relative weakness of planning ministries in relation to others and of planning sections within executing ministries. Correspondingluy, too few resources were devoted to training economic and policy analysts. In their critiques of governmental decisionmaking, the donors were not unmindful that inappropriate governmental decision making could also plausibly explain poor results from their own aid projects.

3. The Bank and the Fund argued that distorted relations between state and society underlay inappropriate public policies. They asserted the necessity of "structural adjustment" to correct for over-reliance upon the public sector, overcentralization within the public sector, and under-reliance upon small producers within the private sector. One particular target of their critique, however, was less

---

[5] Accelerated Development, op.cit.
[6] Robert Bates, Markets and States in Tropical Africa (Berkely: University of California Press, 1981).

the public sector per se than the parastatal corporations, modeled in part upon colonial predecessors, that realized none of the advantages of either private enterprise or public administration: though structurally semi-independent of government in order to be able to operate on business principles, they were in fact characteristically drains on public revenue but without real public accountability. The Bank and the Fund initially criticized not just the deemphasis on private sector development in general but, more specifically, the loss of efficiency within the private sector itself, especially in agriculture. Governments' policies and procedures took a path of least resistance in favoring excessively politically influential large farmers rather than restructuring the private sector to support small producers whom research had shown to be far more efficient if also somewhat more risk averse.

4. The Bank and the Fund found that African peoples themselves had assumed too little direct responsibility for providing the collective goods they appeared to value most highly. They contended that governments had failed to nourish civic responsibility in allowing society's structural dependence upon government for primary and secondary education, primary health care, and housing. The incidence of taxation compounded the problem: imposed fees for the collection and marketing of agricultural production discouraged reliance upon these facilities and failure to impose direct taxes to provide for popularly supported education and health facilities deprived these sectors of much needed financial support.

Implicitly, the Bank and the Fund appeared to critique African governments for failing to strengthen the position of local governments whose weakness in the colonial times paralleled that exhibited domestically by the former colonial powers. Local governments, the donors appeared to assume, should possess the tax base to provide locally for schools, clinics, roads, and other infrastructure. Implicit also may have been a critique of central governments for failing to encourage or support civic consciousnesss centered on the activities of local governments as well as on private initiatives.

Beyond criticizing donors and western investors for inadequate infusion of resources for development and industrialized countries for failing to restructure the international economy allegedly biased against less developed country economies, African leaders inveighed against the domestic implications of the Bank/Fund critique.[7] Fundamentally, they contended that Bank/Fund demands for structural adjustment threatened destruction rather than reform of African governments and economies. The very weakness of African governments, they argued, made it impossible to alienate the public through lowered living standards implied by devaluation and termininating of food subsidies, let alone give them the added strength need to undertake the other aspects of structural adjustment. Moreover, they argued that the emphasis on international export competitiveness, through devaluation and privatization at the expense of domestic food production, augured deeper international economic dependence rather than greater strength and self-reliance. They chided the Bank and the Fund for failing to call for intra-African economic restructuring to eliminate colonially established barriers to regional cooperation.

Underlying contrasting donor and African perspectives on the causes of the

---

[7] The United Nations Economic Commission for Africa responded to the Bank critique on behalf of African governments, though in African governments varied in their responses, ranging from principled rejection through pragmatic,skeptical, sometimes grudging cooperation to resigned acceptance.

development crisis lay understated and underexamined philosophical issues of political responsibility. On the one hand, the international banks joined African governments in declaring the relevance of political responsibility to the broad area of political economy rather than simply to the functioning of government per se. Contending theories of the political economy of development have tended to understate the significance of political choice in setting forth contending views of the nature of the development process. Modernization theory, emphasized the implicitly "natural" transition from "traditional" societies to market-centered modern economies, secular and pragmatic political cultures animated by modern technological progress, and political democracies sustaining and sustained by plural societies.[8] World systems and dependency theories emphasized the dark underside of modernization without supplying the revolutionary outcome anticipated by Marx, Lenin, and Mao.[9] From this perspective, African and other developing countries since the beginning of colonialism had been subjected to an expanding world capitalist economy in which they were consigned either to structural dependence, inequality, and underdevelopment or to exclusion and peripheralization altogether with respect to opportunities to compete for capitalism's rewards.

To varying degrees African countries at independence undertook to practice both non-alignment in the Cold War and envisioned and pursued a courses of development distinct from those rooted in both classic liberal and Marxist precepts. The underlying and unifying theme of these "middle roads" to development was the goal of self-reliance. African economies were to be syncretic; they were to mimic neither capitalist nor socialist economies but rather borrow the best from both schools while remaining true to African cultural premises. Fundamentally, this meant that African countries should not only act responsibly in following a charted path of development but should and must choose the path itself. Necessarily, therefore, this choice, which built upon the foundations of African nationalism during the colonial era, made the governments responsible at a very basic level for the futures of their peoples. The scope of such responsibility went beyond procedural responsibility, such as accountability, responsiveness, or due process, within established political and socioeconomic structures, to the existential choice and creation of those structures themselves. Implicitly, definitions of procedural responsibility were to be derivative from the choice of structure.[10]

As the Bank and the Fund openly acknowledge, they and bilateral donors did not initially challenge directly the validity of the development paths chosen by African governments. But beginning in the 1980s, in the face of economic malaise and political decay and turbulence, they did. In so doing they challenged African ideas of political responsibility in two fundamental respects. First, they declared bankrupt courses of development departing from the precepts of modernization theory and the classical liberation on which it has always implicitly rested. In effect, they thereby invalidated the exercise by African governments of the responsibility to choose their own course of development. At the same time they chided those governments whose course departed less from western models for irresponsibility in

---

[8] Representative of modernization theories is Gabriel Almond and G. Bingham Powell, Comparative Politics: System, Process,and Policy, 2nd ed. (Boston: Little Brown, 1978).
[9] Representative of these schools of thought have been Samir Amin, Accumulation on a World Scale (New York: Monthly Review Press, 1974) and Immanuel Wallerstein, The Politics of the World Economy (Cambridge: Cambridge University Press, 1984).
[10] Gilbert, op.cit., outlines several alternative forms of procedural responsibility.

failing to adhere more closely to those models.

Second, they implicitly challenged the idea that the essence of the practice of political responsibility lies in choice. This they did by reducing the scope of western ideas of responsibility from adherence to precepts of fairness rooted in the idea of democracy to principles of cost effectiveness rooted in classical political economy. Personal qualities of competence, efficacy, and accountability associated with the idea of political responsibility became in effect matters of technical, even essentially quantitative expertise in allocating resources. Other valued albeit sometimes conflicting qualities associated with political responsibility such as probity, due process, prudence, and responsiveness were less easily translated into economic terms and were thus implicitly deemphasized.

In short, African governments and the international financial community both failed to address clearly and fully the issue of political responsibility for the African development crisis. African governments asserted broad responsibility for their countries' choice of development paths but stopped short of clearly establishing their procedural implications in day to day governance, making it easier to honor stated development goals only in the breech. The Bank and the Fund for their part shrunk the concept of political responsibility to technical economic behavior in criticizing African governments' policies but declined to address broader dimensions of political responsibility. Thus, in so doing both sides neglected in a fundamental sense to address the politics of development.

Blueprints for an African renaissance: development without political responsibility?

Prior to at least the 1990s a common theme in an evolving dialogue between Bank and the Fund, on the one hand, and African governments, on the other hand was an emphasis upon economic and policy making responsibility. While there were important structural implications in the positions of both sides, the emphasis was upon the policies rather than upon the reform of political and socioeconomic structures per se. Political responsibility for the structural correlates of policy reform was left unaddressed making the term "structural adjustment" associated with Bank/Fund reform initiatives something of misnomer.

Thus, the Bank and the Fund demanded that (1) central governments assume more responsibility for priority setting and project vetting and devolve responsibility for the implementation of development initiatives upon others, particularly private entrepreneurs; (2) local governments assume more responsibility for development in certain sectors, e.g. health, education, and certain infrastructure such as roads; (3) private individuals and groups, disciplined by the market, were to bear more direct entrepreneurial responsibility for economic development activities and to rely upon local and foreign private investors for these purposes; and (4) consumers were to take more direct financial and management responsibility for essential social services, such as health and education, in cooperation with local governments. This reallocation of development responsibilities was to be accomplished within a framework of a diminished public sector, liberalized domestic and international trade, more realistic exchange rates, price deregulation and reduction of food subsidies, and measures to promote domestic saving. A fifth and little noticed dimension of this reassignment of development responsibilities was that small producers, once liberated from discriminatory wholesale price policies were to be left to their own devices and resources in competing with larger and wealthier producers.

The Bank/Fund strategy for reintegrating a burgeoning informal, or black market, economy with the shrinking formal sector was to legitimize the untrammeled functioning of market-based decision making upon which the former relied. In so doing, the Bank and the Fund implicitly assumed either that the functioning of African informal markets corresponded to the assumptions of classical economic theory or that legitimizing informal markets would cause them more nearly to realize such assumptions in practice.

African governments have resisted Bank/Fund "medicine" to varying degrees, and for varying lengths of time, but in the end most have had little choice but to take the pills. As will be noted shortly, they have at the same time been able to influence donor thinking through United Nations channels where they have been less able to do so in direct negotiations with the fund. The core of their objections have been to the scope and forced pace of Bank/Fund reform measures. How, they asked, could they be responsible governments, in fact or appearance, if they were seen to be simply administrative arms of the multilateral international banks? How could they retain or regain the confidence of key constituencies if they asked them to accept economic pain in the service of a conception of the national interest dictated by international banks? How could they retain their legitimacy if they legalized the activities of an informal sector whose hallmark was defiance of formal governance structures. Finally, they accused the Bank and the Fund of irresponsibility in failing to fine tune the timing or the content of structural adjustment packages to accommodate the particular circumstances of individual countries.

For their own part, however, the emphasis of African governments' responses to Bank/Fund prescriptions centered upon alternative policy packages rather than upon a revamped and strengthened structural (or constitutional) framework of responsibility within which to enact what policy measures could be agreed upon. They broadly accepted renewed emphasis upon the agricultural sector, but neither they nor the Bank and the Fund have appeared to give priority to smallholder agriculture as originally proposed. They have generally acquiesced in Bank/Fund monetary policy prescriptions by effecting sharp currency devaluations though they have been somewhat more reluctant to give agricultural exports the priority in relation to domestic food production that Bank and the Fund have demanded. The winding up of parastatals and the devolving of their functions to the private sector is a long term process upon which African countries have embarked with differing levels of vigor and dispatch. At least one notable example of planned decentralization from national to local levels of government. the District Focus program in Kenya, appeared to have made relatively little progress as of early 1993. Examples of local self help in establishing schools and clinics have long been numerous, and the long term effect of Bank/Fund imposed reforms upon its scope and extent were not yet clear as of early 1993.

Prior to the decade of the 1990s the structural focus of Bank/Fund-imposed reforms remained national level bureaucracies. Neither the Bank and the Fund nor African governments addressed the larger question of political responsibility for acquiescing in, and sustaining the required reforms, or for failing to do so. Nor did either party address the issue of how political structures would be reformed within the framework of which ongoing responsibilities for development would be defined and distributed.

In the absence of a larger debate over the framework of politial responsibility for promoting an African economic renaissance, the Bank and the Fund appeared to assume that the reforms they imposed exhibited responsibility because they were efficacious in two senses. First, at least in principle they relied upon expected statistical verifications that their implementation would elicit economic progress. Second, they contended that governments, in implementing the directives, were in the process of making the most efficient use of their administrative capabilities and resources. The claim of efficaciousness in turn rested upon the assumption that implementation of the directives was responsibole because they were based upon competent authority; i.e. the scientific and technical competence of Bank/Fund economists, resting in turn upon professional canons in Carl Friedrich's sense of a "fellowship of science."[11]

If the intellectual justification of Bank-Fund mandated reforms was initially that they reflected objectively valid principles and were for that reason efficacious, they were nonetheless ensnared in a contradiction. African governments were expected to "represent" professional canons of development "science" through following the lead of Bank/Fund economists. But the "fellowship of science" would appear to be founded on a premise of scientific "neutrality" in the Weberian sense of the term. The problem, however, was that African governments were called upon assume to political responsibility for the reforms, including substantial short and medium term risks, against hoped for long term benefits. To a large extent, they were denied flexibility and discretion to tailor implementation of the externally mandated policies to their particular circumstances. Many in African governments have been acutely sensitive to this contradiction between scientific neutrality and political responsibility.

Thus, the heart of the matter is that the Bank and the Fund both assigned and withdrew from African governments responsibility for ameliorating the development crisis afflicting their countries. On the one hand, they fixed responsibility for the development crisis upon African governments as a basis for requiring them, in turn, to reassign domestic responsibilities for development. On the other hand, in asserting their intellectual and administrative authority for what was to be done they in effect diminished African governments' authority, hence their responsibility, for defining and taking appropriate measures. In effect they repeated the error former colonial powers sometimes committed: assuming that traditional rulers could continue to serve their own peoples without loss of legitimacy while at the same also remaining answerable to their colonial masters.

The internally contradictory Bank/Fund implicit theory of responsibility for stimulating development raised an issue of fundamental constitutional significance. Charles Gilbert contended that "the idea of responsibility seems nearly always to stand for...a complex of values" related to "presumptively popular values."[12] Frameworks of responsibility must ultimately be polity-specific and derived from the basic values that move a people to establish and retain political association with one another. In this light the Bank/Fund implicit theory of responsibility underlying its reform directives appeared to place at greater risk not only the legitimacy administering African governments but also already fragile fundamental bases of political association in the continent.

In practical terms the legitimacy of the Bank/Fund approach to reform appeared to be at risk even on its own terms. Insofar as tangible measures of progress did not take place as the result of the imposed reforms, their validity was in

---

[11] Constitutional Government and Democracy (Boston: Little Brown, 1941), p. 65.
[12] Op.cit.

doubt. As noted above, the record to date is mixed at best. Neither the Bank and the Fund nor African governments were likely to benefit much from efforts by each to transfer responsibility for weak results to the other. Underlying, those mixed tangible results lay a deeper issue: the status of the "science" of development itself. The results to date do little to suggest that strict Bank/Fund insistence on adherence to their initiatives is commensurate with the degree of uncertainty certainty about the truth, at least without adaptation to particular African circumstances, of the underlying theory itself.

Already by the end of the 1980s, African governments had begun to conclude that their initial skepticism may have been justified and that structural adjustment as defined principally by the Bank and the Fund was not likely to work. A 1989 report by the United Nations Economic Commission for Africa on the impact of structural adjustment concluded that "both on theoretical and empirical grounds, the conventional S(tructural) A(djustment) P(rograms) have been inadequate in addressing the causes of economic, financial, and social problems facing African countries which are of a structural nature."[13] Specifically, the ECA claimed that (1) credit tightening policies intended to restrain inflation had been ineffective while at the same time producing economic contraction; (2) higher interest rates had induced more speculation than investments, owing in part to the imperfections of African markets; (3) increasing import prices through devaluation had not stimulated demand for local substitutes because of technology-based quality differents between imported and local products; (4) export promotion had been inhibited by continuing industrial country barriers to African goods; (5) local private sectors had lacked capacity to assume the responsibilities devolved upon them through privatization, leaving multinationals and other external investors as the principal beneficiaries; (6) revamped official prices to encourage local production, particularly in agricultural, had been ineffective-- again because of imperfect market conditions; and (7) mandated reductions in public expenditure had adversely effected the quality and scope of essential social services like education, health, and clean water without stimulating compensatory economic growth.

The thrust of the point-by-point ECA attack was that Bank/Fund structural adjustment initiatives themselves had been victims of the very economic stagnation and crisis circumstances they were designed to ameliorate. Its contention was that Bank/Fund structural adjustment programs, as then conceived, were at most objectives or projected consequences of development. In contending that imposed policy had failed to achieve those objectives and intended consequences, the ECA implicitly pointed to the deeper problem: inattention to the structures and processes needed to shape those policies and guide them toward the intended outcomes. In overlooking the structure and process dimensions, the Bank and Fund had also implicitly bypassed the issues of how those structures and processes should be shaped, what guidelines should govern their functioning, who should function in what roles within them, how those individuals should be selected, and--most important of all-- to whom they should be answerable and by what mechanisms. In fairness, however, it is necessary to add that the ECA itself did not draw out these implications of its own critiques, let alone attempt to deal with them.

In short, both the Bank and the Fund, on the one hand, and African countries as represented through the ECA, on the other hand, in failing to address

---

[13] United Nations Economic Commission for Africa, African Alternative Framework to Structural Adjustment Programmes for Socio-Economic Recovery and Transformation (Addis Ababa: UNECA, 1989).

the structure and process dimensions of economic reform, avoided dealing with all the fundamental questions of political responsibility. Fundamentally, this was a debate over policy reform not structure; the term "structural" adjustment was in an important sense a misnomer. Moreover, in failing to address issues of political responsibility, this was an "aresponsible" debate.[14]

Toward an African renaissance: political responsibility and development in the 1990s

In examining the positions of the Bank and the Fund, on the one hand, and African countries, the other, a reader might tend to conclude at this point that the two sides have been engaged in deadlock and confrontation in the 1980s over how to deal with the African development crisis. In fact, however, while negotiations between the the Bank and the Fund and individual governments have been marred by bitter disagreement in many instances, there has been evidence in general terms of some convergence of perspectives. On the one hand, to varying degrees and with differential levels of political commitment and determination, many African governments have adopted Bank/Fund programs for economic stabilization and structural adjustment. On the other hand, the Bank and the Fund along with bilateral donors have come to recognize that the initial focus of reforms has been too narrow. In recognizing that economic policy reforms can only occur in tandem with broader social, environmental, and most recently political reforms, the Bank, the Fund and bilateral donors have broadened the definition of "structural adjustment" to incorporate some African concerns. Moreover, while recognizing the claims of newly liberated Eastern European countries, the Bank and the Fund have continued to place support for African reform high on their agendas, even as Africa has become more peripheral to many industrialized countries in economic, political, and military terms.[15]

The May, 1986 Special Session of the United Nations General Assembly provided a setting for African countries to assert effectively the need for a broadened reform agenda. The Special Session produced the United Nations Programme of Action for Economic and Recovery 1986-1990. Significantly the Programme emphasized food production and food security by contrast to a greater Bank/Fund focus on export promotion, livestock development as well as agricultural production, greater attention to reforestation and other environmental rehabilitation measures, and greater attention to the social dimension of development: the role of women, family planning, refugee support. The Programme recognized the need for additional external support for African economic reform but, at the assistance of the industrialized countries, no specific levels of financial commitment.

In the late 1980s and early 1990s, the World Bank's priorities also broadened from emphasis on specific economic policy reforms to incorporate attention to the distributional effects of policy reforms, the educational and health prerequisites for an economic renaissance, the industrial sector, the environment,

---

[14] That is, the debate was neither "responsible nor "irresponsible," but "aresponsible."
[15] See John Harbeson and Donald Rothchild, eds., Africa in World Politics (Boulder: Westview Press, 1991).

and regional cooperation.[16] As one Bank-sponsored review of structural adjustment policies put it:

> "The range of policy problems to address with structural adjustment continues to widen as environmental and social concerns come to the fore and as the former socialist countries rebuild their economies. Old problems, such as macroeconomic instability and agricultural stagnation, are increasingly recognized as symptoms of deeper needs for adjustment."[17]

The broadened reform agendas of multilateral and bilateral donors as well as African countries pointed to the possibility that fundamental issues of political responsibility for achieving an African economic renaissance would be addressed more directly than in the past. In fact broader, more fundamental international developments pointed in the same direction
A decade of transitions to democracy elsewhere in the developing world, notably in Latin America, capped by the collapse of communist regimes in Eastern Europe led inevitably to on, and within, African countries to follow suit. A significant aspect of decolonization in the 1950s and 1960s was that African nationalist movements became the governments of independent countries on the basis of only external constitutional negotiations with retiring colonial powers. In the late 1980s and early 1990s for the first time, many African countries sponsored domestic constitutional negotiations in the form of national conventions.[18] Transitions to multiparty democracy appeared to be in process, at different stages, in perhaps a majority of sub-Saharan African countries, dramatized by the 1992 Zambian elections in which the 30 year regime of Kenneth Kaunda was defeated and a peaceful transition to an opposition-led regime effected.[19]

These prospects for political liberalization in the form of transitions to multiparty democracy, however, do not in themselves make clear how African countries will address heretofore largely overlooked issues of political responsibility inherent in the campaigns for an African economic renaissance. The long term outcomes of these initiatives for political liberalization, now in their infancy, are by no means clear. There are no guarantees, and indeed some reasons to be skeptical, that processes of political liberalization and economic liberalization will prove to be as mutually reinforcing as prevalent tenets of classical liberal political philosophy would lead us to expect. The long term effects of international pressures for political liberalization and domestic African political processes, remain to be charted. Moreover, the effects of contradictory international pressures need to be sorted out: multilateral and bilateral pressures for democratization yet increasing African peripheralization in the foreign policy agendas of many industrialized countries. But, important as they are, these considerations are not the central ones.

---

[16] The World Bank, Sub-Saharan Africa: From Crisis to Sustainable Growth -- A Long Term Perspective Study (Washington, D.C.: World Bank, 1989).

[17] Vittorio Corbo, Stanley Fischer, and Stephen B. Webb, eds., Adjustment Lending Revisited: Policies to Restore Growth: A World Bank Symposium (Washington, D.C.: World Bank, 1992).

[18] I suggested the significance of the absence of internal constitutional negotiations in "Constitutions and Constitutionalism in Africa: A Tentative Theoretical Exploration" in Dov Ronen, ed., Democracy and Pluralism in Africa (Boulder: Lynne Rienner Press, 1986).

[19] The Carter Center of Emory University has carefully chronicled African progress toward democratization in a periodic publication entitled Africa Demos.

The heart of the problem is that political liberalization does not in itself predict how African countries will define or redefine political responsibility operationally in terms of structures and processes for stimulating an African economic renaissance. Indeed, neither African countries nor the donors have yet appeared to focus on the centrality of political responsibility issues to successful processes of economic and political liberalization.

The yet-to-be-debated issues of political responsibility include the following.

A. International Negotiations. First, what are responsible forms of negotiations between African governments and multilateral (and also bilateral) donors? While the Bank and the Fund are entitled to continue to contend that responsible African government behavior consists in adherence to what the Bank and the Fund define as economically orthodox, the issue is in fact larger and more complex. African governments, particularly newly elected ones, can claim an obligation to choose paths to reform, that continued Bank/Fund efforts to preempt these choices are self-defeating. Having surrendered the power to articulate their own policy directions for more than a decade, democratically elected African governments may be expected to reclaim the power to choose.

Moreover, a debate over responsible African government-Bank/Fund negotiations might lead to calls for a more experimental approach to defining the content of reform: that prudence, a concern for efficacy, and even in a sense respect for due process require careful and much more collaborative evaluation of the effects of reform initiatives.

B. Policy Implementation. Second, where does responsibility lie for the implementation of reforms intended to lift African countries out of their economic malaise? In the earlier days of structural adjustment programming there was a sense in some quarters that the tailoring of these policies to particular African circumstances was the responsibility of African countries themselves.[20] Rather quickly, however, donors came to emphasize that better governance was indeed a key to successful implementation of those policies. However, in the context of initiatives for political liberalization, there has been a tendency for the debate on good governance to flirt with circularity: democracy demands good governance, but definitions of good governance tend not be sharply differentiated from democracy.[21] Because of such circularity the idea of good governance, and its relationship to democracy, lacks operational specificity; i.e. at a minimum specification of a distribution of responsibilities for policy implementation calculated both to reflect regime norms and to achieve the intended policy outcomes.

What distribution of responsibilities for policy implementation will both the normative requirement of consistency with embryonic democratization and the instrumental one of achieving the intended outcomes? Here lies a very important double historical irony. This question has been central to the field of public administration for decades. Since the middle of the 20th century, however, under the influence of Herbert Simon's work, the field of organizational management has

---

[20] This comment is based largely on my own observations while serving as a senior social science analyst in the Agency for International Development from 1979 through 1982.

[21] For an analysis of this interrelationship, see Michael Hyden and Michael Bratton, Governance and Politics in Africa (Boulder: Lynn Rienner, 1992).

tended to treat its subject as generic and unified rather than segmented into subfields of public and business administration. One ironic consequence is that the field of organizational management appears to have become more rather than less detached intellectually from other social sciences, notably political science and economics. This is especially the case in the multidisciplinary study of development. The greater irony is that a potentially very important contribution of organizational management, though long recognized by practitioners of organizational management in both corporate industrial and less developed country settings, has been obscured from the study of political science and political economy.

In essence, in the second half the the twentieth century a fundamentally new understanding of organization has emerged, one that emphasizes contingency, participation, informal decisionmaking networks, decentralization, and the importance of organizational learning.[22] In societal settings of rapid change, traditional Weberian notions of neutral, predictable, top-down, indeed almost deductive policy implementation yield to acceptance that policy implementation must be context driven. To be context driven, decision-making must be decentralized, and decision-making networks must be informal and formed without relationship to formal organizational hierarchies. To be effective, those affected by policy decisions must no longer be passive recipients of administrative decisions but active participants in shaping and adapting those decisions to their circumstances. Mid and lower level administrators abandon the ideology of "neutral" tranmission of policy decisions for active roles as paricipants in shaping their application. Application and validation of these ideas has taken place not only in corporate settings in industrial societies but at the grassroots in less developed regions including Africa. In-depth impact evaluations have strongly established the efficacy of the new management in developing country settings.[23]

The new theory of organization has, thus, spawned a correspondingly new theory of the nature and distribution of responsibility for policy implementation. Largely unrecognized by students of development and of transitions to political democracy in particular, the new theory of organizational responsibility would appear to represent a major contribution to democratic theory as well as to effective policy implementation. A major effect of contemporary organization theory and practice is to diffuse responsibility more widely and more equitably within the

---

[22] Key works include Norman Uphoff, Learning from Gal Oya: Possibilities for Participatory Development and Post-Newtonian Social Science (Ithaca: Cornell University Press, 1992); Graham Allison, The Essence of Decision: Explaining the Cuban Missile Crisis (Boston: Little Brown, 1971); Chris Argyris and Donald Schon, Organizational Learning (Reading, MA: Addison-Wesley, 1978); Milton Esman and Norman Uphoff, Local Organizations: Intermediaries in Rural Development (Ithaca: Cornell University Press, 1984); Albert O. Hirschman, Development Projects Observed (Washington, D.C.: The Brookings Institution, 1967); David Korten, "Community Organization and Rural Development: A Learning Process Approach," 40 Public Administration Review 5 (1980), pp. 480-511; Tom Peters and Robert H. Waterman, In Search of Excellence: Lessons From America's Best-Run Companies (New York: Random House, 1982); Herbert Simon, Administrative Behavior (New York: Free Press, 1945); Dennis Rondinelli, Development Projects as Policy Experiments (London: Methuen, 1983), and Bryant Coralie and Louise G. White, Managing Development in the Third World (Boulder: Westview Press, 1982).

[23] In the early 1980s, the Agency for International Development sponsored a long series of special in depth impact evaluations of selected projects. These evaluations strongly supported the efficacy of participatory development.

organization and also outside the organization to include the organization's constituents: those whom the organization is to serve and lead. Organizations and their constituents are to define collaboratively and experimentally how policies are to be shaped and implemented. The contemporary macro-level focus on democratic transitions has yet to incorporate these more micro-level organizational management findings, of nearly two decades standing, on which the durability of those transitions may well ultimately depend.

C. The Politics of State-Society Relations. A third key issue in the area of political responsibility for economic reform and development concerns the broad area of state-society relations. Many have observed a paradox of the campaign for structural adjustment: in pressing African states to surrender major responsibility for economic development to the private sector both the Bank and the Fund have placed new and heavy responsibilities upon the state itself to effect that transition. An important outcome has been a prevalent statecentric approach to the politics of structural adjustment that has tended to emphasize the autonomy of the state as a prerequisite for economic reform founded nonetheless on the centrality of the private sector to that end.[24] An important recent study claims, for example, that "the insulation of central decision makers from distributive claims will enhance the state's capacity to launch new initiatives."[25]

The heart of the problem is a simple, familiar tension bordering on conflict between the politics of transitions to multiparty democracy and the politics of economic reform, or structural adjustment in donor terminology. The first presupposes increasing external responsiveness by the state to society; the latter requires much less such external responsiveness in favor of state generated reform policies.[26] The one emphasizes less state autonomy, the other more. Underlying the debate over state autonomy are unarticulated issues concerning the nature of the state and the basic political "rules of the game." The state autonomy literature implicitly reduces the idea of the state to that of government, treats society as in some sense government's competitor for power, and fails to make a place either for rules of the game governing that "competition" or for processes of defining and sustaining those rules. In short, it obscures the issue of political responsibility for government-society interactions. Given the fragility of political orders in much of Africa and the requirements for an end to the continent's economic malaise, this is indeed a serious oversight. Nor is it clear that this issue is being addressed in practical terms in the course of democratization movements; i.e., it is very possible for multiparty elections to become a single end in itself as distinct from institutionalizing a set of rules of the game, or constitution, of which routinized free and competitive elections would be one key component.

An alternative would be to reserve the term "state" for such constitutional

---

[24] See for example Stephen Haggard and Robert R. Kaufman, eds., The Politics of Economic Adjustment: International Constraints, Distributional Conflicts and the State (Princeton: Princeton University Press, 1992) as well as earlier volumes edited by Joan Nelson, Fragile Coalitions: The Politics of Economic Adjustment (1990) and Economic Crisis and Policy Choice (1990). More society-centric literature has had relatively less impact on the adjustment debate as of early 1993.
[25] Haggard and Kaufman, op.cit.
[26] Gilbert, op.cit., specifies a two by two matrix based on formal v. informal responsibility and external v. internal responsibility

rules of the game ("regime" would be an alternative) and to operationalize the reemergent idea of civil society as the instrumentality by which rules of the game are established and sustained. A key concept in the history of political philosophy, the idea of civil society, has recently been resurrected in the context of transitions to democracy in Latin America, Eastern Europe, and Africa.[27] But in this recent empirical usage, it remains very underspecified. Often it seems to treat "civil society" almost as synonymous with society at large. However, a common element among the disparate definitions of civil society in political philosophy is that it refers to societal processes for defining the state, in the sense of the constitutional rules of the game, including how political processes should relate to those of society at large.[28] Development of such a civil society may then hold a key to the locus of responsibility for the nature of the modern state.

Conclusions

The conclusion emerging from the foregoing analysis is that in fundamental respects the question of political responsibility for development in African countries, including processes of both economic and political liberalization, has been inadequately addressed. In seeking to define the the agenda for reform and in critiquing that agenda, both international donors and African countries have neglected to address underlying questions of political responsibility. Emerging initiatives for democratization in conjunction with economic reform make more evident the need to identify and deal with issues of political responsibility. But even within the framework of increasingly normatively oriented discussion of political change in African countries, key normatively-based issues of political responsibility remain to be specified and addressed. The foregoing analysis leads to the conclusion that a more disciplined focus on issues of political responsibility is important, not only to an intellectual understanding, but to the fruition of the quest for an African economic and political renaissance.

---

[27] Representative of this burgeoning civil society literature is Vladimir Tismaneau, In Search of Civil Society: Independent Peace Movements in the Soviet Bloc (New York and London: Routledge, 1990); Michael Bratton, "Beyond the State: Civil Society and Associational Life in Africa," 41 World Politics 3 (1989), pp. 407-429; Jean Francois Bayart, "Civil Society in Africa," in Patrick Chabal, ed., Political Domination in Africa: Reflections on the Limits of Power (Cambridge: Cambridge University Press, 1986); Peter Ekeh, "Colonialism and the Two Publics in Africa," in Chabal, ed., op.cit.; John Keane, ed., Civil Society and the State: A New European Perspective (London: Verso, 1988), and Alfred Stepan, Rethinking Military Politics: Brazil and the Southern Cone (Princeton: Princeton University Press, 1988).
[28] Naomi Chazan, John Harbeson, and Donald Rothchild, eds., Civil Society and the State in Africa (Boulder: Lynne Rienner, 1992).

CHAPTER TEN

RESPONSIBLE TRANSNATIONAL CORPORATIONS?

JONATHAN F. GALLOWAY

What does it mean for a corporation to be responsible? There is no one answer to this question, even within the bounds of a single discipline. Economically, a firm could be responsible if it supported mercantilist principles, but this would be seen as behaving irresponsibly according to laissez-faire assumptions. Politically, a transnational corporation (TNC) could be seen as acting responsibly if it is accountable to the constitutional principles of the state. On the other hand, acting patriotically could be seen as an illegal and unethical act from the point of view of international norms and codes of conduct. Morally, a firm could be seen as above reproach if the consequences of its bottom-line planning result, through the invisible hand, in the greater good. On the other hand, beneficial consequences may not be enough to merit approbation from another ethical perspective - one that considers the explicit intentions of the firm. The many meanings of responsibility remind us of the twelve values connected with the concept according to the analysis of Charles E. Gilbert.[1]

What has interested me theoretically is not only what it means for a TNC to act responsibly according to existing models but to clearly distinguish the levels at which TNCs operate, ending with the planetary perspective that is appropriate to our age. Today, a new synthesis is needed, which I call world political economy.

The life history of a TNC looks something like this.[2] The firm starts out within the boundaries of a territorial state. It is chartered in that state or in a sub-unit such as the state of Delaware. After it captures a working share of the domestic market, it then begins to export its products abroad. To serve its foreign markets, it then sets up manufacturing plants (or, in the case of banks, branches) abroad. After awhile, it integrates its operations regionally and perhaps globally in terms of multiple sourcing, transfer pricing and labor contracts. It may look at each of its markets from a national perspective, but political boundaries begin to get in the way of economic rationality. The law of supply and demand, which does not assume the existence of the state, takes precedence over the law of comparative advantage, which presupposes the existence of national economies. Eventually, if economic logic supersedes nationalistic imperatives, what we see is a convergence of national economies and integration at the world level. The basic actors become individuals,

---

[1] Charles E. Gilbert, "The Framework of Administrative Responsibility," The Journal of Politics, Vol. 21 (1959), pp. 373-407, 374-378. These values are responsiveness, flexibility, consistency, stability, leadership, probity, candor, competence, efficiency, prudence, due process and accountability. In this essay, I emphasize leadership, efficiency, prudence and accountability.

[2] Raymond Vernon, Sovereignty at Bay (New York: Basic Books, 1971), pp. 66-70.

firms, industries and parts of governments linked to other parts of governments locally and internationally and not states linked to other states as monolithic rational actors pursuing holistic policies. As Charles Kindleberger writes, "The nation state is just about through as an economic unit."[3]

In this scenario, national political economy is transformed into international political economy, which is, with the waning of national economies, replaced with regional and then world political economy. In the first two levels of theory and practice, the basic unit of analysis is the state; in world political economy, the basic units of analysis are individuals, industries, firms and factions within governments. What matters is not the international division of labor based on core and peripheral countries but the world division of labor based on the classical factors of production - land, labor and capital - plus technology.

The original contribution of this vantage point is to look at the world political economy -not international political economy - in terms of a pluralistic political processes and economic markets operating at the global level - and not just within and between nations. And, just as the nation or the nation state is not the primary unit of analysis, the world economy is not the sum of national economies. The whole is more than the sum of its parts. Global policy, to the extent there is any, is not the sum of national policies between states in an interdependent world. Rather, there is another level of analysis - analysis at the world level per se - in an integrated, not interdependent, world political economy.

Measures of such an integrated world political economy are world direct foreign investment, joint ventures, the development of world money, illegal immigration, the size of the world underground economy; measures of interdependence, on the other hand, are trade statistics, coordinated macro-economic policies and aid patterns.

The accumulated stock of world direct foreign investment was $830 billion at the end of 1986. This can be taken as an indication of dominant economies controlling other economies as is done in the dependency literature, or it can be taken as a measure of industries integrating worldwide. The latter perspective needs to be taken if observers are not to become slaves to defunct theories. Similarly, joint ventures between firms from different countries can be analyzed from an interdependency perspective, i.e., how dependent are two national economies on each other? or, from a global industries perspective, as indicators of integration and rationalization in industry structure worldwide. The poverty of much of the debate on declining hegemony and de-industrialization is that it does not even entertain the possibility of anything other than a state-centric bias.

Another measure of integration is the tendency of national currencies to become world currencies. For instance, the U.S. dollar is not an expression purely of the wealth of the U.S. economy within its borders; it is a world currency beyond the control of U.S. monetary authorities. A fourth measure of world integration is the mobility of labor as a factor of production. If labor moves not according to national immigration laws but the economic demand for labor, then a national economy is not composed only of its own national labor force but an illegal work force as well. A fifth measure of integration is the world underground economy. Each national economy has its own off-the-books economic transactions. For instance, it is estimated that the underground economy in the United States is ten percent of the G.N.P., in Italy, twenty-five percent. Some of this black market

---

[3] Charles P. Kindleberger, American Business Abroad (New York: Yale University Press, 1969), p. 207.

activity is international, e.g., the drug trade, so if this industry has worldwide sales of $200 billion a year, this should be added to measure the size of the world economy beyond the books of national economies. We should call a world political economy perspective a fourth image beyond Kenneth Waltz's three images.[4] At this level of analysis, we notice not only economic theory and practice within and between states but beyond them.

Similarly, cultures do not just exist inside nations but beneath, around and over them. It is often assumed that each nation has its own homogeneous culture or national character. But there are many cultures that can transcend and supersede national boundaries. As there can be a culture associated with a nation, there can also be a culture associated with a corporation, e.g., IBM's culture, or with an industry, e.g., the culture of the oil industry. As there are civil societies within states, there is also a world civil society beyond states.

Following Robert Gilpin, let us look at world political economy in terms of three existing theoretical approaches to political economy.[5] These are liberalism, mercantilism and Marxism. Then, we shall examine these economic theories in light of several theories of political accountability and corporate social responsibility in order to return to our initial question, "What does it mean for a corporation to be responsible?"

Liberalism

From the vantage point of liberalism as an economic doctrine, the multinational corporation (MNC) would be constrained in its operations by two laws - one, the law of supply and demand,[6] the other, the law of comparative advantage.[7] The first law assumes the existence of a market, ideally a competitive and not an oligopolistic or monopolistic market. Each firm or individual seeking his or her own advantage, creates through an invisible hand the wealth of a nation. This is the story simply put of what today is called micro-economics. We need not concern ourselves with whether MNCs intend to be moral or deliver goods to the market of high quality and at a fair price. What we are interested in is market efficiency via the consequences of corporate behavior in a competitive environment. The analogy to the competitive market in world politics is the structure of the balance of power and the analogy in American government is the "interior structure of the government" as Madison pointed out in Federalist No. 51.[8] In these two cases, however, the structure of the system is clearly oligopolistic - not competitive because the basic

---

[4] Kenneth N. Waltz, Man, The State and War: A Theoretical Analysis (New York: Columbia University Press, 1959); cf. Robert C. North, War, Peace, Survival: Global Politics and Conceptual Synthesis (Boulder: Westview Press, 1990). His fourth image emphasizes environmental concerns but not global industries in the world political economy. My fourth image analysis emphasizes both.

[5] Robert Gilpin, The Political Economy of International Relations (Princeton: Princeton University Press, 1987).

[6] Adam Smith, An Inquiry Into the Nature and Causes of the Wealth of Nations, Canan edition (Chicago: The University of Chicago Press, 1976), p. 65.

[7] David Ricardo, The Principles of Political Economy and Taxation (Cambridge: Cambridge University Press, 1951), pp. 134-136.

[8] James Madison, "The Federalist No. 51," in The Federalist (New York: Random House, n.d.), p. 336.

units of the system are so few. Perhaps a synthesis of these levels is best reached in Clausewitz's observation, "It would be better, instead of comparing (war) with any Art, to liken it to a business competition, which is also a conflict of human interests and activities; and it is still more like State Policy, which again, on its part, may be looked upon as a kind of business competition on a grand scale."[9] In brief, accountability and efficiency are found in the structure of competition, not in the initial intentions of the actors. These values, corresponding to two of Gilbert's meanings of responsibility, are political and economic. They can be seen in terms of integrated measures of power and wealth rather than separating the two spheres as is sometimes done.

But what are the political and economic boundaries of the market? This is where David Ricardo's law of comparative advantage comes in. Under this law, it is assumed that the factors of production are immobile between nations but perfectly mobile within them. As I read this law, there is no room for transnational corporation. There is room for trade but not for direct foreign investment, which would mean that capital moves beyond state boundaries. Thus, the boundary of the market is the territorial border of the state. Each firm can be a patriotic citizen of its own state. However, under the law of supply and demand, to cite Adam Smith, the division of labor is not constrained by national boundaries but by the extent of the market.[10] Thus, there can be a world division of labor, and world or global markets and global industries. I believe Thomas Jefferson recognized this in its negative - not its positive - aspects when he wrote, "Merchants have no country. The mere spot they stand on does not constitute so strong an attachment as that from which they draw their gains." So, if IBM draws gains from around the world, who is to say it is a U.S.-based MNC making foreign investments and not a world corporation trying to overcome the parochialism of state sovereignty. In the latter perspective the accountability of the firm is not to its home country but to the world - if there is a competitive market. Let's examine another case. A Japanese firm makes a joint venture with an American firm in order to help the Japanese economy a la an industrial strategy by the Ministry of International Trade and Industry (MITI). Its intentions are mercantilistic. But the consequences may not be. The consequences may involve breaking down barriers between national economies and the gradual creation of a world economy. This would be the logic of liberalism.

Let's look at another case. Toyota invests in England. Is its auto plant part of the Japanese economy, the British economy, Europe's, or the worldwide automobile industry? The latter answer should certainly be entertained for analytical comprehensiveness. The purest market case would be an illegal firm, e.g., the Medellin Cartel, in an illegal industry, e.g. the cocaine industry, integrating the world underground economy which may account for 10-25% of world product.

The clearest case of a contemporary "liberal" writer who rejects intentional altruism by the state or the firm as a basis for social responsibility is Milton Friedman. He has this to say about corporate social responsibility: "Few trends could so thoroughly undermine the very foundations of our free society as the acceptance by corporate officials of a social responsibility other than to make as

---

[9] Carl von Clausewitz, On War (New York: Penguin Books, 1980), pp. 202-203.
[10] Smith, op.cit., p. 21.

much money for their stockholders as possible."[11] Corporations behave responsibly when they follow government laws not when they go beyond them. Going beyond the laws of a country is unnecessary because after this point, the laws of economics take over. Of course, if the economic law is one that assumes that national economies are the basic units of the world economy, then the law would be comparative advantage and its various emendations, e.g., the Heckscher-Ohlin principle. However, if the law is supply and demand, the world economy can be seen as composed of industries and firms and individuals. Eventually, the stockholders would not be national stockholders but world stockholders. There would be world money, world stock exchanges and "our free society" would be a world civil society!

Marxism

Under Marxism, the MNC would be constrained in its behavior by four laws. First is the law of concentration which posits a logic moving towards monopoly; i.e., the natural state of market is not competitive as under liberalism; rather, it is monopolistic. The second law is the law of declining rate of profit, which is related to the third law, the law of crisis and discontinuity: i.e., the natural state of capitalism is one of disequilibrium and not equilibrium as it posited by liberalism. The fourth law, deriving from Lenin, is the law of unequal development, which explains inequality between nations, firms, banks and industries.

These laws operate at the world level. A world market comes into existence not a series of national markets. Thus Karl Marx and Friedrich Engels write in *The Communist Manifesto*, "The need of a constantly expanding market for its products chases the bourgeoisie over the whole surface of the globe. All old-established national industries have been destroyed or are daily being destroyed... In place of the old local and national self-seclusion and self-sufficiency, we have intercourse in every direction, universal inter-dependence of nations."[12] Firms in the market such as the British East India Company are through their trade in poison - the opium trade - creating the conditions for revolution in China, and India and as Marx wrote in 1853, "...whatever may have been the crimes of England she was the unconscious tool (cf. "invisible hand") of history in bringing about that revolution."[13]

Clearly, a Marxist does not have much to say in favor of the honesty of companies or states in the world capitalist society. Nevertheless, capitalism sets the stage for socialism and thus the activities of MNCs can be applauded in terms of their consequences.

At a more concrete level, Marx examines specific industries and sees differences between industries in their contribution to basic human needs. Marx and Engels write in *The German Ideology*, "The 'history of humanity' must always be studied and treated in relation to the history of industry and exchange."[14] Take, for

---

[11] Milton Friedman, Capitalism and Freedom (Chicago: The University of Chicago Press, 1962), p. 133.
[12] Kenneth N. Waltz, "The Myth of National Interdependence," in Charles P. Kindleberger, ed., The International Corporation (Cambridge: M.I.T. Press, 1970).
[13] Karl Marx, "The British Rule in India," in Robert C. Tucker, ed., The Marx-Engels Reader, 2nd edition (New York: W. W. Norton & Co., 1978), p. 658.
[14] Karl Marx and Frederick Engels, The German Ideology (New York: International Publishers, 1960), p. 18.

instance, "the case of sugar and coffee which have proved their world-historical-importance in the nineteenth century by the fact that the lack of these products, occasioned by the Napoleonic Continental system, caused the Germans to rise against Napoleon, and thus became the real basis for the glorious wars of Liberation of 1813."[15] Or, take the case of cotton. Marx writes:

> Direct slavery is just as much the pivot of bourgeois industry as machinery, credits, etc. Without slavery you have no cotton; without cotton you have no modern industry. It is slavery that gave the colonies their value; it is the colonies that created world trade, and it is world trade that is the pre-condition of large-scale industry. Thus slavery is an economic category of the greatest importance.[16]

To understand Marx's approach to the responsibility of the TNC, one must first understand the system as a whole, i.e., capitalism. One must understand particular industries and how corporations act within those sectors. One must not look at corporate policies of social responsibility but at actual behavior in terms of working conditions and wages within the system and industry.

Mercantilism

Under mercantilist assumptions, the transnational firm is clearly the instrument of the state rather than the other way around. Both liberalism and Marxism ignore the staying power of the nation state and the nation state system. To assume that the firm is rendering national sovereignty obsolete[17] or that sovereignty is at bay,[18] is to be unaware of the historical evidence and the power of the state and the state system.[19]

The dominant school in political economy today is neo-mercantilism. Its purely political counterpart is realism and neo-realism. It is assumed that the world economy is made up of national economies. The law of supply and demand stops at national boundaries and when it doesn't and it is to the disadvantage of the state or at least the states that matter,[20] then states will pursue trade and investment policies which maximize power over wealth.[21] Thus, as an example, the U.S. CIA overthrew the government of Mossadegh in Iran in 1953 and then encouraged U.S. firms to move into the market that had been created politically. International regimes are created by states.[22] For example, the European Economic Community was the deliberate creation of European states and depends for its daily existence upon their

---

[15] Ibid., pp. 38-39.

[16] Karl Marx, The Poverty of Philosophy (Moscow: Foreign Languages Publishing House, n.d.), p. 107.

[17] Kindleberger, op.cit.

[18] Vernon, op.cit.

[19] Waltz, op.cit.

[20] Kenneth N. Waltz, Theory of International Politics (Reading, MA: Addison-Wesley, 1979), p. 72.

[21] Friedrich List, The National System of Political Economy (London: Longmans, Green, 1916).

[22] Robert O. Keohane, After Hegemony: Cooperation and Discord in the World Political Economy (Princeton: Princeton University Press, 1984).

continuing support and collaborative effort. TNCs cannot be divorced from the system of sovereign states. Even if a free trade regime is established along GATT principles and its logic might lead to the decline of sovereignty, this decline will never actually occur because of the autonomy of the state. The accountability of the firm is guaranteed by political checks and balances and the market, but the market is set up politically and thus, when push comes to shove, power matters. There are no economic laws under mercantilism which guarantee this outcome because the basis of economics is state power. For instance, when Japan trades cars with the United States, the boundaries of the market, e.g., "voluntary export restraints," are established politically - not by the law of supply and demand or the law of comparative advantage. Economics is political economics and political economics is a series of games. The best way to understand this reality is by studying game theory and not looking for timeless laws or formulas. This perspective accounts for the dominant tendency among contemporary students of international political economy to study the prisoner's dilemma.[23] Reality is seen as an iterated series of encounters between discrete, rational actors rather than the result of systemic imperatives.

The world political economy perspective

I call my perspective a world political economy approach because I believe that the international political economy school emphasizes the nation, as its name implies, or the state, or more usually the government. (The state is often defined as the government - leaving out the people!) Going back to R. M. MacIver, we may note that "...the state is greater and more inclusive than government. A state has a constitution, a code of laws, a way of setting up a government, a body of citizens."[24] Or, as Max Weber writes, "The state is a human community which exercises the legitimate monopoly of violence in a given territory."[25] Continuing this definitional line to be more inclusive and precise, I think that there is an additional level to the state, the nation and the government. This level is not composed just of international organizations, regimes, or the balance of power system but of TNCs as worldwide interest groups, legal and illegal global industries and a civil society and culture that does not exist solely within countries but beneath, around and beyond them. The following graphic indicates three different ways of viewing the parts of the whole world economy:

---

[23] Ibid.
[24] R.M. MacIver, The Web of Government (revised edition), (New York: The MacMillan Co., 1965), p. 24.
[25] Max Weber, "Politics as a Vocation," in H. S. Gerth and C. Wright Mills, eds., From Max Weber: Essays in Sociology (New York: Oxford University Press, 1958), pp. 77-128.

MODELS OF THE WORLD ECONOMY

	Model A	Model B	Model C
World Composed of:	National Economies	Industries	Multinational Corporations
	USA	Autos	Ford
	Japan	Computers	IBM
	Germany	Oil	Shell
Measures:	GNP	Shipments	Sales

Which theory is more correct? This depends on questions one wishes to address. For instance if one wants to ask questions about the bases of national power during war, Model A would be more correct. If one wants to understand the history of industrial society, Model B would be the place to begin. And, if one wants to understand market strategies on a world basis, Model C would be the place to commence. What one must avoid is a persuasive definition of the world economy which leaves out one or two of the models. In addition one should avoid the fallacy of composition which would see the whole as the sum of the parts of one model or all three models. There are laws of behavior for each model, but are there laws derived from a theory which links all three models?

As John Burton writes," the study of world society is a much wider study than the relations of units within it."[26] I took this perspective in looking at the International Telecommunications Satellite Organization (INTELSAT).[27] This organization was initially established by international agreement in 1964 and now has 121 member nations and corresponding private and public entities operating communications satellites in the geostationary orbit at 22,300 miles above the equator. I saw this commercial international organization chartered by states and operated in a transnational subculture of telecommunications agencies as a geocentric firm because of its abilities to integrate national economies at the world and outer space level. Reality is not interdependence between nations but integration beyond them in the world political economy. This integration is technical and economic, however. It is not political or cultural although it can become a base for these forms so integration.

In a more recent article I note that INTELSAT "enables peoples, firms and groups within and beyond...nations to integrate into the world market. No other industry is organized this way...[28] Although they are world industries, the oil, computer, automobile, cocaine and others are not set up by treaty and run by transnational organizations as cost-sharing cooperatives. Perhaps INTELSAT realizes at the world level Gilbert's ideals and ideas on accountability, efficiency,

---

[26] John W. Burton, World Society (New York: Cambridge University Press, 1972), p. 19.
[27] Jonathan F. Galloway, "Worldwide Corporations and International Integration: The Case of INTELSAT," International Organization Vol. XXIV, No. 3 (Summer 1970), pp. 503-519.
[28] Jonathan F. Galloway, "INTELSAT'S Markets and the New Competitors," International Journal, Vol. XLII, No. 2 (Spring 1987), pp. 256-275.

leadership and representation.[29] The public interest at the world level is realized by intention and through beneficial consequences within an organization that contains representatives from all kinds of states - North-South-East and West - and fulfills a definite need in terms of standards of economic efficiency and political participation.

My second article on TNCs came out in 1971.[30] In this piece I looked at multinational firms as worldwide interest groups and I developed three hypothesis for examination - one that MNCs were reinforcing the integration of the western world; second that MNCs were aiding, but with negligible consequences so far, the convergence of the East with the West (what with glasnost, perestroika and the end of the Cold War, this may be more likely now); and, third, that MNCs were integrating the less developed countries into the world economy but in an unbalanced manner leading to underdevelopment. While MNCs could be tools of their home governments (mercantilism), or control the governments (Marx), or be good citizens of all state sin which they operate (TNC perspective), I also posited that MNCs could be autonomous interest groups in the world economy. Today this might be called a fourth image perspective at the level of world political economy. The following chart indicates this fourth image:

FOUR IMAGES OF POLITICAL ECONOMY AND FOUR THEORIES

	Mercantilism	Liberaism	Marxism	World Political Economy
Ist image (individual)	power struggle	truck, barter and exchange	needs	synthesis of first three
2nd image (state system)	raison d'etat	liberal state	instrument of ruling class	industrial state
3rd image (state system)	balance of power system	interdependence of nationstates	imperialism	integration of states and nations
4th image (planet)	none!	world civil society	communism	planet earth and global industries

In 1972, I wrote:

> The nation-state, especially the great and superpowers, will not be replaced, but the dynamics of the oligopolistic, technological, and profit imperatives could very well make multinational enterprises their coterminous and contiguous partners. It is thus incorrect to stress a conflict between states

---

[29] Gilbert, op.cit., and "Operative Doctrines of Representation," American Political Science Review, Vol. LVII, No. 3 (September 1963), pp. 604-618.

[30] Jonathan F. Galloway, "Multinational Enterprises as Worldwide Interest Groups," Politics & Society, Vol. 2, No. 1 (November 1971), pp. 1-20.

and corporations or economics and politics for what we are viewing is a penetrated system of symbiotic relationships where the important boundaries are increasingly functional and associational rather than territorial.[31]

As territory wanes in importance certain transnational factors of production are increasingly brought into play. In 1973, I brought this perspective to bear with respect to labor as a transnational factor of production. Rather than looking at national labor unions in a comparative perspective, I attempted to see whether labor was organizing transnationally sector by sector. While labor is not as mobile as capital across national boundaries, I found that there is some coordination and institutionalization at the world level in the International Trade Secretariats, especially in the automobile industry, and that this movement attempts to develop labor practices which are consistent not only in developed countries but also in selected cases in less developed countries as well.[32]

My current work continues the interest in TNCs, global industries and world political economy. Further, I have always been interested in the normative and ethical aspects of liberal, Marxist, neo-mercantilist and world political economy perspectives. Thus in a 1979 article on sanctions against South Africa, Robert Baade and I wrote "Our value commitment is to a South African state and government which represents all its people and guarantees their human rights."[33] Part of this value commitment can be achieved (from a world political economy perspective) at the grassroots level through actions by nongovernmental groups such as churches, labor unions and corporations. From a mercantilist perspective, the result can be attained by state policies or coordinated state policies through the U.N. and other intergovernmental organizations.

In discussing the depletion of the ozone layer in 1989 I wrote:

> The 1987 Montreal Protocol on Substances That Deplete the Ozone Layer to the 1985 Vienna Convention for the Protection of the Ozone Layer moves forward the urgent task of preserving the ozone shield so that harmful ultraviolet rays from the sun do not reach the earth's surface. The ozone layer is a natural phenomenon, a common resource, produced by the laws of nature, not the activities of mankind. But the logics of mankind's activities on earth--economic, political, technological and legal--threaten this life-protecting barrier. On the other hand, these same logics, differently conceptualized and implemented, offer a way out of our current chronic crisis. Consensus building and cooperation by scientists, environmentalists, statesmen and lawyers may well enable us to manage the problem to the benefit of this generation, and, most importantly, future generations.[34]

---

[31] Jonathan F. Galloway, "The Military-Industrial Linkages of U.S. Based Multinational Corporations, International Studies Quarterly, Vol. 16, No. 4 (December 1972), pp. 491-510.

[32] Jonathan F. Galloway, "The Multinationalization of Labor: U.S. Perspective," in Kurt Tudyka, ed., Multinational Corporations and Labor Unions (Nijmegen: Werkuitgave Sun, 1973), pp. 197-208.

[33] Robert A. Baade and Jonathan F. Galloway, "Economic Sanctions Against South Africa," Alternatives, Vol. IV, No. 4 (March 1979), pp. 487-505.

[34] Jonathan F. Galloway, "International Law and the Protection of the Ozone Layer," Proceedings of the Thirty-First Colloquium on the Law of Outer Space (Washington: American Institute of Aeronautics and Astronautics, 1989), pp. 274-278.

This consensus building occurs not only nationally and internationally but at the level of world society insofar as these actors form transnational linkages, which they do.

Over the past two years I have been concerned with illegal TNCs in illegal global industries, i.e., the Medellin and Cali "cartels" in the cocaine trade. Here we see the pure operation of the law of supply and demand unconcerned with ethics and law except as a cost of doing business and an unintentional source of large profits. The operation of illegal industries is fascinating in terms of its implications for the study of world political economics at the level of the state and governmental policy. From the perspective of legitimate governments the responsible meaning of honest policy is clear - the "War on Drugs" - but in terms of consequences, responsibility meaning prudence is not so obvious. Rather, we seem to be in a surreal world of magic realism, tragedy, paradox and social decay. From the perspective of the drug syndicates, the world society is a Hobbesian state of nature. Yet the analogies between illegal industries and legal industries such as tobacco, alcohol and gambling bring us back to questions about the moral health of our societies locally, nationally and at the world level. It alerts us to the perspective that not all industries are equal in their effects. Rather, we seem to be in a surreal world of magic realism, tragedy, paradox and social decay. They alert us to the perspective that not all industries are equal in their contributions to mankind. A political economy worthy of its name should be able to distinguish between the cultures and the products of various industries and not just examine the industries from the point of view of sales, profits, employment and growth. Thus, we should look at TNCs not just in terms of host-home country relationships and questions of power bargaining but in terms of the consequences of the industries' products and practices on human values.

In an article I wrote in 1972 on linkages between the MNCs and the military-industrial complex, "optimism" about the decline of territory as a significant factor in World Politics gives way to pessimism[35]. We see not only military-industrial complexes within and between nations but within the fabric of world society. Frequent stories of fraud, bribery, deceit and "accidents" tell us that the norms of this world corporate culture are not prudence, probity, candor or accountability.[36] Instead they are an unpleasant combination of the arrogance, futility and folly of power.

In my study, I tabulated the military sales and foreign sales as a percentage of total sales of selected U. S. firms, rank ordered a comparison of defense linked and multinational industries by Standard Industrial Classification numbers, and undertook a comparison of government sales and domestic sales in six industries.[37] In light of this examination and case study evidence, I made several observations. One concerned conversion. With successful arms control agreements (and now with the end of the Cold War), conversion from military to civilian expenditures is rational, but reason runs up against entrenched interests which have been present so long that they are structural parts of certain industries, most particularly the aerospace industry. James R. Kurth points to the continuity of top defense contractors and a "follow-on imperative" by which "about the time a production line phases out of one major defense contract, it phases in production in a new one,

---

35 Galloway, op.cit., 1972.
36 Gilbert, op.cit.,1959, pp. 376-77.
37 Galloway, op.cit., 1972.

usually within a year."[38] He says this occurs regardless of periods of detente and "the most formidable obstacle (to restructuring defense) is not the Soviet army but the American aerospace industry."[39]

In light of the follow-on imperative and other reasons, moving beyond the nuclear and military culture seems unlikely, unless, the U. S., the Russian Federation, Germany, Japan and other powers take on the role of world leaders in directing attention at ending arms races, preventing further environmental degradation, and serving as peacemakers through the United Nations in trouble spots in the Middle East and elsewhere. Leadership is a public good and what the world requires now is global - not national - leadership. For instance, the protection of the environment has been a major agenda item at a number of conferences since the end of the Cold War, e.g. the United Nations Conference on Environment and Development in Rio in June, 1992. Further, the United States, Russia and other states are beginning to cooperate on the war on drugs.

In contrast to this view emphasizing top-down leadership is the perspective that in fact the Cold War is over - the people know it - and the leaders will gradually catch up with them in recognizing the obsolescence of war, bloated military budgets, arms races and nuclear deterrence. Responsibility in terms of leadership can come at the grassroots level and through transnational movements as well as from governments. In this regard, we may note the historical movement against slavery as well as the contemporary environmental movement and the role of peoples' revolutions in the democracy movement in Eastern Europe. The idea that Madison started with was that founders could structure interest, passion and the form of government to work for the public good. That is what I am trying to do at the world level with the theory of world political economy.

Corporate social responsibility today

At the risk of being procrustean, let me outline TNC social responsibility by reference to the following matrix:

	good intentions	bad intentions
good consequences	INTELSAT (communications satellites)	Rockefeller's Standard Oil (monopoly - competition)
bad consequences	Dupont (CFCs)	Medellin Cartel (cocaine)

This way of organizing our assessments looks at responsibility in terms of deontological and utilitarian ethical theories. The distinctions are too sharp in the sense that any corporation has within itself and overt ime bad and good policies and outcomes but the above pedagogical devise is a good first step in the analysis. It is a

---

[38] James R. Kurth, "The Military-Industrial Complex Revisited," in Joseph Kruzel, ed., American Defense Annual, 1989-1990 (Lexington: Lexington Books, 1989), pp. 195-215, 199.
[39] Ibid., p. 214.

good foil to one dimensional evaluations or selective use of case studies.

When I ask my students for examples of corporate social responsibility, all I receive are cases of neglect, fraud, blackmail, criminal conspiracies, and worse. We can think of the East India Co. and the opium trade, I.T.T. and Chile, Union Carbide and Bhopal, Pemex and corruption, Nestle's and infant formula sales in less developed countries, Exxon and the Exxon Valdez, United Fruit and Guatemala, Rockefeller and the Robber Barons, and the Medellin cartel and cocaine. Few contrary examples are offered. When I mention Texaco funding the Saturday afternoon opera, my students look at this not as charity but a form of advertising. When I mention DuPont's decision to cease producing chloroflurocarbons by the year 2000 (now earlier), my students say the company should do it now. I should say that some of my students are not only International Relations majors but Business majors - so these students are choosing to enter a profession that they evidently do not admire. But they are realistic about it. They do not to believe in liberalism and the invisible hand. They appear to believe in fair trade and neo-mercantilism. Fortunately, I think to myself, these students are not acting or playing mercantile or mercenary "games" with their professor in their undergraduate educational experience; at least I like to think so. Many students have supported the stand for college divestment from TNCs doing business in South Africa, but maybe this was because they were caught up in symbolic political economy - not real political economy. On graduation day 1989 at Lake Forest College, some students wore green arm bands to protest the commencement speaker, Sam Skinner, the Secretary of Transportation, who was seen as responsible for procrastination in dealing with the oil spill in Prince William Sound. So my students seem to be taking implicitly the position that social reality is destitute of morality while they, on the other hand, without being self-righteous, have an innate moral sense. Are they Rousseauians!

My argument is that responsibility at the world level does not have to rely on the conscious intentions of individuals, states, corporations or international organizations. Realists often equate morality with being moralistic and self-righteous and certainly this cautionary perspective merits our continued respect. However, the notion of a world public good (not national public goods, e.g., defense, which may be incompatible with the general interest of mankind) does require some synthesis of deontological and consequentialist ethical theories. The founder of post-war realism, Hans J. Morgenthau, recognized that vulgar realism was atavistic when he wrote in 1980, "If you look at the concrete problems, you realize that most of them transcend national boundaries and that the concept of the national state as the organizing principle of the political world is as obsolete today as the feudal principle of organization was two hundred years ago."[40] Let me outline my own synthesis beyond realism by extending the arguments of Madison in numbers 10 and 51 of The Federalist.

Paraphrasing Madison in Federalist No. 51, we may say that for a firm to be responsible it must exist in a structure of economic power in which greed must be made to counteract greed. The profit of the firm must be connected with the wealth of the nation, then - my addendum - with the wealth of the world. It may be a reflection of human nature that the structure of the market must be made to control the abuses of the corporation, but what is the corporation itself but a reflection of

---

[40] Hans J. Morgenthau, "Constraints on Presidential Leadership in Foreign Policy," in James Sterling Young, ed., <u>Problems and Prospects of Presidential Leadership in the Nineteen-Eighties</u> (Lanham: University Press of America, 1980), p. 24.

man's instinct "to truck barter and exchange."[41] If men were angels, no corporations would be necessary. If angels were to provide for the wealth of nations, neither external nor internal controls on corporate behavior would be necessary. In framing a political economic system which is to be operated by competing firms and factions, the great difficulty lies in this: you must first enable the corporation to produce wealth; and in the next place oblige it to account for negative externalities. A dependence on consumer sovereignty and a competitive market is, no doubt, the primary control on the firm, but experience has taught mankind the necessity of auxiliary precautions.

Continuing with this line of reasoning and paraphrasing No. 10, we may write - again with apologies to Madison - there are two methods of curing the mischief of the transnational corporation: the one by removing its causes, the other by controlling its effects. Let us agree to control the effects because we cannot change economic man, nor can we change (although we can modify) the various and unequal distributions of property which have existed throughout the ages in all societies. Within a national economy, the propensity towards animosity and Plato's criticism of a "City of Pigs" can be controlled by a well constructed republican government, but we now see world markets and global industries. We cannot easily, if ever, have a world government much less a world democracy, as the world lacks the prerequisites of democracy. We must rely on progressively extending the market beyond the borders of the so-called "sovereign" states and have it encompass all mankind. In this way, the competitive economic prerequisites of a large commercial republic can be put in place globally for our posterity to contemplate and act upon. Factions will remain. So will injustice, dishonor, avarice, licentiousness and fear,[42] but the maladies which a world market will produce are more likely to taint a particular industry and firm then the entire world of industries and MNCs.

Conclusions

From four political economy perspectives -- Liberalism, Marxism, Mercantilism, and World Political Economy (a synthesis of the first three) -- we can come to some conclusions about the responsibility of transnational corporations. In the liberal perspective, responsibility lies in the efficient consequences of the firm's behavior in a competitive market. If the world market is more apt to be competitive than any national market or any neo-mercantilist orderly marketing arrangement, then, on the basis of microeconomic reasoning, TNCs in such an efficient market will produce more beneficial consequences regardless of their basic individual corporate strategies. At the national level, we cannot expect the firm to provide for public or collective goods. The government must do this. At the world level, there is no government and thus public goods can only be provided by ad hoc arrangements, institutionalized regimes, or world grassroots movements.

From a Marxist perspective one would not expect the TNC to behave morally or prudently. As an unconscious tool of historical forces, the firm may favor progress but - and this is an enduring value of a Marxist perspective - this depends on the industry involved. The cotton industry is associated with slavery and the opium trade with poisonous degradation. On the other hand, Marx associates the telegraph and railroad industries with the increasing interdependence of nations.

---

[41] Smith, op.cit., p. 17.
[42] Plato, The Republic of Plato, trans. Allan Bloom (New York: Basic Books, 1968), Book VIII.

Responsibility lies then not only in the consequences but also the character and culture of each industry in and of itself. For instance, the computer industry makes profits. So does the tobacco industry. The one makes profits without selling products which clearly produce illness and death; the other does not.

From a mercantilist interpretation, the responsibility of the TNC would lie in its service to state power which, with a tendency to regress towards reductionism, is defined as government power. This is the most conspicuous perspective in political economy today what with all the books about declining American hegemony, the rise of the Japanese and de-industrialization in post-industrial, industrialized democracies. (There is obviously some confusion here!) To the extent that the world economy is seen as the sum of all the nations' GNPs and the economic power of all these nations is relative, then the responsibility of the firm fits within the "patriotic" constraints of protectionism and fair trade - not free trade. The basic role of the TNC is not transnational but national in a world where market share matters more than the wealth of all nations together in a non zero-sum game.

In synthesizing these three theories, unlike Robert Gilpin who emphasizes mercantilism in the balance,[43] I put more weight on the liberal's microeconomic law of supply and demand and the Marxist perspective on differences between particular industries.

I also think a synthesis has to be an act of leadership as well as a result of economic laws, political formulas and the forces of history. Past syntheses such as those of Hegel and Marx are too deterministic. Marx sees a synthesis dialectically and his thinking integrates and criticizes English political economy, French socialism and German idealism; but his synthesis downplays the continuing role of national power. Gilpin's synthesis downplays Marx's dialectical approach methologically and is in danger of projecting current national power models into the future. But trend is not destiny and it would not be prudent to be too "realistic." Politics is sometimes the art of the possible but as we look at the future, given our environmental concerns in particular, politics should be the art of making possible what is necessary. I believe in the neo-mercantilist's emphasis on the positive contribution of a hegemon exercising world leadership needs to be noted as long as this leadership serves mankind and not "free trade imperialism" or the "development of underdevelopment." On another note, however, responsibility often lies not in the conscious imperatives of corporate behavior or governmental or intergovernmental policy but in the consequences of that behavior or policy based on the structure of the world political economic market. The more competitive the market, politically and economically, the more responsible is the corporation. Added to this, however, one must look at the culture and products of individual industries in and of themselves. In terms of the consequences to smokers and to communicators, respectively, a corporation in the tobacco industry is less responsible than one in the telecommunications industry. The Medellin "cartel" is more irresponsible than the OPEC "cartel." As the world economy becomes more integrated as measured by joint ventures, intracorporate trade, world corporate investment and world money, a firm which acts patriotically in terms of the national interest and neo-mercantilist principles may not only be acting myopically and atavistically but irresponsibly in terms of world labor, world capital and world resources. In particular, firms should be concerned with their employees' working conditions and income worldwide, with global banking and stock markets, and with

---

[43] Gilpin, op.cit., pp. xi, 384, 408.

the proper use of depletable natural resources and the environmental consequences of corporate growth. If they are not -- and there is no Smithian, Madisonian or Marxian reason why they will be -- then the accountability of the firm rests on the workings of the market, sometimes the workings of governments and often on the auxiliary precautions, enlightened interests and prudence of the people. Prudence requires seeing and acting with the TNC at four levels -- human nature and psychology within the corporation, political economy within states, international political economy between states, and world political economy beyond the limited powers of individuals, states and the state system.

CHAPTER ELEVEN

"CONSCIENCE" IN WORLD POLITICS

RICHARD W. MANSBACH

There is a widely-held image of "political man" -- one that is closely associated with the Machiavellian tradition -- which assumes that, at best, international leaders act from amoral and expedient motives. This version of Machiavellian man was vividly depicted by Marlowe in The Jew of Malta:

> To some perhaps my name is odious,
> But such as love me guard me from their tongues;
> And let them know that I am Machiavel,
> And weigh not men, and therefore not men's words.
> Admired I am of those that hate me most.
> Though some speak openly against my books,
> Yet they will read me, and thereby attain
> To Peter's chair: and when they cast me off,
> Are poisoned by my climbing followers.
> I count religion but a childish toy,
> And hold there is no sin but ignorance.
> Birds of the air will tell of murders past!
> I am ashamed to hear such fooleries.
> Many will talk of title to a crown:
> What right had Caesar to the empery?
> Might first made kings, and laws were then most sure
> When like the Draco's they were writ in blood.

The ethical dimension of international life

In the absence of a moral rudder, continues the conventional argument, the efforts of leaders to amass power and assure their own tenure inevitably produce excesses of the worst kind. According to this argument, there is a significant difference between the domestic and international political arenas. Leaders have greater freedom internationally than domestically; their power-based instincts are less constrained, and the stakes of the game may be very high. By contrast, the behavior of prominent individuals in domestic politics is fortunately largely tamed by the limitations imposed upon them by complex and conservative bureaucracies, institutionalized roles, and the numerous institutions and processes that force politicians to be responsive to the needs and wishes of those to whom they are formally and informally responsible.

Put differently: It is widely believed that idiosyncratic behavior by leaders is largely precluded in well-ordered domestic settings like the United States by role accountability which is assured by the presence of appropriate formal institutions.[1] Similar institutions do not and cannot exist internationally so that leaders are accountable only in the most tenuous ways for their acts.[2] Thomas Hobbes, for example, constructed his leviathan as a limitation on behavior within the state but implied that only the existence of countervailing power internationally could limit the behavior of states and their surrogates. In subsequent analyses by generations of international relations scholars, informal institutions like balance of power are identified as the sole barriers to the expansive appetites of states and their surrogates.

It is in the international realm, then, that we are told to expect the "naturally" aggressive and amoral tendencies of Machiavellian man[3] to be fully visible.[4] In fact, there is remarkably little evidence for this assumption. Dreadful deeds are, of course, performed on the international stage, especially during wartime, but they are surely matched by similarly atrocious acts carried out by leaders against their own citizens.[5] More to the point, it would appear that such deeds, though they attract great attention, are comparatively rare in international politics. Despite the repeated use of evocative but unfortunate metaphors to describe the international system as a "jungle" and the like, world politics is actually characterized by cooperation and peace far more often than it is by treachery and violence. Why is this the case, and what does it suggest about international realities?

Surely Harry Truman's explanation for supporting the recognition of the new state of Israel in 1948 seems out of place in a "jungle":

> The fate of the Jewish victims of Hitlerism was a matter of deep personal concern to me. I have always been disturbed by the tragedy of people who have been made victims of intolerance because of their race, color, or religion.... The plight of the victims who had survived the mad genocide of

---

[1] See, for example, Charles E. Gilbert, "The Framework of Administrative Responsibility," The Journal of Politics, 21 (1959), p. 404.

[2] For a time after World War II, it was widely hoped and, by some, believed that the Nuremberg and Tokyo war crimes trials might constitute precedents for accountability in foreign-policy behavior. Such postwar optimism has faded and is being replaced by a more cynical view of the trials. See, for instance, Richard H. Minear, Victors' Justice: The Tokyo War Crimes Trial (Princeton, NJ: Princeton University Press, 1971).

[3] Not everyone would agree that Machiavelli and the realist tradition are related in the manner depicted here. See, for example, Edward Vose Gulick, Europe's Classical Balance of Power: A Case History of the Theory and Practice of One of the Great Concepts of European Statecraft, (New York: W.W. Norton, 1955), pp. 42-46.

[4] The argument is repeatedly heard that George Bush concentrates his energies in the foreign-policy area because Democratic majorities in both houses of Congress make it difficult for him to work his will domestically. By contrast, the relative absence of institutional impediments in the international arena will, these pundits assume, permit greater scope for the President's political instincts.

[5] The behavior of Pol Pot's Khmer Rouge, of Argentina's military, of Guatemalan death squads, and many others towards their own citizens constitutes savage testimony against the myth of domestic civility. Instead, that myth reveals the peculiar persistence of Eurocentricity in political science and political philosophy. Indeed, the worst atrocities are committed in civil, not interstate, wars. "Laws of war" have existed historically that govern the treatment of prisoners of war, and these have usually been faithfully observed whether for reasons of reciprocity or ideology. By contrast, captured soldiers in civil wars can rarely expect tolerable treatment.

Hitler's Germany was a challenge to Western civilization, and as President I undertook to do something about it.[6]

The advice which Robert F. Kennedy claims to have given his brother at the height of the Cuban missile crisis when discussion was taking place in the National Security Council's "Executive Committee" about the possibility of an American air strike against Soviet missile sites has a similar resonance. "I now know," wrote Kennedy, "how Tojo felt when he was planning Pearl Harbor."[7] This sounds remarkably unlike the widely accepted depiction of Robert Kennedy as a hardheaded realist. And, almost two decades later, Ronald Reagan, we are told, prior to taking office as president, was aghast to discover that the United States enjoyed no protection against a Soviet nuclear attack. The strategy of mutual assured destruction, he concluded, was immoral, and so the initial decision was taken in the direction of the strategic defense initiative ("Star Wars").

Are these alleged preoccupations with the moral implications of important issues merely fictions created by prominent figures for later autobiographies and/or public consumption, or do they reflect more profound concerns for the ethical bases of political action on the part of Truman, Kennedy, Reagan, and other political leaders?[8] And, if similar sentiments are routinely echoed by foreign-policy practitioners more generally and are rooted in genuine moral concern and awareness, would this not appear to deny basic "power politics" or "realist" assumptions about "human nature" and resulting behavior in a putatively anarchic system? Finally, if there is a widespread preoccupation with the morality and legitimacy of political outcomes in international relations, from whence does it arise and how is it inculcated among foreign-policy elites?

In this essay, we shall argue that foreign-policy leaders are, as a rule, instructed by something akin to what we think of as "conscience" which, although it varies significantly by social and cultural milieu,[9] exercises a powerful restraining influence on foreign-policy behavior. By conscience, we mean an internalized and self-conscious conception of right and wrong and of the blameworthiness of the individual's own conduct. The concept also connotes a recognition of an obligation to do or to be that which is more widely perceived to be appropriate and good and also connotes the presence of remorse if this obligation is ignored.

---

[6] Harry S. Truman, Years of Trial and Hope (Garden City, NY: Doubleday and Company, 1956), p. 132. Truman's personal policy preference was certainly fortunate from an electoral point of view.

[7] Robert F. Kennedy, Thirteen Days: A memoir of the Cuban missile crisis (New York: W.W. Norton, 1968), p. 9.

[8] It is extraordinary the lengths to which leaders will go to justify their ofttimes unjustifiable behavior before the court of world opinion. Even Hitler, the antithesis of moral man in politics, found it necessary to stage justifying "incidents" on the German-Polish frontier prior to the German invasion of Poland on September 1, 1939. See Alan Bullock, Hitler: A study In Tyranny (rev. ed.) (New York: Harper & Row, 1964), p. 546.

[9] Ethical systems are, of course, deeply embedded in culture; and differences among clashing cultures may disguise the fact that leaders are endeavoring to behave according to ethical norms as they understand them. For example, Japanese brutality toward captured European and American servicemen in World War II was, in part, a reflection of the contempt toward those who surrendered engendered in them by Shinto. But their moral code was entirely alien to Western observers. Indeed, incompatibility among ethical systems is likely to generate greater violence during conflicts than amoral cost-benefit behavior.

In short, it is our view that what is popularly described as "superego" plays an important role in global politics. "It was my dream," wrote Jimmy Carter, "not only to be elected President, but to be a good President."[10] Despite the absence of the sort of obvious institutional barriers to arbitrary behavior provided by constitutional systems, international relations is, nevertheless, characterized by coherent though constantly changing norms and by a search for legitimacy on the part of decisionmakers. They genuinely care about how history will depict them and seem to sense that kind treatment will depend on more than public relations. It is at least partly for this reason that political leaders, even though they may have adopted militant rhetoric for electoral reasons, are prone to become more conciliatory toward the end of their terms. All wish to be remembered as "men of peace."

Although an appearance of morality often serves the domestic political ends of statesmen and may also serve to enhance the general odor of state behavior, it would be a serious mistake to dismiss references to law and ethics as solely instrumental. In fact, the observance of ethical standards may serve a variety of interests, not merely those that are "defined in terms of power."[11]

Our claim that the individual conscience of national leaders and the norms that underlie it have an impact on foreign-policy outcomes by no means implies that such outcomes are "good" by our light. The wide divergences among underlying norms precludes this.[12] Indeed, leaders who are driven by personal moral beliefs may be more easily tempted to extremes, may prove very difficult negotiators and unwilling compromisers, and may, therefore, be unusually dangerous.[13]

At a deeper level, realists, too, are creatures of conscience. What offends them are those whose norms are different -- those with less specialized training, those with different ideological commitments, and those who are the products of non-European ethical systems. Thus, the great British diplomatist and consummate realist Sir Harold Nicolson wistfully recalls the "old days" when "the conduct of foreign affairs was entrusted to a small international elite who shared the same sort of background and who desired to preserve the same sort of world."[14] It appears, then, that even though individual motivation is extremely difficult to plumb, international leaders of different backgrounds actually have scruples and seem genuinely proud of the fact.

---

[10] Jimmy Carter, Keeping Faith: Memoirs of a President (New York: Bantam Books, 1982), p. 66.

[11] Hans J. Morgenthau, Politics Among Nations: The Struggle for Power and Peace, 6th ed., revised by Kenneth W. Thompson (New York: Alfred A. Knopf, 1985), p. 5. Realists would presumably respond that statesmen who reveal what we are calling "conscience" are only seeming to be so as Machiavelli advises they must and that, at best, motivation will remain opaque.

[12] For instance, the Ayatollah Khomeini's death "sentence" upon Salmon Rushdie for allegedly insulting Islam in The Satanic Verses was probably triggered more by internalized norms (which are perceived as abhorrent in the West) than by utilitarian considerations.

[13] See Eric Hoffer, The True Believer (New York: Harper & Row, 1951). It is this sort of argument that underlies the preference of realists to keep foreign policy in the hands of a small trained elite. There is, however, a tendency on the part of realists and others to confuse the personal scruples of individuals with ideology. Although the two concepts may in practice shade into one another, using them interchangeably muddies the waters.

[14] Sir Harold Nicolson, Diplomacy, 3rd ed. (New York: Oxford University Press, 1964), p. 138. Of course, Nicolson's norms are class-based and Eurocentric.

Ethics and the classical tradition

According to the "classical tradition"[15] in international relations scholarship, it is believed that there exists what Hans Morgenthau describes as an "ineluctable tension between the moral command and the requirements of successful political action" which entails that "universal moral principles cannot be applied to the actions of states in their abstract universal formulation."[16] For Machiavelli and for self-described realists in the centuries that followed, immutably evil human nature and/or the crushing pressures of "necessity" preclude moral (or immoral) behavior in international relations. "Reason of state"[17] was regarded by Machiavelli and the tradition that invokes his name as the only reliable guide to ethics in state behavior. Such "necessary" behavior could not, the argument goes, be judged by conventional standards. The behavior of leaders acting as the surrogates of states is, therefore, neither moral nor immoral; such conventional categories simply do not apply to an international arena in which the survival of collect critics is at stake. In Hans Morgenthau's words, "a foreign policy guided by moral abstractions... is bound to fail."[18]

Realists in the tradition of Morgenthau emphasize the role of human nature (having been deeply influenced by Machiavelli and Hobbes), whereas structural realists (or "neorealists" if one prefers)[19] stress the critical role of what Kenneth Waltz calls "modified anarchy."[20] The former would constitute a compellant and the latter a permissive cause of amorality. What such scholars have in common is the claim that one must differentiate between the public duty of statesmen (for which "prudence" is regarded as the highest of virtue) and their private preferences (in which what we call "conscience" presumably plays a role). In Machiavelli's words: "The fact is that a man who wants to act virtuously in every way necessarily comes to grief among so many who are not virtuous."[21]

In reality, leaders often do not behave as though the end justifies the means. Unexpectedly perhaps, they place limitations on their actions and do so repeatedly, limitations that cannot be explained fully by reference to "prudence" or reciprocity. Realists themselves recognize this, and it is this recognition that underpins their virulent criticism of statesmen like Woodrow Wilson whose behavior reflects what

---

[15] K.J. Holsti, The Dividing Discipline: Hegemony and Diversity in International Theory (Boston: Allen & Unwin, 1985), p. 5.

[16] Morgenthau, Politics Among Nations, op.cit., p. 12.

[17] Perhaps the best summary of this tradition is Friedrich Meinecke, Machiavellism (New Haven: Yale University Press, 1957).

[18] Hans J. Morgenthau, "The Mainsprings of American Foreign Policy," in James M. McCormick, ed., A Reader in American Foreign Policy (Itasca, Ill: F.E. Peacock Publishers, 1986), p. 48.

[19] See Robert O. Keohane, ed., Neorealism and Its Critics (New York: Columbia University Press, 1986).

[20] Kenneth N. Waltz, Theory of International Politics (Reading, MA: Addison-Wesley, 1979), p. 114. The structural argument is, perhaps, best summarized in Waltz's description of Rousseau's stag-hare metaphor. Waltz, Man, the State and War: A Theoretical Analysis (New York: Columbia University Press, 1959), pp. 167 ff.

[21] Niccolo Machiavelli, The Prince, trans. George Bull (Baltimore: Penguin Books, 1961), p. 91.

Morgenthau disparagingly calls "legalism-moralism."[22] In fact, foreign-policy behavior in the United States and elsewhere does not and has never fully reflected the putatively "scientific" realist version of an amoral "national interest".[23] Thus, the preferred "realist" Middle East policy in 1948 was that held by "some men in the State Department who held the view that the Balfour Declaration could not be carried out without offense to the Arabs" and "that the Arabs, on account of their numbers and because of the fact that they controlled such immense oil resources, should be appeased."[24] President Truman, as we have seen, marched to a different drummer.

It is the repeated failure of reality to confirm realist predictions and prescriptions that has led usually thoughtful scholars like Morgenthau to indulge in wrathful jeremiads. Referring to what "has been variously described as 'utopianism,' 'sentimentalism,' 'moralism,' the 'legalistic-moralistic approach'," Morgenthau thunders: "What challenges the national interest here is a mere figment of the imagination, a product of wishful thinking, which is postulated as a valid norm for international conduct, without being valid there or anywhere else."[25]

The intensity of the metaphor suggests that what is really taking place is a conflict among competing intellectual and political norms and not, as realists like Morgenthau would have it, a conflict between political "science" and political "witchcraft." This conflict is not a recent phenomenon; it is evident, for example, in the competing norms present in Thucydides. And, the clash between "realist" and "idealist" norms occurs in every epoch and reflects the political exigencies of the time.[26] It is, at root, more an ideological clash than it is a scientific dispute.

Nevertheless, it is indeed fortunate for humankind that what we call conscience seems to be operative among leaders and does impede the formulation and implementation of foreign policy. The practical effect of those norms is to guide leaders in making policy decisions by instructing them as to what is and what is not permissible in world politics. Those limits, of course, change in time and by place; but this is equally true of what is regarded as private virtue. Mahatma Gandhi's resort to passive resistance was successful, for example, because the norms of British leaders would not sanction the use of violence against unarmed civilians. It

---

[22] Morgenthau, Politics Among Nations, op.cit., pp. 14 ff. See also George F. Kennan, American Diplomacy 1900-1950 (Chicago: University of Chicago Press, 1951).

[23] Realists are prone to educe erroneous generalizations from the behavior of a relatively few diplomats and statesmen in eighteenth and nineteenth century Europe. See, for instance, Henry A. Kissinger, A World Restored-Metternich, Castlereagh and the Problems of Peace 1812-22 (Boston: Houghton Mifflin, 1957).

[24] Harry S. Truman, Years of Trial and Hope, op.cit., p. 164. It is interesting that "oil power" was no more successfully employed in 1973 despite the organization of Arab oil-producing states into AOPEC and the greater dependence of the industrialized West on Middle East oil by that time. See Roy Licklider, Political Power and the Arab Oil Weapon: The Experience of Five Industrial Nations (Berkeley, CA: University of California Press, 1988).

[25] Hans J. Morgenthau, Politics in the Twentieth Century, abridged ed. (Chicago: University of Chicago Press, 1971), p. 223. Undoubtedly, the most sophisticated and persuasive critique of so-called "utopian" thought and policy is E.H. Carr, The Twenty Years' Crisis, 1919-1939 (New York: St. Martin's Press, 1939).

[26] See Yale H. Ferguson and Richard W. Mansbach, The Elusive Quest: Theory and International Politics (Columbia, SC: University of South Carolina Press, 1988), pp. 79-108.

is improbable that a similar strategy could have succeeded in many other settings.[27]

One error of the realists was to impose a utility model on the making of foreign policy and to assume that rational choice analysis could be used (or ought to be used) as an explanation of behavior. By contrast, it would appear that "seemingly irrational choices sometimes make good sense once we realize that a person may be willing to renounce utilitarian and social rewards in order to avoid the pain of self-disapproval for violating internalized moral standards."[28] Historians are prone to the same error when they reconstruct the past in ways that "make sense" of it.

But, perhaps, the principal error of the classical tradition of realpolitik was to confuse the search by actors for influence to achieve political ends with those ends themselves. Few will quarrel with the importance of influence (or "power" if that is the preferred term) in any political arena, but it is all too easy to forget that its utility is instrumental rather than intrinsic. The utility of influence in international politics is to enhance the basic values of those whom leaders represent.[29] Such basic values are probably universal in scope, but they are ranked differently by different societies and in different historical contexts. The ordering of values largely defines the ethical content of political roles in different societies. It is, in part, for this reason that political conscience reveals itself to have quite distinct faces in different societies and/or in different historical epochs. Context matters greatly, and contextual comparisons can help reveal the differing impact of conscience on foreign policy in different milieus.

Collective values and individual norms

Leaders of societies that are enjoying prosperity and that are able to sustain relatively high cultural and economic levels are likely to foster a conservative outlook among both citizens and leaders. Societies such as these are less concerned with overcoming value deprivation than with preventing it. Consequently, foreign-policy officials in such countries may regard "peace" very highly because wars are inherently risky enterprises in which the prospects for value deprivation are high.[30]

---

[27] A comparison of state responses to Martin Luther King's civil rights movement in the United States in the 1960s and to the anti-apartheid movement in South Africa in the 1980s makes the point. The key difference between the two situations lies less in formal institutions and laws than in informal social norms that structure and inform the consciences of individual leaders of the two societies.

[28] Irving L. Janis and Leon Mann, Decision Making: A Psychological Analysis of Conflict, Choice, and Commitment (New York: The Free Press, 1977), pp. 8-9. The sharpest and most coherent critique of the rationality assumption in international politics remains Robert Jervis, Perception and Misperception in International Politics (Princeton, NJ: Princeton University Press, 1976).

[29] See Richard W. Mansbach and John A. Vasquez, In Search of Theory: A New Paradigm for Global Politics (New York: Columbia University Press, 1981), pp. 58 ff. One of the best analyses of base values in a political context remains Harold J. Lasswell and Abraham Kaplan, Power and Society (New Haven, Conn.: Yale University Press, 1950), pp. 55-56.

[30] A similar logic lies behind the argument that predicted a growing convergence between the U.S. and Soviet political systems. For a recent analysis of how technological change contributes to value convergence, see Joel C. Moses, "The Political Implications of New Technology for the Soviet Union," in Donna Bahry and Moses (eds.), Communist Dialectic - The Political Implications of

Such leaders may find it difficult to understand the willingness of leaders of societies that are relatively backward or that have been deprived of key values like freedom and respect to assume great risks. Lyndon Johnson's inability to comprehend the reasons behind North Vietnamese reluctance to negotiate in the face of American bombing reflects such an incommensurability of values. American and Israeli difficulty in understanding Palestinian behavior reveals a similar inability to empathize.

Indeed, the "suicidal" foreign-policy behavior of societies from time to time -- Hungary in 1956, the island of Melos according to Thucydides, or Japan in 1945 -- suggests that survival may not always and inevitably be seen as the most important of values by some leaders in some contexts. Such leaders may be prepared to gamble and even sacrifice survival for other values like equality or independence. If, like Mao Tse-tung or the Ayatollah Khomeini, they can persuade their adversaries that they hold an idiosyncratic value hierarchy that encourages them to take significant risks, they will have potent bargaining power indeed.[31]

Not only do hierarchies of values vary significantly but so also do the sources of what we are calling conscience. For this reason, the norms that such conscience instills in leaders and the course of action it suggests that leaders adopt to obey the dictates of conscience are also likely to vary dramatically. It is the collision among such norms and resulting misunderstandings that are commonly pointed out as characteristic of interstate relations in contrast to relations among groups in well-ordered domestic societies. In reality, similar collisions occur within individual societies that are characterized by groups at different levels of development. It is not the absence or presence of central authority that determines the compatibility or incompatibility of norms but rather the homogeneity or heterogeneity of the society in question--whether domestic or international.[32] There is, then, a cultural matrix -- in the broadest sense of the idea -- that helps to determine whether norms will compete or will reinforce each other.

We may illustrate the different sources of conscience in global politics by extending to this arena David Riesman's analysis of "the changing American character."[33] In Riesman's words, some political leaders are still "tradition-directed," some are "inner directed," and, at least in the West, many are "outer-directed." The sources of role definitions vary markedly among these three, and, as a consequence, so do the nature and content of those norms that are the bases of conscience in foreign-policy leaders. There will also be significant variation among systems in terms of those relevant others (role validators) who are formally or informally responsible for overseeing adherence to role norms and,

---

Economic Reform in Communist Countries (New York: New York University Press, 1990). For a more skeptical view of the convergence thesis, see Zbigniew Brzezinski and Samuel P. Huntington, Political Power: USA/USSR (New York: Viking Press, 1965). Many of the Gorbachev and Yeltsen reforms, if they prove longlasting, will show Brzezinski and Huntington to have been poor seers indeed.

[31] See Thomas C. Schelling, The Strategy of Conflict (Cambridge, MA: Harvard University Press, 1980), pp. 187 ff.

[32] We are using homogeneity as shorthand for what we have called "similarity" elsewhere; that is, "the extent to which actors perceive that they share the same political, economic, cultural, religious, linguistic, demographic, geographical, ethnic, racial, or other significant characteristics." Mansbach and Vasquez, In Search of Theory, op.cit., p. 207. See also pp. 207-213.

[33] David Riesman with Nathan Glazer and Reuel Denney, The Lonely Crowd: A Study of the Changing American Character (Garden City, NY: Doubleday & Co., 1955).

therefore, the expectations that are associated with roles.[34]

In the contemporary global system, there persist numerous societies --especially in the developing world -- "where the activity of the individual member is determined by characterologically grounded obedience to traditions."[35] Role norms in such societies in part emerge from potent traditional sources such as religion and family, and they may impose a stultifying but stabilizing conformity upon society. It is not surprising, then, that the norms expressed by leaders such as Iran's Ayatollah Khomeini are incomprehensible to leaders whose role conceptions are dramatically different in source and content. Under such circumstances, the sort of conflict and mutual misperception so characteristic of the so-called Rushdie affair, should be expected. Whatever one's judgment of the affair, it would be an error to assume that Iran's spiritual leader lacked conscience or was merely malevolent. Intellectually and politically, it is probably more profitable to seek the sources of the Ayatollah's norms in order to make sense of them.

By contrast, "inner-directed types" from societies that Riesman describes as "transitional" are provided moral guidance, at least in part, early in their lives and are encouraged as individuals toward "inescapably destined goals."[36] Such individuals are likely to be characterized by personal ethical views, which they espouse frequently, that may or may not be compatible with the views that are encouraged by role validators. In other words, from time to time the strongly held personal norms of such leaders may come into conflict with the role norms articulated by electorates, bureaucracies, mullahs, and other validators. Woodrow Wilson and John Foster Dulles epitomize "inner-directed" leaders whose personal moral preferences asserted themselves strongly in foreign-policy decisions.[37] In the case of Wilson, this was perhaps most evident in his unyielding but unsuccessful fight for his vision of the League of Nations. For his part, Dulles's rigid anti-communism and refusal to permit anything to soften his demonic image of the Soviet Union have suggested to some observers that he "was the archetype of the inner-directed person."[38]

Riesman's final category -- "other-directed" individuals -- are the products of relatively affluent and modern societies. Riesman depicts them as conformists who, possessed of weak egos, are supinely responsive to those around them. He judges such individuals harshly:

> What is common to all the other-directed people is that their contemporaries

---

[34] We should differentiate between backward and forward role linkages. Backward links consist of validators and norms that were responsible for placing an individual in his/her current position. Forward links consist of those who will be responsible for maintaining an individual in his/her present position or for advancement. Role holders must be sensitive to both, and acute conflict may result if (as in rapidly changing societies) a significant gap grows between the expectations of the two sets of validators.

[35] Riesman, The Lonely Crowd, op.cit., p. 26.

[36] Ibid, p. 30.

[37] A significant amount of psychobiographical analysis exists for both these individuals. The reader may begin to get the flavor of their moral commitments and the roots of these commitments in Alexander George and Juliette George, Woodrow Wilson and Colonel House (New York: Dover, 1964), and David J. Finlay, Ole R. Holsti, and Richard R. Fagen, Enemies in Politics (Chicago: Rand McNally, 1967), pp. 25-96.

[38] Finlay, Holsti, and Fagen, op.cit., p. 46.

are the source of direction for the individual.... This source is of course "internalized" in the sense that dependence on it for guidance in life is implanted early. The goals toward which the other-directed person strives shift with that guidance....[39]

For leaders who are "other-directed," virtually the sole source of role norms will be the expectations of those whom such leaders perceive to be responsible for having recruited them in the first place and upon whom they believe their continued success depends. Unable to bring personal ethics to the issues they confront, they will conform; they are the careerists.

At first blush, our emphasis on the importance of role in determining conscience may seem to contradict the idea that conscience is highly personal and idiosyncratic. In fact, role and society are major sources of norms that, once internalized, appear as personal attributes. This is especially the case for leaders who will have had, in most cases, prior experience in their societies' principal political institutions and who will have earned the approbation of those institutions in the course of promotion.[40] One cannot imagine, for example, a Pope in the Vatican who did not inherit the key norms of the Catholic Church or an American president who did not reflect the values of the electorate and, to some extent, a major political party.

Role norms in authoritarian societies tend to arise from relatively limited strata of the population -- perhaps a ruling party and the narrow elites that provide personnel and support to that party. If these bases of support are broadened quickly, conflict and turmoil of the sort that we are currently witnessing in Czechoslovakia and South Africa is liking to arise. In time, however, we would expect the individual norms of leaders to evolve in the direction of these new sources of societal support. Leaders in democratic or open societies are likely to internalize norms from the broader society to which they are responsible. Another comment by Robert Kennedy regarding his attitude during the Cuban missile crisis illustrates what we mean:

> With some trepidation, I argued that, whatever validity the military and political arguments were for an attack in preference to a blockade, America's traditions and history would not permit such a course of action.... Our struggle against Communism throughout the world was far more than physical survival -- it had as its essence our heritage and our ideals, and these we must not destroy.[41]

Role norms and expectations are, however, not entirely generated from within the foreign-policy leader's own society. They emerge from the international system as well.[42] The relative absence of hierarchy and decentralization of authority

---

[39] Riesman, et.al., The Lonely Crowd, op.cit., p. 37.

[40] It is this assumption that underlies operational-code analysis. See, for example, Alexander George, "The 'Operational Code': A Neglected Approach to the Study of Political Leaders and Decision-Making," International Studies Quarterly 13 (June 1969), pp. 190-222.

[41] Robert F. Kennedy, Thirteen Days, op.cit., pp. 16,17.

[42] Arguably, international society will be a more important source of role norms for leaders of relatively small countries because such countries will be more dependent than large countries on their external environment. See James N. Rosenau, "Pre-Theories and Theories of Foreign Policy,"

in world politics permit and sometimes encourage individual actors to resort to self-help. This condition does not, however, preclude the existence of a global society which transmits to and, in some measure, even enforces norms upon individual leaders.[43]

Despite the absence of world government, "order," declares Hedley Bull, "is part of the historical record of international relations;... modern states have formed, not only a system of states but also an international society."[44] Such order, he continues, "is not any pattern or regularity in the relations of human individuals or groups, but a pattern that leads to a particular result, an arrangement of social life such that it promotes certain goals or values."[45] What Bull is correctly suggesting is not simply that global actors are predictable but that en groupe they pursue common values. Conflict may and often does ensue as individual actors take dramatically different paths toward their common ends, but such conflict should not be allowed to obscure the existence of those common "goals or values."

For specific issue-areas, individual political leaders are provided cues as to what behavior is appropriate by international regimes -- informal "networks of rules, norms, and procedures that regularize behavior and control its effects."[46] The norms in this context "are standards of behavior defined in terms of rights and obligations."[47] Once embedded in custom, such norms inform leaders of how they ought to behave in selected issue areas under stipulated conditions. Adherence to such norms will elicit approval from other actors in the regime; violation will bring disapproval or worse. It is generally argued that compliance with international regimes arises from the utilitarian considerations of collectivities[48], and this is doubtlessly true in large measure. Yet, if regimes survive for extended periods of time, we would expect that collective utilitarian considerations would be reinforced and even replaced by those individual visions of right and wrong that we call conscience. Thus, whatever the original utilitarian motives that lay behind British support for free trade in the nineteenth century, these were in time woven into the psyches of generations of British statesmen who unthinkingly supported the free-trade norm. Even such apparently utilitarian realist institutions as balance of power were actually promoted most fervently by those who had internalized their virtue. In other words, the goals of the balance (e.g., the independence and survival of states) came to be regarded as values to be sought by any right-thinking people, and the institution that promoted these values was an ethical thing-in-itself. It was in this spirit that Lord Brougham saw the balance of power as "a species of general

---

in Rosenau, The Scientific Study of Foreign Policy (New York: The Free Press, 1971), p. 113.

[43] See Yale H. Ferguson and Richard W. Mansbach, The Elusive Quest: Theory and International Politics (Columbia, SC: University of South Carolina Press, 1988), pp. 186-211.

[44] Hedley Bull, The Anarchical Society: A Study of Order in World Politics (New York: Columbia University Press, 1977), p. 24.

[45] Ibid, p. 4. See also Adam Watson, The Evolution of International Society in Comparative Historical Analysis (London: Routledge, 1992).

[46] Robert O. Keohane and Joseph S. Nye, Power and Interdependence, 2nd ed. (Glenview, Ill.: Scott, Foresman &. Co., 1989), p. 19.

[47] Stephen D. Krasner, "Structural causes and regime consequences: regimes as intervening variables," International Organization 36:2 (Spring 1982), p. 186.

[48] See, for example, Robert O. Keohane, After Hegemony: Cooperation and Discord in the World Political Economy (Princeton, NJ: Princeton University Press, 1984), pp. 98-109.

law, which supersedes...an appeal to the sword...."[49]

Conscience and responsibility

The impact on individual leaders of conscience is greater to the extent that they feel they are responsible for their own acts. If leaders are persuaded that their choices are severely limited, the impact of conscience-based norms will be reduced and perhaps even negated. There is significant psychological evidence for this, the most dramatic of which may be the experiments conducted by Stanley Milgram at Yale in the 1960s. The repeated willingness of increasingly unhappy subjects to administer painful electric shocks to simulated victims at the command of an experimenter led Milgram to wonder whether orientation to authority leads to "short-circuiting of the shame-guilt system."[50]

Since distance serves to attenuate perceptions of responsibility, we would expect, as Milgram found, that greater distance between a decisionmaker and those who bear the consequences of his/her decisions will limit feelings of regret or guilt. This explains, in part, why soldiers who do not see their victims (e.g., airmen and artillery gunners) suffer fewer emotional conflicts than those who are closer to the enemy (e.g., infantrymen). It should also caution us about the dangers that modern military technology may pose. Developments ranging from computers to missiles produce greater psychological distance between those making decisions and those who are effected by them. As psychological distance grows, the impact of conscience is reduced, and decisions may be less sensitive.

International politics itself provides numerous illustrations of these phenomena. Analysis of the 1914 crisis, for example, reveals an extraordinary relationship between making key decisions with potentially sanguinary consequences and the denial by those officials of responsibility for those decisions. "It was found," declare Ole Holsti and his colleagues, "that decision-makers of each nation most strongly felt themselves to be the victims of injury precisely at that time when its leaders were making policy decisions of the most crucial nature."[51] As nations moved closer to the abyss, leaders came increasingly to view their actions as thrust upon them by the actions of others. Holsti explains these findings in terms of dissonance reduction -- to which we shall turn shortly -- on the part of leaders who realized, at some level, the serious nature of their decisions.[52]

It is more difficult for those at the very highest echelons of authority than for those who are lower in the hierarchy to evade the pressures of conscience. Those at the top will find it difficult to escape the profound sense of responsibility for one's actions that is a prerequisite of conscience. They may do so, as the outbreak of World War I shows, but the necessary intellectual and emotional gymnastics are considerable. And, if they know their adversaries personally or share personal ties

---

[49] Henry Brougham, "Balance of Power," in M.G. Forsyth, H.M.A. Keens-Soper, and P. Savigear (eds.), The Theory of International Relations: Selected Texts from Gentili to Treitschke (New York: Atherton Press, 1970), p. 273.

[50] Cited in Roy L. Prosterman, Surviving to 3000: An Introduction to the Study of Lethal Conflict (Belmont, CA: Duxbury Press, 1972), p. 99.

[51] Ole R. Holsti, Robert C. North, and Richard A. Brody, "Perception and Action in the 1914 Crisis," in J. David Singer (ed.), Quantitative International Politics: Insights and Evidence (New York: The Free Press, 1968), p. 137.

[52] Ole R. Holsti, Crisis, Escalation, War (Montreal: McGill University Press, 1972), pp. 17-18.

with them, it will be even more difficult for them to ignore conscience-based norms. Examination of the flurry of letters between the royal cousins, Tsar Nicholas II of Russia and Kaiser Wilhelm II of Germany ("The Nicky-Willy letters"), in the days before the outbreak of the First World War reveal the reluctance they shared in going to war against one another and their distaste for possibly doing harm to their respective dynasties[53]. In general, one of the major factors contributing to the moderate climate of eighteenth-century European politics was the existence of "personal and dynastic loyalties."[54] Leaders of the time were united by blood, marriage, language, culture, and ideology; and they enjoyed one another's company. Such ties -- rarely mentioned by structural realists -- probably contributed as much or more to limiting the diplomacy of the age as did systemic factors.

By contrast, those who function within large bureaucracies may be able to escape a sense of guilt for the consequences of their choices by shifting responsibility to higher authority ("superior orders"[55]), on others who participated in decisions ("groupthink"[56]), or on the collective institution of which they are a part ("bureaucratic politics"[57]). In other words, we would expect that the impact of conscience will be greater upon those at the very top of the pyramid of authority who will be less able to escape recognition of responsibility for their own acts.

The psychological mechanism that seems to be operative is what Leon Festinger called "cognitive dissonance."[58] What Festinger called dissonance exists when two beliefs patently contradict each other. Psychological discomfort is a consequence of recognition of such beliefs, and individuals who suffer such discomfort will seek to reduce dissonance in one or more of a number of possible ways.[59] These alternatives all entail either rationalizing the value of one of the beliefs at the expense of the other or denying the relevance or even the existence of one of the beliefs.

Conscience is the residence of an individual's most deeply held beliefs. Therefore, behavior that appears to require violating such beliefs will be difficult to initiate without considerable cognitive self-manipulation. Denial of responsibility for

---

[53] Kenneth N. Waltz provides a memorable example of dynastic ties during an earlier era: "Francis I, when asked what differences accounted for the constant wars between him and his brother-in-law Charles V, supposedly answered: 'None whatever. We agree perfectly. We both want control of Italy!'" Man, the State and War: A Theoretical Analysis, op.cit., pp. 187-188.

[54] Richard N. Rosecrance, Action and Reaction in World Politics: International Systems in Perspective (Boston: Little Brown, 1963), p. 233.

[55] The efforts of Colonel Oliver North to depict himself as a minor player who was merely carrying out the implicit and explicit wishes of his political superiors in the Iran-Contra affair illustrates the point as did the testimony of Adolph Eichmann during his trial in Israel. What is extraordinary about such individuals is not that they use the defense of superior orders to exculpate their behavior but that they apparently come to believe genuinely that they are not guilty.

[56] See Irving L. Janis, Victims of Groupthink (Boston: Houghton and Mifflin, 1972).

[57] See Morton H. Halperin, Bureaucratic Politics and Foreign Policy (Washington, D.C.: Brookings, 1974).

[58] Leon Festinger, A Theory of Cognitive Dissonance (Stanford, CA· Stanford University Press, 1957).

[59] See Jervis, Perception and Misperception in International Politics, op.cit., pp. 382-406. A valuable and suggestive model of the sources and consequences of decisional stress is elaborated by Janis and Mann, Decision Making, op.cit., pp. 45-80.

the behavior or denial of freedom of action are among the most effective of ways to reduce painful guilt. "The less the decision is felt to be voluntary...," observes Jervis, "the less the dissonance....By contrast, the belief that one has had an opportunity to influence a decision increases feeling of choice and so increases dissonance."[60]

Those who are persuaded by the power-politics literature are less apt to find themselves constrained by conscience because they come to believe that their behavior is necessitated by forces beyond their control. In this way, realists can themselves avoid the painful effects of cognitive dissonance. If "anarchy," "power vacuums," "imbalance of power," "necessity of state," or some other distant structural attribute is perceived to govern one's acts, then a sense of personal responsibility is dissipated; and conscience can be kept at bay. The irony is that the norms that are institutionalized by realism may provide an excuse for leaders to behave in unconscionable ways, and the doctrine thereby becomes a self-fulfilling prophecy. It is precisely this sort of muddled thinking -- a belief that powerful external forces had attenuated Hitler's responsibility -- that led the historian A.J.P. Taylor to conclude that the outbreak of World War II "is a story without heroes; and perhaps even without villains.."[61] If, then, one of the functions of education is socialization of clients, the continued popularity of the classical tradition might be viewed as an effective means of circumscribing individual conscience in emerging generations of leaders.

Conclusions: analytic problems and opportunities

The issues we are raising pose a number of serious analytic problems that defy simple solution. In order to substantiate the claim that individual conscience is a key factor in world politics, we should be able to point to outcomes that were different owing to the presence of this factor. Examination of the historical record, for example, suggests that American policy in the Cuban missile crisis and in the recognition of the state of Israel was partly shaped in response to the conscience of leaders. Other significant illustrations might include Neville Chamberlain's loathing of war and consequent willingness to reach agreement with Hitler at Munich in 1938, Jimmy Carter's advocacy of human rights[62], American nonintervention in the 1954 Dien Bien Phu crisis[63], and Western action to halt the Serbian dismemberment of Bosnia-Herzegovina in 1992.

Clearly, counterfactual claims such as these resist falsification and so must remain speculative. If we are correct, however, immutable structural forces of the kind identified by realists as determining foreign-policy behavior will prove less important than previously believed. This conforms to our own assumption that,

---

[60] Jervis, op.cit., pp. 400, 401. Jervis also notes paradoxically that, if an individual feels irresponsible for an action, "he will be less prone to avoid or distort information than he would if he had acted freely."

[61] A.J.P. Taylor, The Origins Of The Second World War (Greenwich, Conn.: Fawcett Publications, 1961), p. 22 (emphasis added).

[62] See Jimmy Carter, Keeping Faith, op.cit., pp. 141-151.

[63] President Dwight D. Eisenhower reportedly told those advisors who recommended the use of nuclear weapons to aid the French: "You boys must be crazy. We can't use those awful things against Asians for the second time in less than ten years. My God!" Cited in Joseph S. Nye, Jr., Nuclear Ethics (New York: The Free Press, 1986), p. 5.

while the global distribution of resources tells us what is possible in human affairs and so sets parameters for behavior, it is the distribution of attitudes (including the norms that constitute the consciences of leaders) that determine what is probable.

One of our key analytic difficulties is that, conscience, like most other psychological phenomena, cannot be directly observed. We may see what we regard as the traces of conscience, but it may reasonably be argued that what we are observing is the consequence of some other phenomenon. As noted earlier, leaders inevitably have reason to claim that they keep faith with their own beliefs, and motives are virtually impossible to fathom with any degree of confidence. Fortunately, the natural sciences have also confronted and overcome similar problems with subjective phenomena.

Additionally, the sort of data about individual leaders that we would like to have is notoriously difficult to obtain. Leaders are not willing to lie on couches for the sake of science. Indeed, if they do so for therapeutic reasons, they may be pilloried as the sad case of Senator Thomas Eagleton reminds us. And, as our experience with psychobiography suggests, data collection can be extremely difficult and tedious, especially as we are looking at one individual at a time.[64] For the most part, usable data become available only after a leader has died or retired so that we are limited to postdiction.

Nevertheless, methodological issues should not be permitted to drive theory and analysis. Whether or not sufficient tools are available to falsify theory is ultimately irrelevant to the utility of that theory as explanation. We should avoid the understandable propensity of engaging in broad but vacuous system-level analysis because of difficulty in acquiring data about phenomena at other levels. The issue of fathoming motive remains the most troubling, yet tacit assumptions about motivation -- often clothed as assumptions about "human nature" -- haunt realist analyses as well.

In all events, our contention is minimal. We are simply arguing, along with Joseph Nye, that: "Ethical considerations often move people, at least in part. Most leaders do not live wholly by the word, but neither do they live solely by the sword. Mixed motives are a fact of human life. It is as mistaken to dismiss the ethical dimension as it would be to ignore the pragmatic aspect in the motives of leaders."[65]

The underlying assumption of this analysis has been that people produce change; structures do not, though they may facilitate or inhibit such change. Tolstoyean forces of the sort that the classical tradition in international politics views as determining behavior may exist, but, since they will remain relatively immune to our manipulation, they are theoretically unsatisfactory. That which is objective and measurable is only part of the reality we seek to comprehend and perhaps the lesser part at that. We must take seriously what Raymond Hopkins calls the "subjective dimension" of international politics and pay "much greater attention to personalities,

---

[64] Moreover, the application of insights from psychological experiments, like the one referred to earlier conducted by Milgram, must be treated with care. It is not only possible but likely that "leaders" are different than "subjects" so that insights about the latter may, at best, have heuristic value.

[65] Ibid, p. 5.

norm setting and collective beliefs...in international political analysis."[66] Only in doing so will we once again be observing human behavior rather than the artifacts of that behavior. And, in the last analysis, we must believe in the importance of individual conscience if we are to cope effectively with the mounting threats to our survival as a species.

---

[66] Raymond F. Hopkins, "Interests and Regimes: The Subjective Dimension of International Politics." Paper delivered at the 1987 Annual Meeting of the American Political Science Association (September 1987), p. 30.

REFERENCES

Allison, Graham, The Essence of Decision: Explaining the Cuban Missile Crisis (Boston: Little Brown, 1971).
Allum, Percy A., Italy: Republic without Government? (New York: W.W. Norton, 1973).
Almond, Gabriel and Sidney Verba, The Civic Culture (Princeton: Princeton University Press, 1963).
Anderson, John and Hilary Hevenor, Burning Down the House: MOVE and the Tragedy of Philadelphia (New York: W.W. Norton and Co., 1987).
Appleby, Joyce, Liberalism and Republicanism in the Historical Imagination (Cambridge, MA: Harvard University Press, 1992).
Argyris, Chris and Donald Schon, Organizational Learning (Reading, Mass.: Addison-Wesley, 1978).
Assifa, Hizkias and Paul Wahrhafitg, Extremist Groups and Conflict Resolution: The MOVE Crisis in Philadelphia (New York: Praeger, 1988).
Bailyn, Bernard, The Ideological Origins of the American Revolution (Cambridge, MA: Belknap Press of Harvard University Press, 1967).
Baranski, Zygmunt G.and Robert Lumley, eds., Culture and Conflict in Postwar Italy: Essays on Mass and Popular Culture (London: Macmillan, 1990).
Bates, Robert, Beyond the Miracle of the Market (New York: Cambridge University Press, 1989).
Beitz, Charles R., "Procedural Equality in Democratic Theory: A Preliminary Examination," in J. Roland Pennock and John W. Chapman, eds., Liberal Democracy (New York: New York University Press, 1983).
Bell, Derrick, Faces at the Bottom of the Well (New York: Basic Books, 1992).
Bellah, Robert, et.al., Habits of the Heart: Individualim and Commitment in American Life (Berkeley: University of California Press, 1985).
Bennis, Warren, Why Leaders Can't Lead (San Francisco: Jossey-Bass, 1989).
Berger, Peter L. and Richard J. Neuhaus, To Empower People: The Role of Mediating Structures in Public Policy. (Washington: American Enterprise Institute, 1977).
Block, Peter, The Empowered Manager: Positive Political Skills at Work (San Francisco: Jossey-Bass, 1987).
Bowser, Charles W., Let the Bunker Burn: The Final Battle with MOVE (Philadelphia: Camino Books, 1989).
Brest, Paul, "The Fundamental Rights Controversy: The Essential Contradictions of Normative Constitutional Scholarship," 90 Yale Law Journal (1981).
Bryant, Coralie and Louise G. White, Managing Development in the Third World (Boulder, Colorado: Westview Press, 1982).
Bull, Hedley, The Anarchical Society: A Study of Order in World Politics (New York: Columbia University Press, 1977).
Callaghy, Thomas, The State-Society Struggle: Zaire in Comparative Perspective (New York: Columbia University Press, 1984).
Carter, Jimmy, Keeping Faith: Memoirs of a President (New York: Bantam Books, 1982).
Chazan, Naomi, John Harbeson and Donald Rothchild, eds., Civil Society and the State in Africa (Boulder, CO: Lynne Rienner, 1992).

Cohen, Ronald, ed., Satisfying Africa's Food Needs (Boulder: Lynn Reinner Publishers, 1988).
Connolly, William, The Terms of Political Discourse (Princeton: Princeton University Press, 2nd ed., 1983).
Cooper, Kerry and Donald Fraser, Banking Deregulation and the New Competition in Financial Services (Cambridge, MA: Ballenger Publishing Co., 1986).
Corbo, Vittorio, Stanley Fischer, and Stephen B. Webb, eds., Adjustment Lending Revisited: Policies to Restore Growth, A World Bank Symposium (Washington: World Bank, 1992)
Dahl, Robert A., Dilemmas of Pluralist Democracy: Autonomy vs. Control (New Haven: Yale University Press, 1982).
Davidson, Chandler, ed., Minority Vote Dilution (Washington: Howard University Press, 1984).
Dixon, Robert G., Democratic Representation (New York: Oxford University Press, 1968).
Douglas, James, Why Charity? The Case for a Third Sector (Beverly Hills: Sage Publications, 1983).
Dreze, Jean and Amartya Sen, Hunger and Public Action (New York: Oxford University Press, 1989).
Edwards, David V., Creating a New World Politics (New York: McKay, 1973).
Edwards, David V., The American Political Experience (Englewood Cliffs: Prentice-Hall, [four editions] 1979, 1982, 1985, 1988).
Ely, John Hart, Democracy and Distrust (Cambridge, MA: Harvard University Press, 1980).
Esman, Milton and Norman Uphoff, Local Organizations: Intermediaries in Rural Development (Ithaca: Cornell University Press, 1984).
Etzioni, Amitai, The Active Society (New York: Free Press, 1968).
FDIC, Mandate for Change - Restructuring the Banking Industry (Washington: 1988).
Ferguson, Yale H. and Richard W. Mansbach, The Elusive Quest: Theory and International Politics (Columbia, SC: University of South Carolina Press, 1988).
Festinger, Leon, A Theory of Cognitive Dissonance (Stanford, CA: Stanford University Press, 1957).
Finlay, David J., Ole R. Holsti, and Richard R. Fagen, Enemies in Politics (Chicago: Rand McNally, 1967).
Foster, R.Scott, ed., New Economic Role of American States - Strategies in a Competitive World Economy (New York: Oxford University Press, 1988).
Frieder, Larry et.al., Commercial Banking and Interstate Expansion - Issues, Prospects and Strategies (Ann Arbor, MI: UMI Research Press, 1985).
Friedman, Milton, Capitalism and Freedom (Chicago: The University of Chicago Press, 1962).
Friere, Paulo, Pedagogy of the Oppressed, translated by Myra Bergman Ramos (New York: Seabury Press, 1988).
Fukuda, K. John, Japanese-Style Management Transferral (London: Routledge, 1988).
Galloway, Jonathan F., "Multinational Enterprises as Worldwide Interest Groups," Politics & Society, Vol. 2, No. 1 (November 1971).
Galloway, Jonathan F., "The Multinationalization of Labor: U.S. Perspective," in Kurt Tudyka, ed., Multinational Corporations and Labor Unions (Nijmegen: Werkuitgave Sun, 1973).

Galloway, Jonathan F., "INTELSAT'S Markets and the New Competitors," International Journal, Vol. XLII, No. 2 (Spring 1987).
Galloway, Jonathan F., "International Law and the Protection of the Ozone Layer," Proceedings of the Thirty-First Colloquium on the Law of Outer Space (Washington: American Institute of Aeronautics and Astronautics, 1989).
Gilbert, Charles E., "The Framework of Administrative Responsibility", The Journal of Politics, Vol. 21, No. 3 (August 1959).
Gilbert, Charles E., "Operative Doctrines of Representation," American Political Science Review, Vol. 57 (September 1963).
Gilpin, Robert, The Political Economy of International Relations (Princeton: Princeton University Press, 1987).
Ginsborg, Paul, A History of Contemporary Italy: Society and Politics 1943-1988 (London: Penguin Books, 1990).
Glickman, Harvey, ed., The Crisis and Challenge of African Development (New York: Greenwood Press, 1988).
Goode, W. Wilson, with Joann Stevens, In Goode Faith (Valley Forge, PA: Judson Press, 1992).
Gormley, William T., Taming the Bureaucracy: Muscles, Prayers, and Other Strategies (Princeton: Princeton University Press, 1989).
Gurwitt, Rob, "Curing the Thrift Industry Will Mean a Loss of State Regulatory Powers," Governing (June 1989).
Hacker, Andrew, Two Nations (New York: Scribner's, 1992).
Haggard, Stephen and Robert R. Kaufman (eds.), The Politics of Economic Adjustment: International Constraints, Distributional Conflicts and the State Coalitions (Princeton: Princeton University Press, 1992).
Halperin, Morton H., Bureaucratic Politics and Foreign Policy (Washington: The Brookings Institution, 1974).
Harbeson, John and Donald Rothchild (eds.), Africa in World Politics (Boulder: Westview Press, 1991).
Hickman, Craig R., The Mind of a Manager, the Soul of a Leader (New York: Wiley, 1990).
Holsti, K.J., The Dividing Discipline: Hegemony and Diversity in International Theory (Boston: Allen and Unwin, 1985).
Hopkins Raymond F., "Interests and Regimes: The Subjective Dimension of International Politics," American Political Science Association Meetings Paper (Chicago: September 1987).
Hopkins, Raymond F., Donald J. Puchala and Ross B. Talbot, eds., Food, Politics, and Agricultural Development (Boulder: Westview, 1979).
Hopkins, Raymond F. et.al., Global Political Economy of Food (Madison: University of Wisconsin Press, 1979).
Huntington, Samuel, Political Order in Changing Societies (New Haven: Yale University Press, 1968).
Hyden, Goren, Ujamaa (Berkeley: University of California Press, 1980).
Janis, Irving L., Crucial Decisions: Leadership in Policymaking and Crisis Management (New York: The Free Press, 1989).
Janis, Irving L., Victims of Groupthink (Boston: Houghton Mifflin, 1972).
Jervis, Robert, Perception and Misperception in International Politics (Princeton: Princeton University Press, 1976).
Jones, Merrick and Pete Mann, eds., HRD: International Perspectives on Development and Learning (West Hartford, CT: Kumarian Press, 1992).

Jones, Russell A., Self-Fulfilling Prophecies: Social, Psychological, and Physiological Effects of Expectancies (Hillsdale, NJ: Lawrence Erlbaum, 1977).
Jonsen, Albert R. and Stephen Toulmin, Abuse of Casuistry: A History of Moral Reasoning (Berkeley: University of California Press, 1988).
Kellner, Hans, Language and Historical Representation: Getting the Story Crooked (Madison: University of Wisconsin Press, 1989).
Kennedy, Robert F., Thirteen Days: A memoir of the Cuban missile crisis (New York: W.W. Norton, 1968).
Keohane Robert O., After Hegemony: Cooperation and Discord in the World Political Economy (Princeton: Princeton University Press, 1984).
Keohane, Robert O., ed., Neorealism and Its Critics (New York: Columbia University Press, 1986).
Keohane, Robert O. and Joseph S. Nye, Power and Interdependence, 2nd ed. (Glenview, IL: Scott, Foresman and Co., 1989).
Kurth, James R. "The Military-Industrial Complex Revisited," in Joseph Kruzel, ed., American Defense Annual, 1989-1990 (Lexington: Lexington Books, 1989).
Lijphart, Arend and Bernard Grofman, eds., Choosing an Electoral System (New York: Praeger, 1984).
Lindblom, Charles E., Politics and Markets (New York: Basic Books, 1977).
Lipton, Michael, Why the Poor Stay Poor: A study of Urban Bias in World Development (London: Temple Smith, 1977).
Lowi, Theodore J., The End of Liberalism: Ideology, Policy, and the Crisis of Public Authority (New York: W.W. Norton, 1969).
MacIver, R.M., The Web of Government (rev. ed.), (New York: The MacMillan Co., 1965).
MacKinnon, Catharine A., Feminism Unmodified (Cambridge, MA: Harvard University Press, 1987).
Mansbach, Richard W. and John A. Vasquez, In Search of Theory: A New Paradigm for Global Politics (New York: Columbia University Press, 1981).
March, James G. and Johan P. Olsen, Rediscovering Institutions: The Organizational Basis of Politics (New York: Free Press, 1989).
Miller, Charles, The Supreme Court and the Uses of History (Cambridge, MA: 1969).
Moore, Barrington, Jr., Social Origins of Dictatorship and Democracy: Lord and Peasant in the Making of the Modern World (Boston: Beacon Press, 1967).
Morgenthau, Hans J., Politics in the Twentieth Century, abridged ed. (Chicago: University of Chicago Press, 1971).
Morgenthau, Hans J., Politics Among Nations: The Struggle for Power and Peace, 6th ed., rev. by Kenneth W. Thompson (New York: Alfred A. Knopf, 1985).
Myrdal, Gunnar, Asian Drama: An Inquiry into the Poverty of Nations (New York: Pantheon Books, 1968).
Nagel, Jack H., Participation (Englewood Cliffs: Prentice-Hall, 1987).
Nicholson, Nigel, et.al., eds., The Theory and Practice of Organizational Psychology (New York: Academic Press, 1982).
Nye, Joseph S., Jr., Nuclear Ethics (New York: The Free Press, 1986).
Okun, Arthur, Equality and Efficiency: The Big Trade Off (Washington: The Brookings Institution, 1975).

Olson, Mancur, The Logic of Collective Action (Cambridge: Harvard University Press, 1965).
Olson, Mancur, The Rise and Decline of Nations -- Economic Growth, Stagflation, and Social Rigidities (New Haven: Yale University Press, 1982).
Osborne, David and Ted A. Gaebler, Reinventing Government: How the Entrepreneurial Spirit Is Transforming the Public Sector (Reading, MA: Addison-Wesley, 1992).
Osborne, David, Laboratories of Democracy (Boston, MA: Harvard Business School Press, 1988).
Ouchi, William G., Theory Z: How American Business Can Meet the Japanese Challenge (Reading, MA: Addison-Wesley, 1981).
Parker, Frank R., Black Votes Count (Chapel Hill: University of North Carolina Press, 1990).
Parker, Richard, "The Past of Constitutional Theory--and its Future," 42 Ohio State Law Review (1981).
Pennock, J. Roland, Democratic Political Theory (Princeton: Princeton University Press, 1979).
Peters, Tom and Nancy Austin, A Passion for Excellence: The Leadership Difference (New York: Random House, 1985).
Pinchot, Gifford III, Intrapreneuring (New York: Harper & Row, 1985).
Pinstrup-Andersen, Per, ed., Food Subsidies in Developing Countries (Baltimore: Johns Hopkins University Press, 1988).
Polsby, Nelson, ed., Reapportionment in the 1970s (Berkeley: University of California Press, 1971).
Putnam, Robert D., Making Democracy Work: Civic Traditions in Modern Italy (Princeton: Princeton University Press, 1993).
Putnam, Robert, Politicians and Politics: Themes in British and Italian Elite Political Culture (New Haven: Yale University Press, 1970).
Rae, Douglas and Douglas Yates, Equalities (Cambridge, MA: Harvard University Press, 1981).
Rosecrance, Richard N., Action and Reaction in World Politics: International Systems in Perspective (Boston: Little Brown, 1963).
Salamon, Lester M., ed., Beyond Privatization: The Tools of Government Action (Washington: Urban Institute Press, 1989).
Schelling, Thomas C., The Strategy of Conflict (Cambridge, MA: Harvard University Press, 1980).
Schon, Donald A., The Reflective Practitioner: How Professionals Think in Action (New York: Basic Books, 1983).
Schwartz, Barry, The Battle for Human Nature: Science, Morality, and Modern Life (New York: Norton, 1986).
Scott, James C., Weapons of the Weak (New Haven: Yale University Press, 1985).
Senge, Peter M., The Fifth Discipline: The Art and Practice of the Learning Organization (New York: Doubleday, 1990).
Shackle, G. L. S., Imagination and the Nature of Choice (Edinburgh: Edinburgh University Press, 1979).
Slights, Camille Wells, The Casuistical Tradition (Princeton: Princeton University Press, 1981).
Smith, David G., "Liberalism and Judicial Review," in J. Roland Pennock and John W. Chapman, eds., Liberal Democracy (New York: New York University Press, 1983).

Staniland, Martin, What is Political Economy? (New Haven: Yale University Press, 1985).
Stepan, Alfred, Rethinking Military Politics: Brazil and the Southern Cone (Princeton: Princeton University Press, 1988).
Taagepera, Rein and Matthew Soberg Shugart, Seats and Votes (New Haven: Yale University Press, 1989).
Thernstrom, Abigail, Whose Votes Count (Cambridge, MA: Harvard University Press, 1987).
Timmer, C. Peter, ed., Agriculture and the State: Growth, Employment, and Poverty in Developing Countries (Ithaca: Cornell University Press, 1991).
Tismaneau, Vladimir, In Search of Civil Society: Independent Peace Movements in the Soviet Bloc (New York and London: Routledge, 1990).
Torstendahl, Rolf, et.al., eds., The Formation of Professions: Knowledge, State, and Strategy (Newbury Park, CA: Sage, 1990).
Tracy, Michael, Agriculture in Western Europe: Crisis and Adaptation since 1880 (London: Jonathan Cape, 1982, 2nd edition).
Truman, Harry S., Years of Trial and Hope (Garden City, NY: Doubleday and Company, 1956).
Tulis, Jeffrey, The Rhetorical Presidency (Princeton: Princeton University Press, 1988).
Tullis, F. Lamond and W. Ladd Hollis, eds., Food, the State, and International Political Economy (Lincoln: University of Nebraska Press, 1986).
Uphoff, Norman, Learning from Gal Oya: Possibilities for Participatory Development and Post-Newtonian Social Science (Ithaca: Cornell University Press, 1992).
Van Til, Jon, Mapping the Third Sector: Voluntarism in a Changing Social Economy (New York: The Foundation Center, 1988).
Waltz, Kenneth N., Man, The State and War: A Theoretical Analysis (New York: Columbia University Press, 1959).
Waltz, Kenneth N., Theory of International Politics (Reading, MA: Addison-Wesley, 1979).
Watson, Adam, The Evolution of International Society in Comparative Historical Analysis (London: Routledge, 1992).
Winter, Richard, Action-Research and the Nature of Social Inquiry (Aldershot: Gower, 1987).
Wolin, Richard, The Terms of Cultural Criticism (New York: Columbia University Press, 1992).
Wood, Gordon S., The Creation of the American Republic, 1776-1787 (Chapel Hill: University of North Carolina Press, 1969).
World Bank, World Development Report, 1992: Development and the Environment (Washington: World Bank, 1992).
World Bank, World Development Report, 1990: Poverty (Washington: World Bank, 1990).
World Bank, From Crisis to Sustainable Growth: A Long-Term Perspective Study (Washington: World Bank, 1989).

INDEX

accountability, 3, 130, 181-183, 199
administration, 6, 8, 13-18, 21-22, 45, 66, 193, 210
Africa, governments, 101, 106, 109-112, 115-116, 177-181, 186-192, 205, 218
agriculture, 107-110, 115-119, 176, 184
   production in, 109, 181, 187
   transformation of, 109
associations, civic, 107
   voluntary, 56, 58-59, 64
authority, 5, 14, 42-43, 109, 122, 125-130, 132, 144, 148, 154, 157, 164, 169, 179, 185, 216, 219-221
autonomy, 62, 127-128, 147-148, 150, 164-165, 191, 199
Baker v. Carr, 81-83
banking, and regulation, 45, 47
   Delaware, 51
capitalism, 197-198
Carter, Jimmy, 24, 215, 226
centralization, 125-126
Christian Democrats (Ital.), 126-127, 134, 138, 148
citizen, citizenship, 62, 91, 94, 96-97, 102, 105-106, 120, 140, 157-158, 163, 199, 201, 210, 215
clientilism, 125, 147, 161
cold war, 177, 182, 201, 204
Colegrove v. Green, 70, 81
Communists, 126-127, 138
comparative advantage, 180, 194-197, 199
competence, governmental, 163-171, 183, 185, 193
constitutions, 91, 118-119, 188
decision-making, theory of, 31-33, 43-44
delegation, devolution, 14, 36-38, 55, 60-64
democracy, 2-3, 11, 13, 45, 55, 57, 60-64, 67, 90-91, 93-94, 101-102
   and economic development, 179, 181, 187, 188-189
   constitutionalism and, 93-94, 104
   "laboratories of..", 45, 59, 75
   liberal, 2, 85, 87-88
   representative, 90-91
deregulation, 13, 45-51, 53, 55
development, 3, 9, 11, 13, 94, 101-103, 107-117, 177-183, 188-189, 192
   agriculture and, 107-112
   democracy and, 188-189
   economic, 101-104, 183-192
   political, 11, 13, 94, 177-183
   regional government and, 127-128
   state and, 111-117
empowerment, 13-17, 95-98
Etzioni, Amitai, 63-64
Federalist, The, 2, 196, 206
food, production of, 108-109, 117-118, 178-181, 183-184, 187

Friedrich, Carl J., 185
Garn-St. Germain Act, 63
Gilbert, Charles E., 1, 6, 22, 45, 59, 64-66, 69-70, 78, 91, 95, 102, 177, 185, 193, 210
Goode, Wilson, 21, 25
Gore, W. L., 15
governance, 122-124
  and economic development, 101-112
Harrington, Michael, 63
Hartz, Louis, 70, 79
Hobbes, Thomas, 213, 216
India, 104, 200, 208
institutionalization, 105-108, 116, 121-122, 134-135, 148, 205
interdependence, 197, 200, 203-204, 210, 222
international economy, 180, 182, 184
International Monetary Fund, 179-187, 189-191
Israel, 213, 224-225
Italian regional government, 121, 124, 179
Japan, 9, 67, 102, 116, 118, 202-203, 207, 219
Johnson, Lyndon B., 58, 216
Kenya, 16, 115, 187
leadership, 9-11, 13-16, 22, 114-115, 204, 207, 209-210
League of Nations, 107, 220
legitimacy, 6, 8, 98-100, 103, 105-106, 117, 173-175, 187-189, 214-215
liberalism, 93, 95, 103, 195-198, 205-206
local government, 125, 156, 181, 183
Machiavelli, Niccolo, 210, 212-213
Madison, James, 2, 7, 103, 157, 196, 204, 206
management, 9-16, 22, 30-32, 39, 42-44, 158-159, 180, 189-191
market, markets, 46-47, 49, 65, 103, 109, 112, 117, 182-184, 186, 193, 197, 199-200, 206-208
Marx, Karl, 182, 197-198, 201, 207
Marxism, 106, 195, 197-198, 201, 206
mercantilism, 195-199, 201, 206-207
Mexico, 50, 105
Mobile v. Bolden, 88-89
modernization, 109, 119, 182
Morgenthau, Hans J., 205-206, 212-214
MOVE, 31, 33-43
national interest, 184, 208, 214
nationalism, 107, 182
Philadelphia, 21-31, 34-42
  police, 37-38
  Special Investigations Commission, 36-39, 41-42
pluralism, 61-62, 99, 101, 144
political development, 111-117
political economy, 111-112, 182-183, 194-196, 199-203, 205-209
political instability, 179
political science, 6-8, 12
regions, regionalism, 46, 48-49, 127-128, 147-148, 154-156, 175-176
regulation, 47-49, 51, 53

representation, 65, 67-68, 70-72
responsibility, 2, 11, 14-18, 31-33, 58, 67-68
    administrative, 6, 8, 13-18, 21-22, 45, 66
responsive government, 1, 3, 46
responsiveness, 2, 3
Reynolds v. Sims, 71-72
Rousseau, Jean-Jacques, 62
Smith, Adam, 195-196
socialism, 197-198
sociology, 18-19
Somalia, 1, 106, 179
Soviet Union, 1, 11, 101, 105-106, 115, 119, 218-219
stability, political, 117-118, 133, 171, 179, 220
state, 102, 125-126, 130, 156, 163-164, 173, 176, 209
    and development, 113-114, 198-199
    and transnationalism, 199-204
Sudan, 106, 179
Taylorism, 10
Thornburg v. Gingles, 73-74, 96
transnational corporations, 201-204
voluntarism, 3, 58-59, 64
    responsible, 58, 67-68
vote dilution, 70-91, 94-95, 97-98, 100-103
Walzer, Michael, 64
welfare state, 111, 117
Wilson, Woodrow, 215, 218-219
World Bank, 101-102, 179-189
world politics, 187, 192, 196, 204, 210-211, 216, 220-224
    and ethical values, 209-212
    and Realism, 213-215
    and responsibility, 221
    and transnational corporations, 201-204
World War II, 102, 125-126, 211-212, 223
Zaire, 105, 112, 116

NOTES ON THE CONTRIBUTORS

Eleanor D. Craig is Associate Professor of Economics at the University of Delaware. In addition to extensive publications she has held numerous governmental positions including service in the cabinet of former Governor duPont of Delaware and as chair of the Delaware Economic and Financial Advisory Council. She has also taught at Rutgers University and at the University of Sophia, Bulgaria.

David V. Edwards is Professor of Government at the University of Texas. Among his books are The American Political Experience (4th edition) and Creating a New World Politics. He has been a Research Associate of the Washington Center for Foreign Policy Research.

Jonathan F. Galloway is Irwin D. and Fern D. Young Professor of Politics at Lake Forest College. His books include The Politics and Technology of Satellite Communications and many articles on space policy and international law.

John W. Harbeson is professor in the Department of Political Science, in the Graduate Center and at City College in the City University of New York. His books include Civil Society and the State in Africa (with Naomi Chazan and Donald Rothchild) and The Ethiopian Transformation: the Quest for the Post-Imperial State.

Raymond F. Hopkins is professor of Political Science at Swarthmore College. Among his books are Food in the Global Arena and Global Food Interdependence: Challenge to American Policy (co-author). He has been a Guggenheim Fellow and a Fellow at the Woodrow Wilson International Center for Scholars.

Richard W. Mansbach is professor and chair in the Department of Political Science at Iowa State University. Among his books are In Search of Theory: A New Paradigm for Global Politics (with John Vasquez) and The Elusive Quest: Theory and International Politics.

Roger B. Moore is an attorney in private practice in the San Francisco area. He specializes in environmental, constitutional, civil rights and international human rights law.

Jack H. Nagel is the Daniel J. Brodsky Term Professor of Political Science and Public Policy and Management at the University of Pennsylvania. His books include Participation and The Descriptive Analysis of Power.

J. Roland Pennock is Richter Professor of Political Science Emeritus at Swarthmore College. He is the author of Liberal Democracy: Its Merits and Prospects. He has been editor of NOMOS, President of the American Society of Political and Legal Philosophy and Vice President of the American Political Science Association.

Robert D. Putnam is professor in the Department of Government at Harvard University. Among his books are <u>Making Democracy Work</u>, <u>Bureaucrats and Politicians in Western Democracies</u> and <u>Hanging Together: The Seven Power Summit</u>. He has served in the National Security Council and has been a Fellow at the Woodrow Wilson International Center for Scholars.

David G. Smith is Richter Professor of Political Science Emeritus at Swarthmore College. He is the author of <u>Paying for Medicare: The Politics of Reform</u> and <u>The Convention and the Constitution</u>.

Jon Van Til is professor of Urban Studies and Public Policy at Rutgers University, Camden. Among his publications is <u>Mapping the Third Sector: Voluntarism in a Changing Social Economy</u>.